# Sunday
## Celebration

### OF THE WORD AND HOURS

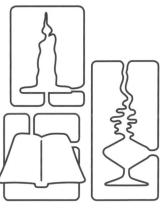

# Sunday Celebration of the Word and Hours

Approved by the National Liturgical Office
for use in Canada

Edited by
**National Liturgical Office**

Published by
**Publications Service**

Canadian Conference of Catholic Bishops
90 Parent Avenue
Ottawa, Ontario
Canada
K1N 7B1

Printed and bound in Canada by Tri-Graphic Printing (Ottawa) Limited

ISBN (Study Edition) 0-88997-338-5
ISBN (Ambo Edition) 0-88997-328-8
Legal Deposit: National Library of Canada, Ottawa

# FOREWORD

## *SUNDAY CELEBRATION OF THE WORD AND HOURS*

Ritual that is truly liturgical is not a spontaneous action that is left to the talent and ingenuity of leaders and planners, or arises from the occasion it marks or celebrates. Rather, it must have a stable, recognizable format that links it with the tradition of prayer and worship of the whole church. In a particular or diocesan church, it should have a unity of shape that clearly speaks of a community gathered with the local bishop and by him linked to the entire church.

The *Ritual for Sunday Celebration of the Word and Hours* has been designed for that purpose and approved by the Bishops of Canada for use in our country. This *Ritual* marks a new step in the process of providing a form for Sunday worship for those communities without a priest that will be common across our country. Care has also been taken that both French and English language editions of this Ritual are similar in format. For a number of years many dioceses have had to face this situation; their experience and work of pioneering local rituals and forms of worship is acknowledged and recognized.

Because the use of these rites is a new experience for many, there will inevitably be questions as to the need and appropriateness of using these rites in particular situations. The pastoral notes that have been developed to accompany the ritual may help both clergy and laity to understand better the full significance of Sunday celebrations of the Word, the place for Holy Communion during these celebrations, and the most appropriate ways to express clearly the deep, basic meaning and value of the Sunday assembly when the Eucharist cannot be celebrated.

The purpose of the ritual book is to provide a liturgical celebration that will nourish the faith and devotion of each local assembly and give every member a genuine experience of being and acting as church. The publication of the Pastoral Notes, in a separate booklet (number 6 of the series *Canadian Studies in Liturgy*), is an important step to achieving the goal of liturgy and assisting in the preparation of these celebrations. These publications are directed not only to the leaders of these liturgical gatherings or to the ministers who will carry them out, but to the entire community so that everyone can be prepared to understand that these are true liturgical actions – official worship of the Church – and as such, they involve the whole assembly (See *Constitution on the Sacred Liturgy* [CSL] no. 26).

† James M. Hayes

Most Reverend James M. Hayes
Archbishop Emeritus of Halifax
Chairman, Episcopal Commission for Liturgy

# EDITORIAL NOTE

The Ritual for the Sunday Celebration of the Word and Hours is intended for liturgical assemblies on Sunday, the Lord's Day, when the Eucharist cannot be celebrated. Its use is primarily intended for lay persons or deacons who lead the prayer at the Sunday worship of communities when there is no priest to preside at the celebration of the Eucharist. There are other occasions for its use: parish or community celebrations of Morning or Evening Prayer; liturgies of the Word in chapels and institutions where it is not pastorally possible to celebrate the Eucharist; or ecumenical celebrations of the Word or Hours. This Ritual is intended for these celebrations, whether led by lay or ordained ministers.

## Terminology

With few exceptions the names of celebrations in the Roman Catholic tradition are not taken from the person who presides, but from the nature of the celebration itself. This tradition recognizes that every liturgy is the celebration of the whole assembly and Church. When the Eucharist cannot be celebrated in a community, the community can still gather to listen to the Word of God, sing the praise of the Most High and intercede for the salvation of the world and the good of all. Thus, even if a priest is not available, the name of the celebration should reflect the nature of the celebration and not the person who leads it. The name *Sunday Celebration of the Word or Hours* honours this tradition, and is the name and title chosen for this Ritual.

The *Directory for Sunday Celebrations in the absence of a priest* uses the term "leader" to designate the ministry of those lay persons who lead the prayer in the absence of a priest. In many places the word "presider" is used as well. For the sake of consistency this Ritual uses the noun "leader of prayer," "lay presider"or "leader" and the verbs "lead" and "preside."

In some cases, more than one term may be used to design liturgical ministers and furnishings. Some names may be used exclusively in some regions of Canada, however, the ritual and pastoral notes tend to use them interchangeably. Some examples are: ambo or lectern; lector or reader; thurible or censer; cantor or leader of song or psalmist.

## Pastoral Notes

The pastoral notes for the celebration of the Word or Hours are contained in two separate publications. The *Liturgical Notes* (*LN*) are printed in this *Ritual* and concern the actual celebration and its preparation. Additional notes for the formation and training of ministers, especially the leader of prayer, are printed with the *Liturgical Notes* in number 6 of the *Canadian Studies in Liturgy* (May 1995) published by the Canadian Conference of Catholic Bishops. This publication is intended as a companion volume to the *Ritual.* The notes concerning the formation and training of leaders of prayer are entitled *Formation Notes* (*FN*).

# TABLE OF CONTENTS

# DIRECTORY FOR SUNDAY CELEBRATIONS

## IN THE ABSENCE OF A PRIEST

Congregation For Divine Worship

Prot. 691/86

The *Directory for Sunday Celebrations in the Absence of a Priest* is a response to the convergence of several factors. The first of these is the fact that it is not everywhere and always possible to have a complete liturgical celebration of Sunday (no. 2). A second factor is the request over the past few years from several conferences of bishops that the Holy See issue guidelines for this de facto situation (no. 7). A third factor is a matter of experience: in the light of the actual situation and its circumstances the Holy See and many bishops in their local Churches have already turned their attention to Sunday celebrations in the absence of a priest. The *Directory* has profited from such experience in regard to its assessment of the advantages and at the same time the possible limitations of the sort of celebration in question.

The fundamental point of the entire *Directory* is to ensure, in the best way possible and in every situation, the Christian celebration of Sunday. This means remembering that the Mass remains the proper way of celebrating Sunday, but also means recognizing the presence of important elements even when Mass cannot be celebrated.

The intent of the present document is not to encourage, much less facilitate unnecessary or contrived Sunday assemblies without the celebration of the eucharist. The intent rather is simply to guide and to prescribe what should be done when real circumstances require the decision to have Sunday celebrations in the absence of a priest (nos. 21-22).

The first part of the *Directory* is completely devoted to a summary of the meaning of Sunday and its point of departure is art. 106 of the Constitution on the Liturgy *Sacrosanctum Concilium* (no. 8).

The second part prescribes the conditions necessary for the decision in a diocese to schedule as a regular occurrence Sunday assemblies in the absence of a priest. From a practical and directive point of view this is the most important part of this document. The document envisions the collaboration of the laity in the cases in question; this is an example of responsibilities

The third part of the *Directory* is a brief description of the rite for Sunday celebrations of the word along with distribution of communion.

As with similar documents, the application of this *Directory* depends on all the bishops, each acting in accord with the situation of his Church; in matters involving norms for an entire region, the application of the *Directory* depends on the conference of bishops.

What matters above all is ensuring that communities involved in the situation in question have the opportunity to gather together on Sunday, and in a way that coincides with the celebration of the liturgical year (no. 36), and that unites such communities with a community that is celebrating the eucharist with their own parish priest (pastor) (no. 42).

As Pope Paul VI (no. 21) and Pope John Paul II (no. 50) have stated, the purpose of all pastoral endeavour concerned with Sunday is that it be celebrated and regarded in accord with Christian tradition.

## Preface

1.  From the day of Pentecost, after the coming of the Holy Spirit, the Church of Christ has always faithfully come together to celebrate the paschal mystery on the day called "the Lord's Day" in memory of the Lord's resurrection. In the Sunday assembly the Church reads in all the Scriptures those things that concern Christ1 and celebrates the eucharist as the memorial of the death and resurrection of the Lord until he comes.

2.  But a complete celebration of the Lord's Day is not always possible. There have been and still are many of the faithful for whom "because of the lack of a priest or some other serious reason, participation in the eucharistic celebration is not possible."[2]

3.  In some regions, after their first evangelization, the bishops have put catechists in charge of gathering the faithful together on Sunday and, in the form of a devotional exercise, of leading them in prayer. In such cases the number of Christians grew and they were scattered in so many and such widely separated places that a priest could not reach them every Sunday.

4.  In other places the faithful were completely blocked from gathering on Sunday, either because of the persecution of Christians or because of other severe restrictions of religious freedom. Like the Christians of old, who held fast to the Sunday assembly even in the face of martyrdom,[3] the faithful today, even when deprived of the presence of an ordained minister, also strive to gather on Sunday for prayer either within a family or in small groups.

5.  On other grounds today, namely, the scarcity of priests, in many places not every parish can have its own eucharistic celebration each Sunday. Further, for various social and economic reasons some parishes have many fewer members. As a consequence many priests are assigned to celebrate Mass several times on Sunday in

---

[1]  See Luke 24.17
[2]  Codex Iuris Canonici, 1983 (hereafter, CIC), can. 1248, §2.
[3]  See *Acta Martyrum Bytiniae*, in D. Ruiz Bueno, *Actas de los Martires*, Biblioteca de Autores Cristianos (BAC) 75 (Madrid, 1951), 973

many, widely scattered churches. But this practice is regarded as not always satisfactory either to the parishes lacking their own parish priest (pastor) or to the priests involved.

6.     In some local Churches, then, because of the conditions indicated, the bishops have judged it necessary to arrange for other Sunday celebrations in the absence of a priest, so that in the best way possible the weekly gathering of the faithful can be continued and the Christian tradition regarding Sunday preserved.

It is by no means unusual, particularly in mission territories, for the faithful themselves, aware of the importance of the Lord's Day and with the help of catechists and religious, to gather to listen to the word of God, to pray, and, in some cases, even to receive communion.

7.     The Congregation for Divine Worship has considered these matters, reviewed the documents already published by the Holy See,[4] and acceded to the wishes of the conferences of bishops. Therefore the Congregation regards it as opportune to recall elements of the teaching on the meaning of Sunday, to lay down the conditions for the lawfulness of such celebrations in dioceses, and to provide guidelines for carrying out such celebrations correctly.

It will be the responsibility of the conferences of bishops, as circumstances suggest, to determine these norms in greater detail, to adapt them to the culture and conditions of their people, and to report their decisions to the Apostolic See.

## CHAPTER I

### Sunday and Its Observance

8.     "By a tradition handed down from the apostles and having its origin from the very day of Christ's resurrection, the Church celebrates the paschal mystery every eighth day, which, with good reason, bears the name of the Lord's Day or Sunday."[5]

9.     Evidence of the gathering of the faithful on the day which the New Testament itself already designates as the Lord's Day[6] appears explicitly in documents of the first and second centuries.[7] Outstanding among such evidence is the testimony of Saint Justin: "On this day which is called Sunday, all who live in the cities or in the country gather together in one place."[8] But the day of gathering for Christians did not coincide with the day of rest in the Greek or Roman calendar and therefore even the gathering on this day was a sign to fellow citizens of the Christians' identity.

10.     From the earliest centuries pastors had never failed to counsel their people on the need to gather together on Sunday. "Because you are Christ's members, do not scatter from the church by not coming together...do not neglect your Saviour or separate him from his members. Do not shatter or scatter the Body of Christ...."[9] Vatican Council II recalled this teaching in the following words: "On this day Christ's faithful must gather together, so that, by hearing the word of God and taking part in the eucharist, they may call to mind the passion, resurrection, and glorification of the Lord Jesus and may thank God, who 'has begotten them again unto a living hope through the resurrection of Jesus Christ from the dead' (1 Peter 1.3)."[10]

11.     Saint Ignatius of Antioch pointed out the importance of the Sunday celebration for the life of the faithful: "Christians no longer observe the sabbath day, but live according to the Lord's Day, on which our life was restored through Jesus Christ and his death."[11] In their "sense of the faith" *(sensus fidelium)* the faithful, now as in the past have held the Lord's Day in such high regard that they have never willingly omitted its observance even in times of persecution or in the midst of cultures alien or hostile to the Christian faith.

12.     The following are the principal requisites for the Sunday assembly of the faithful.

    a. the gathering of the faithful to manifest the Church, not simply on their own initiative but as called together by God, that is, as the people of God in their organic structure, presided over by a priest, who acts in the person of Christ;

    b. their instruction in the paschal mystery through the Scriptures that are proclaimed and that are explained by a priest or deacon;

    c. the celebration of the eucharistic sacrifice, by which the paschal mystery is expressed, and which is carried out by the priest in the person of Christ and offered in the name of the entire Christian people.

13.     Pastoral efforts should have this aim above all that the sacrifice of the Mass on Sunday be regarded as the only true actualization of the Lord's paschal mystery[12] and as the most complete manifestation of the Church: "Hence the Lord's Day is the first holy day of all and should be proposed to the devotion of the faithful and taught to them . . . . Other celebrations, unless they be truly of greatest importance, shall not have precedence

---

[4]     See SC Rites, Instruction *Inter Oecumenici* (26 September 1964), no. 37: *Acta Apostolicae Sedis* (hereafter, AAS) 56, (1964), 884-885; *Documents on the Liturgy*, 1963-1979: *Conciliar, Papal, and Curial Texts* (hereafter, DOL) 23, no. 329. CIC, can. 1248, §2.

[5]     Vatican Council II, Constitution on the Liturgy *Sacrosanctum Concilium* (hereafter, SC), art. 106: DOL 1, no. 106. See also ibid., Appendix, Declaration of the Second Vatican Ecumenical Council on Revision of the Calendar: DOL 1, no. 131.

[6]     See Revelation 1.10. See also John 20.19,26; Acts 20.7-12; 1 Corinthians 16.2; Hebrews 10.24-25

[7]     Didache 14, 1: F.X. Funk, ed., *Doctrina duodecim Apostolorum* (1887), p. 42

[8]     Saint Justin, *Apologia* I, 67: PG 6, 430

[9]     *Didascalia Apostolorum* 2, 59, 1-3: F.X. Funk, ed., *Didascalia et Constitutiones Apostolorum* (1905) vol. 1, p. 170

[10]     SC, art. 106: DOL 1, no. 106

[11]     Saint Ignatius of Antioch, *Ad Magnesios* 9, 1: F.X. Funk, ed., *Didascalia Constitutiones Apostolorum* (1905) vol. 1, 199

[12]     See Paul VI, Address to bishops of central France, 26 March 1977: AAS 69 (1977), 465; "The goal must always be the celebration of the sacrifice of the Mass, the only true actualization of the Lord's paschal mystery" (tr., DOL 449, no. 3842)

over the Sunday, the foundation and core of the whole liturgical year."[13]

14. Such principles should be set before the faithful and instilled in them right from the beginning of their Christian formation, in order that they may willingly fulfill the precept to keep this day holy and may understand why they are brought together for the celebration of the eucharist by the call of the Church[14] and not simply by their personal devotion. In this way the faithful will be led to experience the Lord's Day as a sign of the divine transcendence over all human works, and not as simply a day off from work; in virtue of the Sunday assembly they will more deeply perceive themselves to be members of the Church and will show this outwardly.

15. In the Sunday assembly, as also in the life of the Christian community, the faithful should find both active participation and a true spirit of community, as well as the opportunity to be renewed spiritually under the guidance of the Holy Spirit. In this way, too, they will be protected against the attractions of sects that promise relief from the pain of loneliness and a more complete fulfillment of religious aspirations.

16. Finally, pastoral effort should concentrate on measures which have as their purpose "that the Lord's Day becomes in fact a day of joy and of freedom from work."[15] In this way Sunday will stand out in today's culture as a sign of freedom and consequently as a day established for the well-being of the human person, which clearly is a higher value than commerce or industrial production.[16]

17. The word of God, the eucharist, and the ministry of the priest are gifts that the Lord presents to the Church, his Bride, and they are to be received and to be prayed for as divine graces. The Church, which possesses these gifts above all in the Sunday assembly, thanks God for them in that same assembly and awaits the joy of its complete rest in the day of the Lord "before the throne of God and before the Lamb."[17]

## CHAPTER II

### Conditions for Holding Sunday Celebrations in the Absence of a Priest

18. Whenever and wherever Mass cannot be celebrated on Sunday, the first thing to be ascertained is whether the faithful can go to a church in a place nearby to participate there in the eucharistic mystery. At the present time this solution is to be recommended and to be retained where it is in effect; but it demands that the faithful, rightly imbued with a fuller understanding of the Sunday assembly, respond with good will to a new situation.

19. The aim is that the riches of Sacred Scripture and of the Church's prayer be amply provided to the faithful gathered on Sundays in various ways even apart from Mass. For the faithful should not be deprived of the readings that are read at Mass in the course of a year, nor of the prayers of the liturgical seasons.

20. Among the forms of celebration found in liturgical tradition when Mass is not possible, a celebration of the word of God is particularly recommended,[18] and also its completion, when possible, by eucharistic communion. In this way the faithful can be nourished by both the word of God and the body of Christ. "By hearing the word of God the faithful learn that the marvels it proclaims reach their climax in the paschal mystery, of which the Mass is a sacramental memorial and in which they share by communion."[19] Further, in certain circumstances the Sunday celebration can be combined with the celebration of one or more of the sacraments and especially of the sacramentals and in ways that are suited to the needs of each community.

21. It is imperative that the faithful be taught to see the substitutional character of these celebrations, which should not be regarded as the optimal solution to new difficulties nor as a surrender to mere convenience.[20] Therefore a gathering or assembly of this kind can never be held on a Sunday in places where Mass has already been celebrated or is to be celebrated or was celebrated on the preceding Saturday evening, even if the Mass is celebrated in a different language. Nor is it right to have more than one assembly of this kind on any given Sunday.

22. Any confusion between this kind of assembly and a eucharistic celebration must be carefully avoided. Assemblies of this kind should not take away but rather increase the desire of the faithful to take part in the celebration of the eucharist, and should make them more eager to be present at the celebration of the eucharist.

23. The faithful are to understand that the eucharistic sacrifice cannot take place without a priest and that the eucharistic communion which they may receive in this kind of assembly is closely connected with the sacrifice of the Mass. On that basis the faithful can be shown how necessary it is to pray that God will "give the Church more priests and keep them faithful in their love and service."[21]

---

[13]  SC, art 106: DOL 1, no. 106

[14]  See SC Rites, Instruction *Eucharisticum mysterium*, (25 May 1967), no. 25: AAS 59 (1967), 555: DOL 179, no. 25

[15]  SC, art. 106: dol 1, NO. 106

[16]  See "Le sens du dimanche dans une société pluraliste. Réflexions pastorales de la Conférence des évêques du Canada," *La Documentation Catholique*, no. 1935 (1987), 273-276

[17]  Revelation 7.9

[18]  See SC, art 35, 4: DOL 1, no. 35

[19]  The Roman Ritual, *Holy Communion and Worship of the Eucharist outside Mass*, no. 26

[20]  See Paul VI, Address to bishops of Central France, 26 March 1977: AAS 69 (1977); "Proceed judiciously, but without multiplying this type of Sunday assembly, as though it were the ideal solution and the last change" (tr., DOL 449, no. 3842

[21]  *The Roman Missal (Sacramentary)*, Masses and Prayers for Various Needs and Occasions, I. For the Church, 9. For Priestly Vocations, prayer over the gifts.

---

24. It belongs to the diocesan bishop, after hearing the council of presbyters, to decide whether Sunday assemblies without the celebration of the eucharist should be held on a regular basis in his diocese. It belongs also to the bishop, after considering the place and persons involved, to set out both general and particular norms for such celebrations. These assemblies are therefore to be conducted only in virtue of their convocation by the bishop and only under the pastoral ministry of the parish priest (pastor).

25. "No Christian community is ever built up unless it has its roots and centre in the eucharistic liturgy."[22] Therefore before the bishop decides on having Sunday assemblies without celebration of the eucharist the following, in addition to the status of parishes (see no. 5), should be considered: the possibility of recourse to priests, even religious priests, who are not directly assigned to the care of souls and the frequency of Masses in the various parishes and churches.[23] The preeminence of the celebration of the eucharist, particularly on Sunday, over other pastoral activities is to be respected.

26. Either personally or through his representatives the bishop will, by an appropriate catechesis, instruct the diocesan community on the causes requiring provision of these celebrations, pointing out the seriousness of the issue and urging the community's support and cooperation. The bishop is to appoint a delegate or a special committee to see to it that these celebrations are carried out correctly: he is also to choose those who are to promote these celebrations, and to see to it that these people receive the necessary instruction. But the bishop's concern is always to be that several times a year the faithful involved have the opportunity to participate in the celebration of the eucharist.

27. It is the duty of the parish priest (pastor) to inform the bishop about the opportuneness of such celebrations in his territory, to prepare the faithful for them, to visit them during the week, and at a convenient time to celebrate the sacraments for them, particularly the sacrament of penance. In this way the communities involved will come to realize that their assembly on Sunday is not an assembly "without a priest," but an assembly "in the absence of a priest," or, better still, an assembly "in expectation of a priest."

28. When Mass cannot be celebrated the parish priest (pastor) is to ensure that holy communion be given. He is also to see to it that there is a celebration of the eucharist in due time in each community. The consecrated hosts are to be renewed often and kept in a safe place.

29. As the primary assistants of priests, deacons are called in a special way to lead these Sunday assemblies. Since the deacon has been ordained for the nurture and increase of the people of God, it belongs to him to lead the prayers, to proclaim the gospel, to preach the homily, and to give communion.[24]

30. In the absence of both a priest and a deacon, the parish priest (pastor) is to appoint lay persons, who are to be entrusted with the care of these celebrations, namely, with leading the prayers, with the ministry of the word, and with giving holy communion.

Those to be chosen first by the parish priest (pastor) are readers and acolytes who have been duly instituted for the service of the altar and of the word of God. If there are no such instituted ministers available, other lay persons, both men and women, may be appointed; they can carry out this responsibility in virtue of their baptism and confirmation.[25] Such persons are to be chosen in view of the consistency of their way of life with the Gospel and in the expectation of their being acceptable to the community of the faithful. Appointment is usually to be for a definite time and is to be made known publicly to the community. It is fitting that there be a celebration in which prayers are offered to God on behalf of those appointed.[26]

The parish priest (pastor) is to see to the suitable and continuous instruction of these lay persons and to prepare with them worthy celebrations (see Chapter III).

31. The lay persons appointed should regard the office entrusted to them not so much as an honour but as a responsibility and above all as a service to their brothers and sisters under the authority of the parish priest (pastor). For theirs is not a proper office but a supplementary office, since they exercise it "where the need of the Church suggests in the absence of ministers."[27]

Those who are appointed to such an office "should do all of, but only, those parts which pertain to that office."[28] They should carry out their office with sincere devotion and the decorum demanded by such a responsibility and rightly expected of them by God's people.[29]

32. When on a Sunday a celebration of the word of God along with the giving of holy communion is not possible, the faithful are strongly urged to devote themselves to prayer "for a suitable time either individually or with the family or, if possible, with a group of families."[30] In these circumstances the telecast of liturgical services can provide useful assistance.

33. Particularly to be kept in mind is the possibility of celebrating some part of the liturgy of the hours, for

[22]  Vatican Council II, Decree on the Ministry and Life of Priests *Presbyterorum ordinis*, no. 6: DOL 18, no. 261

[23]  See SC Rites, Instruction *Eucharisticum mysterium* (25 May 1967), no. 26: AAS 59 (1967), 555; DOL 179, no. 1255

[24]  See Paul VI, Motu proprio *Ad pascendum* (15 August 1972), no. 1: AAS 64 (1972) 534; DOL 319, no. 2576

[25]  See CIC, can. 230, §3

[26]  See the Roman Ritual, *A Book of Blessings*, ch. 4, I, B

[27]  CIC, can 230, §3

[28]  SC, art. 28: DOL 1, no. 28

[29]  See SC, art. 29: DOL 1, no. 29

[30]  CIC, can. 1248, §2

example, morning prayer or evening prayer, during which the Sunday readings of the current year can be inserted. For "when the people are invited to the liturgy of the hours and come together in unity of heart and voice, they show forth the Church in its celebration of the mystery of Christ."[51] At the end of such a celebration communion may be given (see no. 46).

34.    "The grace of the Redeemer is not lacking for individual members of the faithful or entire communities that, because of persecution or a lack of priests, are deprived of celebration of the eucharist for a short time or even for a long period. They can be moved by a deep desire for the sacrament and be united in prayer with the whole Church. Then when they call upon the Lord and raise their minds and hearts to him, through the power of the Holy Spirit they enter into communion with Christ and with the Church, his living body . . . and therefore they receive the fruits of the eucharist."[52]

## CHAPTER III

### Order of Celebration

35.    The order to be followed in a Sunday celebration that does not include Mass consists of two parts, the celebration of the word of God and the giving of holy communion. Nothing that is proper to Mass, and particularly the presentation of the gifts and the eucharistic prayer, is to be inserted into the celebration. The order of celebration is to be arranged in such a way that it is truly conducive to prayer and conveys the image not of a simple meeting but of a genuine liturgical assembly.

36.    As a rule the texts for the prayers and readings for each Sunday or solemnity are to be taken from *The Roman Missal (Sacramentary)* and the *Lectionary for Mass*. In this way the faithful will follow the cycle of the liturgical year and will pray and listen to the word of God in communion with the other communities of the Church.

37.    In preparing the celebration the parish priest (pastor) together with the appointed lay persons may make adaptations suited to the number of those who will take part in the celebration, the ability of the leaders (animators), and the kind of instruments available for the music and the singing.

38.    When a deacon presides at the celebration, he acts in accord with his ministry in regard to the greetings, the prayers, the gospel reading and homily, the giving of communion, and the dismissal and blessing. He wears the vestments proper to his ministry, that is, the alb with stole, and, as circumstances suggest, the dalmatic. He uses the presidential chair.

39.    A lay person who leads the assembly acts as one among equals, in the way followed in the liturgy of the hours when not presided over by an ordained minister, and in the case of blessings when the minister is a lay person ("May the Lord bless us . . ."; "Let us praise the Lord . . ."). The lay person is not to use words that are proper to a priest or deacon and is to omit rites that are too readily associated with the Mass, for example, greetings – especially "The Lord be with you" – and dismissals, since these might give the impression that the lay person is a sacred minister.[33]

40.    The lay leader wears vesture that is suitable for his or her function or the vesture prescribed by the bishop.[34] He or she does not use the presidential chair, but another chair prepared outside the sanctuary.[35] Since the altar is the table of sacrifice and of the paschal banquet, its only use in this celebration is for the rite of communion, when the consecrated bread is placed on it before communion is given.

Preparation of the celebration should include careful attention to suitable distribution of offices, for example, for the readings, the singing, etc., and also to the arrangement and decoration of the place of celebration.

41.    The following is an outline of the elements of the celebration.

    a.    Introductory rites. The purpose of these is to form the gathered faithful into a community and for them to dispose themselves for the celebration.

    b . of the word. Here God speaks to his people, to disclose to them the mystery of redemption and salvation; the people respond through the profession of faith and the general intercessions.

    c.    Thanksgiving. Here God is blessed for his great glory (see no. 45).

    d.    Communion rites. These are an expression and accomplishment of communion with Christ and with his members, especially with those who on this same day take part in the eucharistic sacrifice.

    e.    Concluding rites. These point to the connection existing between the liturgy and the Christian life.

The conference of bishops, or the individual bishop himself, may, in view of the conditions of the place and the people involved, determine more precisely the details of the celebration, using resources prepared by the national or diocesan liturgical committee, but the general structure of the celebration should not be changed unnecessarily.

42.    In the introduction at the beginning of the celebration, or at some other point, the leader should make mention of the community of the faithful with whom the parish priest (pastor) is celebrating the eucharist on that

---

[51]    General Instruction of the Liturgy of the Hours (hereafter, GILH), no. 22: DOL 426, no. 3452

[52]    Congregation for the Doctrine of the Faith, *Epistle...on certain questions regarding the minister of the eucharist*, 6 August 1983: AAS 75 (1983), 1007

[33]    See GILH, no. 258: DOL 426, no. 3688; see also The Roman Ritual, *A Book of Blessings*, nos. 48, 119, 130, 181

[34]    See The Roman Ritual, *Holy Communion and Worship of the Eucharist outside Mass*, no. 20: DOL 266, NO. 2098

[35]    See GILH, no. 258: DOL 426, no. 3688

Sunday and urge the assembly to unite itself in spirit with that community.

43.     In order that the participants may retain the word of God, there should be an explanation of the readings or a period of silence for reflection on what has been heard. Since only a priest or a deacon may give a homily,[36] it is desirable that the parish priest (pastor) prepare a homily and give it to the leader of the assembly to be read. But in this matter the decisions of the conference of bishops are to be followed.

44.     The general intercessions are to follow an established series of intentions.[37] Intentions for the whole diocese that the bishop may have proposed are not to be omitted. There would also often be intentions for vocations to sacred orders, for the bishop, and for the parish priest (pastor).

45.     The thanksgiving may follow either one of the ways described here.

1. After the general intercessions or after holy communion, the leader invites all to an act of thanksgiving, in which the faithful praise the glory and mercy of God. This can be done by use of a psalm (for example, Psalms 100, 113, 118, 136, 147, 150), a hymn (for example, the *Gloria*), a canticle (for example, the *Canticle of Mary*), or a litanic prayer. The leader and the faithful stand, and facing the altar, together recite the thanksgiving.

2. Before the Lord's Prayer, the leader of the assembly goes to the tabernacle or other place where the eucharist is reserved and, after making a reverence, places the ciborium with the holy eucharist on the altar. Then while kneeling before the altar he or she together with all the faithful sing or recite a hymn, psalm, or litany, which in this case is directed to Christ in the eucharist.

But this thanksgiving is not in any way to take the form of the eucharistic prayer, the texts of prefaces of eucharistic prayers from *The Roman Missal (Sacramentary)* are not to be used, and all danger of confusion is to be removed.

46.     For the communion rite the provisions given in the Roman Ritual for communion outside Mass are to be observed.[38] The faithful are to be frequently reminded that even when they receive communion outside Mass they are united to the eucharistic sacrifice.

47.     For communion, if at all possible, bread consecrated that same Sunday in a Mass celebrated elsewhere is used; a deacon or lay person brings it in a ciborium or pyx and places it in the tabernacle before the celebration. Bread consecrated at the last Mass celebrated in the place of assembly may also be used. Before the Lord's Prayer the leader goes to the tabernacle or place where the eucharist is reserved, takes the vessel with the body of the Lord, and places it upon the table of the altar, then introduces the Lord's Prayer – unless the act of thanksgiving mentioned in no. 45, 2 is to take place at this point.

48.     The Lord's Prayer is always recited or sung by all, even if there is to be no communion. The sign of peace may be exchanged. After communion, "a period of silence may be observed or a psalm or song of praise may be sung."[39] A thanksgiving as described in no. 45, 1 may also take place here.

49.     Before the conclusion of the assembly, announcements or notices related to the life of the parish or the diocese are read.

50.     "Too much importance can never be attached to the Sunday assembly, whether as the source of the Christian life of the individual and of the community, or as a sign of God's intent to gather the whole human race together in Christ.

"All Christians must share the conviction that they cannot live their faith or participate – in the manner proper to them – in the universal mission of the Church unless they are nourished by the eucharistic bread. They should be equally convinced that the Sunday assembly is a sign to the world of the mystery of communion, which is the eucharist."[40]

On 21 May 1988 this Directory, prepared by the Congregation for Divine Worship, was approved and confirmed by Pope John Paul II, who also ordered its publication.

Office of the Congregation for Divine Worship, Solemnity of the Body and Blood of Christ,

2 June 1988.

Paul Augustin Cardinal Mayer, OSB
Prefect

Virgilio Noé
Titular Archbishop of Voncaria
Secretar

---

[36]     See CIC, can. 766-767
[37]     See General Instruction of the Roman Missal, nos. 45-47: DOL 208, nos. 1435-1435
[38]     See The Roman Ritual, *Holy Communion and Worship of the Eucharist outside Mass*, ch. 1: DOL 266, nos. 2092-2103
[39]     Ibid., no. 37
[40]     John Paul II, Address to the bishops of France on the occasion of their *ad limina* visit, 27 March 1987

EPISCOPAL COMMISSION FOR LITURGY
CANADIAN CONFERENCE OF CATHOLIC BISHOPS

# PASTORAL LETTER
## SUNDAY CELEBRATIONS OF THE WORD:
## GATHERING IN THE EXPECTATION OF THE EUCHARIST

### INTRODUCTION

For some years now, a number of Christian communities have no longer been assured of the regular presence of a priest to preside at the Sunday Eucharist. Indeed, this situation became so widespread that on 30 June, 1988, at the specific request of the Holy Father, the Congregation for Divine Worship published a *Directory for Sunday Celebrations in the Absence of a Priest.*[1]

This novel situation calls for previously unforeseen pastoral arrangements to sustain the Sunday assembly. In the absence of the pastor or another priest, deacons or lay man and women are called to lead the Sunday prayer of the community. These celebrations are appropriately call "Sunday Celebrations of the Word", for this indicates their specific liturgical character. However, to recognize clearly their relationship to the Eucharist, they might also be called by the fuller title, "Sunday Celebrations of the Word in Anticipation of the Eucharist".

Such celebrations are necessary in the circumstances, and in themselves have a positive value. Nonetheless the Church can never accept as inevitable or desirable the situation which gives rise to them. The Eucharist is the very centre of the Church's life. The Second Vatican Council taught this clearly when it said, "The aim and object of apostolic works is that all who are made children of God by faith and baptism should come together to praise God in the midst of his Church, to take part in the sacrifice, and to eat the Lord's Supper".[2] At the same time the Church's constant tradition has always upheld the necessary link between the celebration of the Eucharist and the ministry of the ordained priesthood. Where communities are deprived of the ability to celebrate the Eucharist because of the lack of priests, Sunday Celebrations of the Word must be viewed only as an interim measure, and never as a solution.

We recognize that this situation is a source of real distress for a large number of our Catholic communities. For this reason, we earnestly ask the prayers of the Catholic people of our land that God will provide our Church with the means to have the priests who are needed to preside at the celebration of what is "the source and the apex of the whole Christian life".[3]

Throughout our country, gathering on Sunday for the Eucharist has been an almost constant norm, in fidelity to the tradition going back to the very beginnings of the Church. After Christ's resurrection, his disciples gathered to share "the Lord's Supper" in his memory (1 Cor 11.20). Since then, faithful to Christ's command, the Church assembles each Sunday as for a weekly Easter, and celebrates in the Eucharist his dying and rising.

The bishops have never ceased to recall to all the baptized the importance, indeed the obligation, of assembling each Sunday for the Eucharist. In a 1986 message to the faithful, "The Meaning of Sunday in a Pluralistic Society,"[4] the Canadian bishops clearly reaffirmed the call to keep Sunday in its fullest sense as the Lord's Day, for it should be for all people, "a day of playfulness and simplicity, of contemplation, of wonder, of praise and enjoyment of life".

In continuing to uphold the Sunday assembly as essential to the Church's life, the 1988 Roman document took account of a variety of questions and situations. Moreover, it provided guidelines for the decisions that are to be made about the form of Sunday celebrations when there is no priest. The *Directory* leaves to each bishop the task of determining the conditions for its application in his own diocese.

The present document, prepared at the request of the Episcopal Commission for Liturgy of the Canadian Conference of Catholic Bishops, is intended to help local churches to implement the principles of the *Directory*. Some theological considerations and other pastoral notes are provided to indicate the directions that Christian communities might take in the preparation of Sunday worship when a priest is lacking.

Although these notes are designed primarily with parish communities in mind, the principles here set forth are also applicable to similar situations – hospitals, prisons, senior citizens' homes, for example – where there are Sunday liturgical celebrations other than the Eucharist.

It is important that these Sunday Celebrations of the Word respect the aspirations of the people of God to "be Church" by remaining truly vital Christian communities. It is hoped that they will sustain and foster a true love of the Scriptures. Let them also stir up a burning desire for the Eucharist, that saving mystery which makes us one in faith through the risen Christ, our one and eternal Pastor.

† Raymond Saint-Gelais
  Évêque de Nicolet
  Président de la Commission
  épiscopal de liturgie
29 August 1992

† Raymond J. Lahey
  Bishop of St. George's
  Chairman, Episcopal
  Commission for Liturgy

---

[1] The complete text was originally published in *National Bulletin on Liturgy*, no. 117 (June 1989), pp.108-119. See also related articles in *National Bulletin on Liturgy*, no 139 (Winter 1994).

[2] *Sacrosanctum Concilium* (Constitution on the Liturgy), no. 10

[3] *Lumen Gentium* (Constitution on the Church), no. 11.

[4] Pastoral Reflections by the Canadian Conference of Catholic Bishops, 4 September 1986.

# CONTENTS OF PASTORAL LETTER

# PART ONE
# THEOLOGICAL CONSIDERATIONS
## SUNDAY IN THE CHRISTIAN CONTEXT

### Significance of Sunday as a Day of Gathering

1.  Church history teaches us that from the very beginning Christians gathered on Sunday. The four Gospels (Mt 28.1; Mk 16.2; Lk 24.1; Jn 20.6) and the Acts of the Apostles (20.6-12) describe the life and practice of the first Christians. They insist on the importance to them of the first day of the week, the day the Risen Lord has revealed to his disciples. From the Resurrection day itself (Jn 20.19; Lk 24.33), Christ's disciples have kept Sunday as a day to gather.

2.  Texts from the first centuries of Christianity give witness to the constancy of this practice. At the beginning of the second century, the *Didache* prescribed: On the . . . Day of the Lord, come together and break bread and give thanks, having first confessed your transgressions, that your sacrifice may be pure."[5] In the same period, Pliny, the Roman governor of Bithynia, noted of the Christians of his region that "it was their habit on a fixed day to assemble before daylight and to recite by turns a form of words to Christ as a God."

Similarly, the writer Justin in his *Apology,* a work written about 150 A.D., said that on Sundays Christians, whether they lived in the towns or in the countryside, gathered for worship in one place.

3.  Linked from the beginning to the Resurrection, the Sunday assembly was a standard feature not only of the apostolic age, but also of the centuries which followed. Christians would accept martyrdom rather than forsake common Sunday worship: "We ought to be together. We cannot live without the Lord's meal; it is more important for us than life itself."[6] Prior to the time of the Emperor Constantine, when Sunday was not yet a day of rest, Christians would gather for the breaking of the bread before taking up their daily work. In Canada, our own ancestors showed the same fidelity to Sunday worship. Especially in less populous areas, and even to relatively recently times, lay people frequently led the local community in Sunday prayer in situations where

Mass might be celebrated only quarterly or even twice a year.

4.  As these few examples show, Christians have always considered the Sunday assembly indispensable. In it is experienced both the encounter with the Risen Lord and the need of his active and life-giving presence until his return in glory. For this reason the Church has always affirmed the vital necessity of the Sunday assembly, which anticipates that new world in which God's people will be gathered and of which they have a part even now.

### Preaching the Word and Sharing the Eucharist

5.  The gathering of the baptized on the Lord's Day is the gathering of a community which celebrates the Eucharist in Christ's memory. If Christians assemble, it is because they have been called together to encounter Christ. This is an encounter in the form of a dialogue. It includes listening, silence, and contemplation, as well as times of prayer, of praise, and of thanksgiving. In this exchange, God's people leave themselves open to God's tender care. They recall and re-live the memory of God's wondrous deeds and steadfast love as they are nourished at "the table of God's Word and of Christ's body."[7]

6.  The Second Vatican Council restored to the Word of God that same importance it held during the first five centuries of the Church.[8] The readings from the Old Testament, from the Gospels, and from the other New Testament writings, together spread before the people of God a marvellous feast, breaking open for them the mystery of salvation in all its splendour. In the proclamation of the Word Christ is present to his people.[9] Including also the singing of the Psalm which contains echoes of the first reading, the acclamation to Christ present in the Word, and the homily which brings word and life together, the liturgy of the Word forms a key moment in the dialogue between God and the gathered Church.

7.  Thus formed by the Word and brought together in a communion of faith, Christians celebrate the liturgy of the

---

[5]  Didache (Teaching of the Twelve Apostles) XIV, 1, quoted in *A New Eusebius: Documents Illustrative of the History of the Church to A.D. 337,* ed. J. Stevenson (London: SPCK 1965) p. 129.

[6]  Pliny, Epistola, X. 96.7, quoted in ibid., p. 13.

[7]  Justin, *Apologia,* I, LXVII, *The Ante-Nicene Fathers: Translations of the Writings of the Fathers down to A.D. 325,* ed. Alexander Rogers and James Donaldson (Grand Rapids: Eerdmans 1979), I, p. 186. The text reads in part: "And on the day called Sunday, all who live in cities or in the country gather together in one place, and the memoirs of the apostles or the writings of the prophets are read, ...the president verbally instructs and exhorts to the imitation of these good things. Then we all rise together and pray, and ...when our prayer is ended, bread and wine and water are brought and the president in like manner offers prayers and thanksgivings...and the people assent, saying Amen; and there is a distribution to each, and a participation of that over which thanks have been given, and to those who are absent a portion is sent by the deacons.... But Sunday is the day on which we all hold our common assembly, because it is the first day, on which God, having wrought a change in darkness and matter, made the world; and Jesus Christ our Saviour on the same day rose from the dead."

[8]  W. Rordorf, *Liturgie, foi et vie des premiers chrétiens,* p. 45.

[9]  *General Instruction of the Roman Missal,* no. 8.

Eucharist. Through the ministry of the priest, acting in the name of Christ and on behalf of the assembly, the Church becomes obedient to the command of the Lord Jesus at the Last Supper: "Take this all of you, and eat it: this is my body . . . . Take this all of you, and drink from it: this is the cup of my blood . . . shed for you and for all. Do this in memory of me." The Church does what Christ did. It brings forward the gifts, gives thanks to God, breaks and shares the bread which has been consecrated, and dispenses the cup of salvation. It is the Eucharist that is the cornerstone of the Church, for here, as the memory of the Lord's deeds is celebrated, they are made sacramentally present. Here the Church is brought into being, formed and renewed. Here Christ's Body grows in unity through that same life of Christ which is shared by each of its members. Christians feed upon that which they are and are called to be, the body of Christ, for the eucharistic body is the foundation of the ecclesial Body: "This bread that we break, is it not a sharing in the body of Christ? Because there is one bread, we who are many are one body, for we partake of the one bread." (1 Cor 10.16-17)

### Building Up the Church and Witness

8.    In welcoming the Word and in giving thanks to the one who saves them, God's gathered people form the Church, the community of disciples and witnesses to the resurrection. The community of believers does not less than give witness in the world to that presence of the Risen Saviour who never ceases to give life to the Church. The faithful thus strive to become a community which has but "one heart and soul." (Acts 4.32)

9.    The life of the first Christian communities shows us that the ideal is not always easy to attain. Voluntary sharing conflicted with individualism (Acts 5. 1-12; 6.1; 2 Cor 8.1-24). At Corinth, some Christians even dared to eat and drink in the presence of their hungry sisters and brothers without sharing their food (1 Cor 11.21). In communities of mixed Jewish and pagan origins, cultural diversity created considerable tensions. Yet, however great, these tensions could never overpower that unity which has its roots in Christ. It is Christ who encounters the community gathered in faith, who is its foundation, who challenges it, and who binds it together. Whenever Christians gather on Sunday they continue to make a statement about Church, responsive to the call of their Lord to live in communion, whatever their roots, or their pinions, their age or social status, their race or culture. Even when those assembled are few, the community is a sign within the world of God's transcendence and love. They make present within a given area the Church of Christ. They proclaim that for them the Risen Lord is life and that his gospel is the light of life. The gathering for Sunday eucharist is the expression of a Church whose mission is in the world. This gathering, the preeminent place of encounter with the Lord is truly a grace, with no less a power than to transform the human condition.

### Gathering in Anticipation of the Eucharist

10.    In certain areas, due to the lack of priests, communities are unable regularly to celebrate the Sunday Eucharist. When they continue to gather on that day, they are not thereby any less responsive to the call of the Risen Christ, but their assembly is not lived out in its fullest form, which is the Eucharist. It is for this reason that we can, in a more particular way, speak here of "Sunday Celebrations of the Word *in anticipation of the Eucharist.*" This should not suggest that they are not authentic liturgical celebrations in themselves nor should it obscure the truth that every other liturgy finds its completion only in the Eucharist. At the same time it must be recognized that while these celebrations look forward to the day when the Eucharist will again be celebrated within the community, they also flow from the Eucharist and are the worship of a community which has been sustained by it. In this context, however, the particular designation "in anticipation of the Eucharist" recognizes the hope of the assembly that it may once more, and soon, celebrate in all its fullness "the mystery of faith."

## STRENGTHS AND LIMITATIONS

A brief look at the strengths and limitations of the Sunday assembly in this form is in order.

### A True Sunday Assembly

11.    When we speak of a non-eucharistic Sunday celebration as an assembly, we recognize an invitation and a response. The Sunday gathering of God's people is important in itself. Each community which assembles to hear God's word is truly Church, and Christ is always present in it. It possesses a common faith and a unity flows from diversity; it is in communion with the Church throughout the world. In this manner, those gathered in Christ's name form the Church in that place and give witness to its presence. When the assembly holds fast to Sunday (the Lord's Day), it does so because it is of vital necessity for personal faith as well as for the faith of the Church, a need experienced since Easter Day itself. Indeed, any celebration of Sunday is always a celebration of the Lord's Paschal Mystery, in which the whole Church dies with Christ, is buried, and rises with him.

### A Liturgical Act

12.    The Sunday celebration of the Word is truly liturgy. It is the saving action of Christ the Head among his people and the work of his Body which is the Church. Gathered on that day when the Church throughout the world keeps memory of the Risen Lord, the faithful of a particular parish proclaim the Father's glory, through the Son, in the communion of the Holy Spirit. This assembly which gathers to celebrate God's Word[10] truly celebrates the liturgy in union with the members of the Church universal.

---

[10]    It is taught in the Constitution on Divine Revelation (*Dei Verbum*): "The Church has always venerated the divine Scriptures as she venerated the Body of the Lord, insofar as she never ceases, particularly in the sacred liturgy, to partake of the bread of life and to offer it to the faithful from the one table of the Word of God and the Body of Christ." no. 21.

### A Gathered Church Gives Thanks and Praise to God

13. This Sunday celebration honours the Father by giving thanks for the salvation so freely given through the death and resurrection of Christ. Those who gather on Sunday to welcome with joy God's saving word truly give thanks to the Father even when circumstances do not permit them to celebrate the Eucharist, the Church's greatest prayer of thanksgiving.

### The Presence of Christ

14. When he ascended into heaven Christ did not cease to be present to his Church. The Second Vatican Council recalled, when it underlined the various modes of his presence, that "to accomplish so great a work Christ is always present in his Church, especially in her liturgical celebrations . . . . He is present in his word, since it is he himself who speaks when the holy scriptures are read in the Church. Lastly, he is present when the Church prays and sings, for he has promised 'when two or three are gathered together in my name there I am in the midst of them' (Mt 18.20)."[11] Thus the assembly which gathers on Sunday is itself a place of Christ's presence; it hears his word, by which Christ becomes present anew.

15. Christ is also present under the form of the bread which has been consecrated at an earlier celebration of the Eucharist when this is given and shared in communion at a Sunday celebration of the Word. But Pope Paul VI reminds us that "this presence is called the real presence not to exclude the other kinds as though they were not real, but because it is real par excellence."[12] Thus even when communion does not take place, the presence of Christ spoken of by Vatican II is truly realized in this form of Sunday celebration, for it is in the full sense a liturgical action.

### Discovering the Ministries and Gifts of the Community

16. Sunday celebrations of the Word require an even greater involvement of the laity than might otherwise be the case. Obviously even apart from the celebration of the Eucharist the important liturgical ministries of hospitality, proclaiming the Word, cantor, choir and music leader, communion, acolyte, environment, etc., are still needed. In the absence of a priest, however, for Sunday celebrations of the Word, some will be called to new ministries: the coordination of other ministries, leadership of the liturgical assembly, and preaching God's Word. In this way the faithful are often helped to rediscover the priestly character of their baptism, which endows them with a mission to acclaim throughout the world the presence of the living God. From the teamwork which is essential to a community preparing such liturgies can flow a new sense of the whole celebrating community as the primary subject of worship: the Body of Christ, united by him and animated by his presence, and yet with its variety of persons and gifts.

### Renewing the Church's Mission

17. The liturgical assembly always comes from the world of daily life, and is sent forth from the liturgy into that world. When on Sundays God's word is proclaimed in the midst of the whole community, when it is heard in faith, and when it is kept in the lives of those who have heard it, the Church is fortified to declare the Gospel in the world around it. Indeed, the power of Christ present in his word refreshes the Church, which experiences the same earthly situation as humanity in general, that it may be "a leaven and kind of soul for human society as it is to be renewed in Christ and transformed into God's family."[13] From its worship, always both summit and source of the Church's activity, comes the mission of the community in, to, and for the world.[14] Thus the Sunday celebration of the Word truly inspires and directs the encounter with human activity and culture, so that Christians, in solidarity with the whole human family, may give witness to Jesus Christ and service to those in need.

### Absence of the Celebration of the Eucharist

18. The rich character of a Sunday celebration of the Word which anticipates a future eucharistic celebration should not lead us to overlook its limitations by contrast with the celebration of the Eucharist itself. It is not the Eucharist, for it does not make present the fullness of Christ's saving action. Deacons or lay persons who lead it are not ordained to act in the name of the Church, and therefore in Christ's person, in the offering of the Eucharist. They are thus unable to do, in his memory, what Christ did – all those things brought together for us in the liturgy of the Eucharist – to take bread and cup, and having given thanks to God, to break the bread and offer the cup that those assembled might receive of them. Even if at a Sunday celebration the eucharistic sacrament is shared, one is not celebrating the Eucharist. For the Eucharist is not only sacramental communion with Christ's body. It presumes the echoing of Christ's words and actions by the bishop or the priest, thereby enabling the Church to make present anew Christ's gift of himself to the Father and to be one with him in his action.

### Absence of Ordained Ministry

19. The Church, the People of God, has as its Head the Christ who brings it together through the strength of his Spirit. The Sunday eucharistic assembly is the premier visible sign of this great mystery. The bishop or priest who

---

[11]  "He is present in his word since it is he himself who speaks when the holy scriptures are read in the Church." *Sacrosanctum Concilium*, no. 7.

[12]  See the recommendations in *Sacrosanctum Concilium*, no. 35 (4), and in the *Directory for Sunday Celebrations in the Absence of a Priest*, nos. 20, 32, 35.

[13]  *Sacrosanctum Concilium*, no. 7.

[14]  *Mysterium Fidei* (Encyclical on the Doctrine and Worship of the Eucharist, 3 September 1965), no. 39

presides at the eucharistic gathering signifies the presence of Christ the Head with his Body, the Church. Presbyter and bishop, by virtue of ordination, also represent the bond of communion between this assembly and the local and universal Church. Because Sunday celebrations of the Word take place in the absence of bishop and priest they lack one of the sacramental signs of Christ's presence and of that communion which is a mark of his Church.

20.    A deacon has as his liturgical ministry to proclaim the Gospel and to direct the Church's prayer. When he is called upon to preside at a Sunday celebration of the Word, it is in consequence of the ministry given him by ordination.[15] Although the homily is normally the ministry of the bishop or priest who presides at the proclamation of the Word, a deacon may give the homily when a priest or bishop is absent.

21.    The lay person who leads Sunday worship has not the sacramental ordination empowering him or her to preside over the building up of the Church and its gathering together. Instead, such lay persons serve their baptized sisters and brothers in virtue of the mission given them in the sacraments of Christian initiation. When ordained ministers are unavailable, lay persons who preside may preach or lead a reflection on the Word of God, provided they have been authorized to do this by the bishop.[16]

## Possibility of Confusion

22.    Obviously something so new to most of the Church can lead to misunderstanding. Some would wonder whether this practice was not a significant move from our tradition as a Eucharistic Church toward a Church of the Word. Others would question whether by having other Sunday celebrations "in parallel" to the Mass, the Eucharist and the priesthood are not thereby devalued. For those more directly involved, there can be further areas of confusion. Although Catholics may readily understand that such celebrations and the Eucharist are "technically" different, they may have difficulty in appreciating the *effective* difference when what is for them the fullest mode of participation in the Eucharist, that is, the reception of communion, takes place in both. In terms of ministries, there is always a danger that the ordained priesthood, when it is not actively involved in the day-to-day pastoring of the community, may be perceived as an intrusion in terms of the lay ministries in place. The reverse, too, is possible. Finally, there can be confusion about the status of communities; are those which are unable to celebrate regularly the Sunday Eucharist somehow second-class to those which do? It is because the possibilities for misunderstanding are so present in this situation that the greatest care must be taken in its implementation.

---

[15]   *Gaudium et Spes* (Constitution on the Church in the Modern World), no. 40

[16]   *Sacrosanctum Concilium*, no. 10.

# PART TWO
# PASTORAL CONSIDERATIONS[17]

## PASTORAL EVALUATION

### Making the Decision

23.   In keeping with the *Directory* (no. 24), "It belongs to the diocesan bishop, after hearing the council of presbyters, to decide whether Sunday assemblies without the celebration of the Eucharist should be held on a regular basis in his diocese. It belongs also to the bishop, after considering the place and persons involved, to set out both general and particular norms for such celebrations. These assemblies are therefore to be conducted only in virtue of their convocation by the bishop and only under the pastoral ministry of the parish priest (pastor)."

### Process for Deciding

24.   Before arriving at a decision, the bishop and his advisers ought to take account of the places of worship within the diocese, the number of eucharistic celebrations in each of the parishes, the possibility of cooperation among the priests of a given area, and the geographic and demographic factors involved. They would need to be aware of the people in such areas capable of leading their Sunday assemblies, and how they might be provided with the necessary resources. Further, they would want to avoid that in the same place there would occur both the celebration of the Eucharist and a Sunday celebration of the Word for the same Sunday (*Directory*, no. 21).

### Implementing the Decision

25.   An appropriate catechesis should be given to the faithful of the parish before such a practice begins (*Directory*, no. 26). This might be done by way of pastoral letters, the parish bulletin, through workshops and special meetings of the community, or through other means of communication appropriate to the particular situation.

26.   The catechetical component of preparation should point out the differences between the two types of the Sunday assembly, especially as it deals with the presider and the nature of the liturgy in each case. It is important that such explanations should be clear enough to eliminate any misunderstanding or confusion (*Directory*, no. 22). The overall information given to the people to prepare them for this reality should present new practice in a balanced manner. The faithful can be helped to see its importance and its value without its drawbacks being minimized. Its character as a celebration "in anticipation of

the celebration of the Eucharist" obviously deserves particular attention.

27.   It will also be essential to provide proper formation for those called to provide a service to the Church in leading these assemblies. Such persons should be aware of the character of a non-eucharistic Sunday celebration, of its structure as distinct from the celebration of the Eucharist, and of the particular role which is theirs. In this way, their words, gestures and demeanour will be tailored to the concrete circumstances and will not engender confusion either as to the nature of the celebration or their own ministry within the Church. Proper liturgical formation for those who lead the Sunday assembly would seek to provide them with the competency and the confidence they require. Indeed it would be preferable if teams of people – presiders, musicians, readers, communion ministers – were prepared together, since in this way a variety of ministries may best be encouraged and the nature of these assemblies as celebrations of the whole Christian community may be made more evident.

### The Form of Celebration

28.   Two forms of liturgical gathering are proposed by the *Directory*: celebration of the Liturgy of the Word, and celebration of the Liturgy of the Hours. Similar to one another because of their scriptural content, each of these celebrations of the Word has distinctive features. The Liturgy of the Word celebrates in a preeminent way the unfolding mystery of Christ and salvation as this is recalled in a structured manner during the course of the liturgical year. Its principal elements are organized in a manner similar to the liturgy of the Word which forms the first part of the eucharistic celebration, although the two are not identical; these features focus the assembly on the mystery of salvation realized in Christ and lived out by the Church. The Liturgy of the Hours is also a celebration of God's Word, but above all it calls the community to praise and wonder. It draws upon the treasury of hymns and psalms which has preserved the content of the traditional prayer of our ancestors in faith.

### With or Without Communion

29.   Vatican II recalled the importance, for "that more complete form of participation in the Mass," of receiving the Body of the Lord from the same eucharistic celebration, for it is both sacrifice and banquet.[18] The instruction

---

[17]   *Lumen Gentium*, no. 29

[18]   *Code of Canon Law*, canon 766; see also Decree no. 6 of the Canadian Conference of Catholic Bishops, 23 October 1984. This decree provides that the diocesan bishop may permit lay persons to preach in such situations.

on the worship of the Eucharist (1967) laid down an even more precise directive that the faithful should receive "hosts consecrated at the Mass," that communion may stand out more clearly through signs as a participation in the sacrifice actually being celebrated.[19] This ought to be the normal practice.

30. Does it follow that communion should not take place apart from the celebration of the Eucharist? Pastoral considerations certainly suggest a more cautious approach. The *Directory* itself provides for communion, although it foresees celebrations without it, and it makes the important point that the faithful are called to gather on Sunday to hear God's Word and to give thanks even when communion will not take place.[20] Before deciding as a practice to have or not to have communion during the Sunday celebrations of the Word, the effects of this on the life and outlook of the community would need careful evaluation.

31. Those involved in the preparation of these celebrations, as well as the local pastor, will have to reflect on the repercussions of a decision one way or the other. A practice varied according to time and circumstances, and carefully presented through an appropriate catechesis, may be preferable to a decision made once and for all either for or against sharing communion within the framework of such celebrations. It is important that the community itself be encouraged to reflect upon the important theological, liturgical and pastoral considerations involved in this decision.


## COMPARISON WITH THE EUCHARIST

### Connection with the Eucharist

32. At the beginning of each Sunday celebration of the Word, it would seem fitting to call to mind the link with celebrations of the Eucharist taking place elsewhere, or with the last celebration of the Eucharist to have taken place in the community. It is in union with these eucharistic assemblies that the local community prepares to give thanks to the Father for the salvation made its own by Christ's dying and rising.

33. The scripture readings proclaimed are those from the liturgical cycle. Thus the faithful are fed at the same table of the Word as their brothers and sisters who take part in the celebration of the Eucharist on the same day.

34. When the distribution of communion takes place, the blessed sacrament should be formally brought into the assembly. A person designated at a Eucharistic celebration in another place might bring the ciborium from there and place it on the altar. A second possibility is that the ciborium be clearly seen to be brought from the tabernacle to the altar before the members of the community are invited to come to share the Bread of Life. In these ways the communion ministers indicate that they are sharing in a prior celebration of the Eucharist in which Christ became present sacramentally to his Church. By the bringing of the blessed sacrament to the altar and by a suitable introduction, the community will understand that communion is always a participation in the celebration of the Eucharist of an assembly previously gathered and is directed always to the communion of the Church itself.

### The Differences

35. Those who prepare these Sunday celebrations of the Word will recognize that the rite is far from identical to the way in which the celebration of Mass takes place. Of the two forms suggested, that of the Liturgy of the Hours more clearly indicates the distinctive nature of this gathering.

36. On the other hand, a Liturgy of the Word in which the biblical texts are proclaimed in the usual order of Sunday worship is more familiar to the assembly. In this form, fellowship with other Christians who are gathered on this same day to celebrate the Eucharist becomes more tangible. As a general principle, to have Sunday celebrations from time to time according to each of the two approved forms will both help to avoid routine and provide the experience of different ways of giving thanks to the Lord.

37. Whatever the form chosen, the preparation of the gifts is always omitted, and the prayer of thanksgiving is always found at a place other than that which is usual for the eucharistic prayer. Further, it should have neither the structure nor the content of the eucharistic prayer; the epiclesis, and the institution narrative are never used. If there is communion, the breaking of the bread and its accompanying chant, "Lamb of God . . .", are omitted, and communion is given from the reserved sacrament or brought from a celebration of the Eucharist elsewhere, and only under the form of bread.

38. It should be added further that the increase in Sunday celebrations of the Word places a new and serious obligation upon those responsible for celebrations for the Eucharist to see that those rites proper to the Eucharist are observed with great emphasis and dignity. These distinctive elements include the preparation of the gifts, the eucharistic prayer, the breaking of the bread and its chant, communion under both forms, and communion from the sacrament consecrated at the same celebration. No less than those who plan Sunday celebrations of the Word, those who prepare eucharistic celebrations must ensure also that the differences between the two are clearly recognized and understood by the community.

39. A further major difference between a Sunday celebration of the Word and a celebration of the Eucharist is the ministerial status of those who lead them. Only a bishop or a priest can preside at the Eucharist. In most cases it will be lay persons who conduct Sunday celebrations of the Word. They act in virtue of their baptism and confir-

---

[19] Chapter 2 of the *Directory* deals with many of these issues.
[20] *Sacrosanctum Concilium*, no. 55

mation, and have been delegated to serve in the absence of a priest, not to replace him. A deacon, however, who fulfils this function acts not by delegation but in virtue of his own ministry.

40.    The non-ordained who lead such celebrations do not use the usual place of the presider at Eucharist. They lead from another place appropriate to the nature of the service they are performing, but also to the nature of this assembly and to their ministry within the Church. Thus the usual presidential chair, a symbol of the ministry of the bishop or priest, would remain empty.[21] It is still important to find a place from which a lay presider can effectively lead the prayer of the assembly, while indicating, even in terms of physical set-up, that the presider gives thanks to the Lord in union with the assembly. A place in the front of the church, in full view, perhaps closer to the ambo than to the altar, would seem appropriate.

41.    Lay presiders greet the assembly and invoke God's blessing using a different formula: one that uses the first person plural. They sit to listen to the biblical readings or to take part in the singing of the psalms, but the position of the chair must not hinder the view of or access to the ambo, since it must be used by other ministers.

42.    The presider would come to the ambo to lead the reflection which follows the proclamation of the readings or to deliver a text prepared by the priest who services the community. Alternatively, another person may be designated to do these things.

43.    The dismissal takes place from the place chosen to lead the assembly, with the use of the form "Let us go in the peace of Christ," or a similar formula.

44.    A deacon may preside from the area used by the ordained presider. However, he should not use the priest's chair, but a chair placed to the right of the presidential chair. A deacon would use the usual formulas proper to the ordained ministry.

45.    The *Directory* (no. 40) leaves it to the bishop to decide upon the form of vesture for the lay person who leads the Sunday celebration of the Word. When deacons are called to preside, they wear the vestments proper to their ministry – the alb and stole.

---

[21]    *Eucharisticum Mysterium* (Instruction on the worship of the Eucharist, 25 May 1967), no. 31; see also the General Instruction of the Roman Missal, no. 56h
[22]    *Directory,* nos 20, 32, 35
[23]    *Directory,* no. 40; *A Book of Blessings,* nos 880-881

# LITURGICAL NOTES

## SUNDAY CELEBRATION
## OF THE
## WORD AND HOURS

# CONTENTS

## LITURGICAL NOTES

# PART ONE
# OPTIONS FOR CELEBRATION

## Form of the Celebration: Word or Hours

1.    Four forms of celebration are included in this Ritual: Liturgy of the Word, Liturgy of the Word with Communion, Morning Prayer and Evening Prayer. It is anticipated that a Liturgy of the Word will be the main celebration of the community in order that the three scripture readings of the Sunday may be proclaimed in the assembly. Morning and Evening Prayer are provided for the times when these may be celebrated in addition to the Sunday Celebration of the Word, and even to the Eucharist, or for the times when a Liturgy of the Word is impossible or not pastorally suited to the occasion. It is NOT recommended that the three scriptural readings of the Sunday be proclaimed at Morning or Evening Prayer nor that the rite of the distribution of Communion be added to Morning or Evening Prayer.

## Symbols and Gestures

2.    The use of gestures at liturgy are not restricted to the ordained ministers of the Church. They are used for the benefit of the ritual action and the prayer of community. They are not indications of status within the community. In addition, everything the leader of prayer does is an expression of the prayer of the community, including every posture, movement, action and gesture; therefore a leader of prayer uses the symbols, walks and carries out the actions and gestures as in any liturgy of the Church. These include the signs of the cross at the beginning and conclusion of the rite and at the proclamation of the gospel; the gestures of greeting and prayer; and the use of incense. These are done in a deliberate, unhurried, reverent manner, visible to the community as expression of its own prayer. [See *Formation Notes* nos. 19-25].

3.    The use of incense in any liturgical celebration is optional. Nevertheless, its use, especially in the procession and enthronement of the Lectionary, is recommended and encouraged. [See *Formation Notes* no. 26 and *Liturgical Notes* nos. 21, 64 and 89].

## Place of the Leader of Prayer

4.    Many customs exist across Canada, however the following options are recommended in order of descending preference. In all cases a leader of prayer does not use the presidential chair, which remains empty. This also includes the case when a deacon presides at the liturgy. In the options provided it is emphasized that wherever a leader of prayer is seated, the leader is always a member of the assembly.

   a) *A chair is placed in the sanctuary:* In this option, importance is attached to the role of the leader of prayer to model the action of the assembly.

The leader of prayer not only can be seen by all when addressing the assembly or inviting them to pray, but also when listening to the Word of God and joining the praises of God. In this option the leader stands and sits in a place where he or she can be seen at all times during the celebration and models the action of the assembly, whether listening, singing or praying in silence, as well as leading the assembly in prayer.

   b) *The leader of prayer sits in the front seats of the assembly:* In this option, the leader of prayer sits in the front seats or pews of the church and walks to a place at the front of the church or in the sanctuary whenever addressing the assembly or leading it in prayer.

## Form of the Gathering Rite

5.    Central to the Sunday Celebration of the Word is the procession and enthronement of the Lectionary, accompanied by ministers carrying candles, which takes place after the opening prayer and before the first reading. During this procession the community sings a song or acclamation, the Lectionary is carried in procession and is solemnly enthroned at the lectern (ambo). The procession and enthronement of the Word of God is incorporated into the ritual since the rite is primarily a liturgy of the Word, and it emphasizes the importance of the Word of God in the life of the community, the presence of Christ in the proclaimed word and the unique nature of the celebration.

6.    In order to emphasize the importance of this procession, it is recommended that entrance procession be scaled down. Three options are suggested below.

   a) *Gathering Song without a Procession:* In this option there is no entrance procession. The celebration begins with an introduction by the leader of prayer and the gathering song. Except for the ministers who carry the candles (and incense) and a lector who carries the Lectionary at the Procession and Enthronement of the Word, the ministers take their places in the church before the celebration begins.

   The Lectionary is placed on a suitably covered table or stand near the entrance of the church, or in another appropriate place from which it can be carried later in procession to the lectern (ambo). The lector who will carry the Lectionary and the servers are seated nearby. At the designated time, the leader of prayer stands and goes to the place from which he or she will preside and begins the celebration with the introductory remarks or another option listed below. All stand and join in the song, psalm or acclamation.

b) *Gathering Song with a Procession with the Cross:* In this option there is a simple procession of the Cross accompanied by candles, carried by servers. Except for a lector who carries the Lectionary at the Procession and Enthronement of the Word, and the ministers who will carry the Processional Cross and the candles (and incense), the ministers take their places in the church before the celebration begins.

The Lectionary is placed on a suitably covered table or stand near the entrance of the church, or in another appropriate place from which it can be carried later in procession to the lectern (ambo). The lector who will carry the Lectionary is seated nearby. The Processional Cross and candles are prepared and placed near the entrance of the church. At the designated time, the leader of prayer stands and goes to the place from which he or she will preside and begins the celebration with the introductory remarks. All stand and join in the hymn, psalm or acclamation. During the gathering song, the processional Cross is brought in procession through the church to the sanctuary. The cross-bearer is accompanied by two ministers carrying candles. The processional Cross is placed in an appropriate place, in or near the sanctuary, visible to the assembly. The candles are placed nearby or at the credence table. At the beginning of the Liturgy of the Word, other servers carrying candles accompany the lector who will carry the Lectionary. If only two servers are available to carry candles, these should remain at the entrance of the church for the procession and enthronement of the Word. It is inappropriate for servers to carry candles from the sanctuary to the entrance in order to accompany the lector.

c) *Gathering Song with Procession of the Ministers and the Cross:* In this option there is the usual procession of the ministers, led by servers carrying the processional Cross and candles. All the ministers join in the procession, except the lector who carries the Lectionary and two other servers who carry candles.

The Lectionary is placed on a suitably covered table or stand near the entrance of the church, or in another appropriate place from which it can be carried later in procession to the lectern (ambo). The lector who will carry the Lectionary and the servers who will carry the candles for the enthronement of the Word are seated nearby. The Processional Cross and candles are pre-pared and placed near the entrance of the church. The ministers stand ready to join in the procession during the gathering song. At the designated time, the leader of prayer, or preferably another minister, begins the celebration with the introductory remarks. A leader of song introduces the song. All stand and join in the hymn, psalm or acclamation.

During the gathering song, the processional Cross is brought in procession through the church to the sanctuary. The cross-bearer may be accompanied by two ministers carrying candles. The other ministers and the leader of prayer follow. The processional Cross is placed in an appropriate place, in or near the sanctuary, visible to the assembly. The candles are placed nearby or at the credence table. The ministers go to their designated places.

After the opening prayer, at the beginning of the Liturgy of the Word, the servers carrying the candles lead the lector who carries the Lectionary. If only two servers are available to carry candles, these should remain at the entrance of the church for the procession and enthronement of the Word. It is inappropriate for servers to carry candles from the sanctuary to the entrance in order to accompany the lector.

## Introductory Remarks

7.    The Introductory Remarks serve not only to remind the community that the Eucharist will not be celebrated, but also that the Sunday Celebration is a duly constituted act of worship of the Church and is celebrated in union with the whole Church under the leadership of the local bishop and the Pope. The remarks are provided mainly for those places where the Celebration of the Word alternates with the Celebration of the Eucharist. Therefore, where the Sunday Celebration of the Word is celebrated Sunday after Sunday, they may be adapted or omitted. One of the following options may be selected. Preference is given to the first option. The Introductory Remarks may be made by the leader of prayer or another minister.[1]

a) *Introductory Remarks Precede the Gathering Song:* Since these remarks are introductory and lengthy in nature, it is recommended that they precede the beginning of the celebration (before the gathering song). In this way they do not inhibit the flow of the rite which leads the assembly to prayer.

b) *Introductory Remarks Follow the Liturgical Greeting:* For pastoral reasons, the Introductory Remarks may be made after the liturgical greeting. Care must be taken that they are not made in an off handed manner, but in a way that leads the community to prayer.

[1]    *Directory,* 42.

## Preparatory or Opening Rite

8.    Many options are provided for the introductory rites as a preparation for the Liturgy of the Word. Only one option is used in any celebration. These may be used to highlight the liturgical season, thus the following recommendations are made:

   a) Easter Season: the use of the Thanksgiving and Sprinkling of Holy Water;

   b) Lenten Season: the use of the Penitential Rite or the sung *Kyrie*;

   c) Christmas Season: the use of the sung *Gloria*;

   d) Advent Season: the Litany of Praise or the sung *Kyrie*;

   e) Ordinary Time: the use of the Litany of Praise is recommended in this season, but due to the length of this liturgical season, a variety of options should be used.

9.    The *Kyrie* is essentially an acclamation of praise to the Lord. Although the *Kyrie* and the Season of Advent are sometimes seen as penitential, the character of both is not directly penitential.

## Form of the Profession of Faith

10.    The use of the Apostles' or the Nicene Creed is recommended for use at a Sunday Celebration of the Word. The use of the baptismal form is provided in an Appendix for use on Easter Sunday, as in the celebration of the Eucharist.

## Leading the Communion Rite

11.    Although only one person leads the prayer of the assembly at any celebration, the Ritual makes provision for a minister of communion to conduct the communion rite, when one is held. This should not be seen as two people presiding over the celebration. The rite of the distribution of communion is a separate rite from the liturgy of the word, and the ministry of the distribution of communion outside the Mass is a ministerial function, not a presidential one. Thus when a minister of communion conducts the communion rite, the leader of prayer remains at the place of presiding and presides over the rite.

12.    This provision is optional, more normative is the situation when the leader of prayer also conducts the prayers of the communion rite. In all cases, the person who conducts the communion rite should do so from the altar, facing the assembly. Leading the prayers of the communion rite from the place of presiding over the Liturgy of the Word is inappropriate, since the liturgy must have one focal point at a time.

   a) When the leader of prayer conducts the communion service, he or she remains at his or her place until the ministers of communion have transferred the vessels containing the holy eucharist to the altar. When all is ready the leader comes to altar and begins the rite of distribution of communion.

   b) When a minister of communion conducts the communion service, the leader of prayer remains at the place of presiding, and in silence continues to preside over the celebration.

13.    Whoever leads the rite of communion concludes it with the prayer after communion, either the minister of communion at the altar or the leader of prayer from the altar or the place of presiding.

## PART TWO

# SUNDAY CELEBRATION OF THE WORD

### Introduction

14.   The liturgy of the word is provided in two formats: one for celebrations of the word, and a second for celebrations of the word with a communion service.

15.   The basic format of the liturgy of the word at the eucharist remains largely intact in the Sunday Celebration of the Word with the first reading, responsorial psalm, second reading, gospel acclamation, gospel and homily (reflection), profession of faith, and general intercessions following in order. However, a proclamation of praise is added to the liturgy of the word and is placed immediately after the intercessions as its concluding prayer. The collection is moved to the concluding rite so that it is not confused with the procession of gifts for the eucharist.

16.   The Ritual uses those ritual gestures and symbols which belong to the Church as a whole and which are part of the Catholic heritage and tradition of the Church: the use of the extended hands during greetings and prayers, incensing of the Lectionary, the carrying of candles and incense, the use of the processional cross and the Lectionary, carried in procession.

### Ministers

17.   In addition to the leader of prayer, the following ministers are needed to assist at the celebration of the Liturgy of the Word.
   a) three lectors to proclaim the first reading, the second reading and the gospel;
   b) a cantor/psalmist to sing the verses of the psalm (and the intentions);
   c) a leader of song to lead the assembly in the singing of the hymn and the canticle;
   d) servers to carry the candles and cross, to assist with the holy water and/or incense if either of these is used, to hold the Ritual for the leader of prayer.
   e) communion ministers, if communion is to be given;
   f) ministers of hospitality;
   g) a person to read the intercessions.

### Preparations

18.   The Ritual is placed in a convenient location for use during the celebration. The Ritual is never carried in the entrance procession.

19.   The Lectionary is placed on a suitably covered table near the entrance of the church or in another appropriate place from which it can be brought in procession to the ambo at the beginning of the liturgy of the word. Candles may be placed near the Lectionary, if this can be safely done. Otherwise the candles are placed near-by.

20.   Hymnals and other participation aids should be placed at the chairs of the ministers.

21.   Incense may be used during the enthronement of the Lectionary and at the proclamation of the gospel.

22.   A container of water with a sprinkler should be placed in the sanctuary near the place of the leader of prayer when the rite of thanksgiving and sprinkling of water is used.

23.   Candles for the servers to carry in the entrance procession and/or at the procession of the word should be placed near the entrance of the church; candles may also be placed at the tabernacle for the procession to the altar at the communion rite.

24.   Vessels for the distribution of communion are placed near the tabernacle.

### INTRODUCTORY RITE

25.   In order to mark the distinct character of the *Sunday Celebration of the Word*, the liturgy contains a short preparatory rite, which helps the assembly focus on the word of God and emphasizes that this is a celebration of the word. The introductory remarks help to situate this celebration within the larger context of the worship of the whole church.

26.   The introductory rites of the *Sunday Celebration of the Word* include: the introductory remarks, the sign of the cross, the liturgical greeting, the preparatory or opening rite and the opening prayer. The introductory remarks may also be placed after the liturgical greeting.

27.   The purpose of the introductory rites is to unify the assembly as a priestly people and to prepare the community to listen to the Word of God. Since they are preparatory, the introductory rites are of secondary importance and, therefore, are to be brief.

28.   The introductory rites are to facilitate the worship of the community, and therefore, the use of non-ritual or informal language into the introductory rites disturbs the flow of the liturgy and hinders the cumulative effect of the rites.

### Music

29.   The important elements of the introductory rites are the gathering song and the opening prayer. This fact should be reflected by always singing a gathering song. Other parts of the introductory rite may be sung depending on the selection of the preparatory rites. In this case singing in the introductory rites should not overshadow the singing of the more important parts of the liturgy of the word. Too much singing at the beginning of the cele-

bration may weary the people before the liturgy of the word begins and may prolong what is meant to be introductory and brief. In a Sunday Celebration of the Word care must also be exercised in balancing the gathering song with the song during the procession and enthronement of the Word. Two hymns placed in close proximity could overburdened the assembly and obscure the importance of the procession of the Word.

## Gathering of the Community

30.    As usual, the celebration begins with the gathering of the assembly, who, by cordially greeting one another, express the fellowship of the Spirit and the love of God that binds all into the one body of Christ. The members of the community may also be welcomed and assisted by ministers of hospitality.

31.    The members of the community take their places in the assembly, as may the ministers. One of the lectors and the ministers who carry the candles and incense gather in the foyer or near the entrance, ready to begin the procession of the word at the appropriate time.

32.    The presidential chair remains empty. A lay person sits in another place, either among the assembly or another place in the sanctuary. A deacon sits at a special chair placed to the right of the presidential chair.

33.    When the time comes to begin the celebration the leader of prayer goes to the place from which he or she will preside. As in any liturgy, whether presided by an ordained or lay minister, the altar and the ambo (lectern) are inappropriate places from which to preside.

34.    A server normally holds the Ritual for the leader of prayer whenever the ritual book is needed. Less preferable is the use of a stand to hold the Ritual as it places a barrier between the leader and the community. The use of several stands is aesthetically unpleasing and diminishes the uniqueness of the ambo (lectern), especially if there is a stand for the leader of song as well as for the leader of prayer.

## Introductory Remarks

35.    The introductory remarks serve to prepare the community to listen to the Word and, if necessary, to inform any members who were not aware that the Eucharist would not be celebrated. This is especially appropriate when a *Sunday Celebration of the Word* is not regularly celebrated. It also functions to remind the congregation that this celebration is a true act of worship of the Church and is celebrated in union with the diocesan bishop, the pastor of the community and the universal church.

36.    The introductory remarks may be given before the celebration begins or after the liturgical greeting. The texts provided for the introductory remarks are optional and may be adapted to the local circumstances and needs. The addition of lengthy explanations or remarks hinders the community from focusing on the presence of Christ

in their midst, over-shadows the more important elements of the introductory rite and reduces the effectiveness of the rite. Additional remarks that need to be made may be announced by a commentator before the celebration begins. These should concern the celebration.

37.    The introductory remarks are not intended to welcome the assembly to the celebration. The welcoming of the assembly properly belongs to the gathering of the community and to the ministers of hospitality. It is inappropriate for the leader of prayer (lay or ordained) to presume to welcome the assembly. However it may be appropriate for the leader to welcome special visitors in the name of the assembly to a particular celebration.

38.    The introductory remarks may be made by the leader of prayer or by another minister.

## Greeting

39.    The liturgical greeting consists of two parts, the sign of the cross and the scriptural greeting itself.

40.    The greeting is a reminder that Christ is present among the assembly. It is a prayerful expression that the assembly may realize the presence of Christ in its midst and act as the body of Christ.

41.    In keeping with the provisions of the *Directory*, no. 39, the form of greeting used by lay ministers is different from the form used by ordained ministers. In addition, the formula of greeting evokes a different response from the assembly. The greetings reflect the nature of the liturgical season; nevertheless, following the Roman tradition, they are scriptural in content.

42.    The purpose of the liturgical greeting is a recognition of the presence of the Lord who is present when two or three are gathered in his name.

43.    Facing the assembly, and with hands extended, the leader greets the people, using one of the formularies provided, either from the Ordinary (the unchanging parts of the rite) found in the centre of the ritual or from the Proper of Seasons (the changeable or seasonal parts of the rite) found at the beginning of the ritual book.

## Preparatory or Opening Rite

44.    Many options are provided as a preparation for the Liturgy of the Word. These may be used to highlight the liturgical season. Each form begins with an invitation to prayer, given by the leader of prayer. A time of silent reflection follows, concluded with a prayer or sung hymn or acclamation. Only one of the following is chosen for use.

45.    The *Rite of Thanksgiving and Sprinkling of Water* reminds the assembly of baptism. As such it is appropriate particularly during the Easter season. During the sprinkling an appropriate hymn or acclamation is sung and the leader moves throughout the assembly. The sprinkling of water is intended to touch all the members of the assembly. This is best achieved when the leader uses a generous

amount of water while moving through the assembly. If the liturgical space allows the assembly to see the baptismal font, the rite of thanksgiving and sprinkling of water may take place from the baptismal area.

46. The *Penitential Rite* prepares the assembly for celebration by way of a confession of sin and is most appropriate for the season of Lent. Two forms are provided. The first, known as the *confiteor* or *I confess*, originates from a private preparation for the eucharist. The second form consists of verses from penitential psalms in a dialogue form.

47. The *Litany of Praise* acknowledges the power of the risen Lord active in the midst of the church. It is suitable for all seasons and occasions, especially Advent and Ordinary Time. Although the *Lord, have mercy* and the Season of Advent are sometimes seen as penitential, the character of both is not directly penitential. The Ritual provides a number of models for the acclamations in the Ordinary and in the Proper of the Seasons.

48. Other invocations may be used, provided they are addressed to Christ and acknowledge his saving power and priestly ministry. The invocations or acclamations may be announced by a minister other than the leader of prayer; they may also be sung. The litany establishes a dialogue between the minister and the community. The *Kyrie* is essentially an acclamation of praise to the Lord. The acclamations should never focus on the community or its sinfulness. Inappropriate are formulas which ask forgiveness for the "the times when . . ."

49. The *Kyrie* or *Lord, have mercy* is an ancient chant acclaiming the Lord and his loving kindness. The Roman Church adopted it from the litanies of the Eastern liturgies. It may be used in its English or Greek forms. This rite is most appropriate during Lent. When sung as a litany the assembly repeats the acclamation of the cantor. This rite is always sung. When it is not sung as part of the preparatory rite, the *Lord, have mercy* may be used as the sung acclamation during the procession and enthronement of the Lectionary.

50. The *Glory to God* or Hymn of Praise is an ancient hymn of joy, expanded from the song of the angels at the birth of Christ. Originally its use was restricted to the most solemn of celebrations. In the Eastern liturgies it is used as the hymn at morning prayer. This rite is particularly appropriate during the Christmas season, solemnities and during the Easter Season. The hymn of praise is by nature a hymn and is always sung. The assembly may sing it in its entirety or by repeating a refrain. When it is not sung as part of the preparatory rite, the Glory to God may be used as the sung acclamation during the procession and enthronement of the Lectionary outside the Advent and Lenten seasons.

51. On some occasions, although rare at a Sunday Celebration of the Word, particular ritual celebrations provide their own opening rites. At funeral and baptismal liturgies, rites of reception are held near the entrance to the church and replace the opening or preparatory rite of the Sunday Celebration of the Word.

**Opening Prayer**

52. Immediately following the preparatory rite, the leader invites the people to pray. All pray silently for a short time, then, with hands outstretched the leader, in the words of the opening prayer, collects or sums up the prayers of the members of the assembly.

53. The opening prayer is the most important element of the introductory rite and so should be the strongest element of the rite.

54. The structure of liturgical prayer is complex and involves both the assembly and the leader of prayer together with silent and verbal prayer.

   a) *Invitation:* The prayer begins with an invitation to the assembly to pray.

   b) *Prayer of the assembly:* Next follows the most important element of the prayer: the prayer of the assembly which takes place in silence. Therefore, the leader of prayer must respect the silence that is part of the rite.

   c) *Collect:* After the silent prayer of the community, the leader exercises a ministry of unity, gathers the prayers of the community into one in a proclaimed prayer that is addressed to God the Father, through his Son, Jesus Christ, in the power of the Holy Spirit. The conclusion of the prayer is an important Trinitarian expression of divine activity and the mystery of our salvation: therefore, it should be prayed with conviction and deliberateness.

   d) *Assent:* The final element of the prayer is the assent expressed by the assembly in the acclamation: *Amen.*

55. The ritual provides two prayers for each Sunday and Solemnity. The first is translated from the Latin. The second, which is proper to each cycle of the Lectionary (Years A, B or C), is an alternate prayer inspired by the readings of the cycle of the particular Sunday .

56. The leader of prayer says this prayer and the other presidential prayers with hands and arms extended in the ancient *orans* position. The open arms embrace the community and reach out to God. The open palms symbolize offering to God and are outstretched to the unseen God, the giver of all blessings and good things. The entire assembly, following Jewish and ancient Christian practice, may wish to assume the *orans* position for the prayer.

## THE LITURGY OF THE WORD

57. The liturgy of the word takes up anew the enduring dialogue between God and the world. In his word Jesus speaks to the assembly, inviting it to share the good news of the paschal mystery. The assembly responds to this good news by a response of joy in silence, song and awe.

58. The liturgy of the word follows as usual, using the three scriptural readings from the Sunday Lectionary, with the responsorial psalm and gospel acclamation. After the time of silence following the homily or reflection,

there follows the profession of faith, the general intercessions, the proclamation of praise and the sign of peace.

59.    Because of the importance of God's word, no other readings, even of a religious nature, may replace or be added to the scriptural texts.

60.    On occasion, when the readings are unusually difficult, a brief introduction to the liturgy of the word may be given. It should highlight the significance and importance of the proclamation of God's salvation. It should not be a homily, exegesis or catechesis. It should never limit or condition the meaning of God's word.

61.    A characteristic of a *Sunday Celebration of the Word* is the enthronement of the Word of God. It is accompanied by the use of incense and candles. The use of incense is optional in any liturgical service; nevertheless, its use adds to the incarnational dimension of liturgy which appeals not only to the mind, but also to the senses. The sight of the incense rising and its pleasant scent help to enwrap the whole person in the liturgical action. It is not appropriate to incense the altar at this or any time during the *Sunday Celebration of the Word*.

**Procession and Enthronement of the Word**

62.    Immediately after the opening prayer, the assembly remains standing, and an appropriate song or acclamation is sung by the community. During the hymn the Lectionary is carried in procession, accompanied by ministers carrying candles and incense, if it is used.

63.    The ministers with the candles walk on each side of the lector carrying the Lectionary. If there is insufficient space to walk on each side of the minister, those carrying the candles walk immediately in front of the Lectionary.

64.    If incense is used, before the procession begins, a minister places a sufficient amount in the censer to last throughout the procession and the enthronement of the Word. The minister swings the thurible while walking before the Lectionary in the procession.

65.    The order of ministers is as follows:

   a) a minister with the lighted censer, if it is used;

   b) two ministers carrying lighted candles;

   c) the lector who carries the Lectionary.

66.    During the procession, an appropriate song is sung. Outside Advent and Lent, the *Glory to God*, and during Lent, the Greek *Kyrie* or the *Lord, have mercy* may be used, if neither was used in the preparatory or opening rite.

67.    Without reverencing the altar, the lector and ministers carrying the candles proceed to the ambo. The lector and the ministers carrying the candles and the incense stand at the ambo, facing the assembly. The lector continues to hold up the Lectionary for all to see, and the bearers of the candles stand on each side of the lector until the processional song is completed.

68.    The procession should be solemn and dignified. Its purpose is to be a visible indication of the unity of the assembly, gathered around Christ present in the assembly and in the proclamation of the Word.

69.    After the song is completed, the reader places the Lectionary on the ambo and incenses it. If the incense is still burning, it is not necessary to place more incense on the coals.

70.    After the incensing of the Lectionary, the leader of prayer speaks to the assembly, using the formula provided in the Ritual. Meanwhile, the lector should step back from the ambo, but remain near it. The leader of prayer may give a brief introduction to the readings, but this is not necessary, and in most cases not desirable. However, if an introduction is given, it must be well prepared and to the point and should help the assembly to open their minds and hearts to the working of the Spirit and the voice of God that will speak to each member of the assembly. It should not tell the assembly what the meaning of the reading(s) is (are), nor should it condition what the assembly will hear.

**Readings**

71.    Ideally, two readers will proclaim the readings before the gospel. They should sit near the ambo, either in the assembly or adjacent to it, so that they do not have to cross the church or sanctuary on the way to the ambo or cause unnecessary delays in the liturgy of the word. The reader approaches the ambo without any bows or signs of reverence. The only exception may be if the reader passes in front of the altar on the way to the ambo. In this case the reader stops before the altar and makes a slight bow.

72.    The readings should always be proclaimed from the Lectionary and not from sheets of paper, missalettes or booklets. The use of the Lectionary is a sign of respect for the Word of God and emphasizes its importance and permanence in the life of the assembly.

73.    As all are seated, the first reader approaches the ambo and opens the Lectionary and locates the proper reading. The lector should pause momentarily, in order to give the congregation sufficient time to get "settled" to listen to the Word of God. When all is quiet, the lector begins the reading without making any reference to chapter and verse, or reading the summary of the reading, or announcing that this is the first reading.

74.    At the end of each reading, the lector pauses momentarily, and then announces the acclamation: *The word of the Lord.* The lector does not hold up the Lectionary. The assembly is acclaiming the *spoken* Word of God, not the book, itself.

75.    A period of silence is observed after each reading, before the responsorial psalm or the gospel acclamation is sung. The lector remains at the ambo for the time of reflective silence, and leaves only as the cantor or psalmist approaches the ambo for the psalm, or the first notes of the music for the gospel acclamation are played. The period of silence is an obligatory part of the celebration, since the word that has been proclaimed must be received in the heart. It should be of sufficient length to allow for genuine reflection, yet not so long as to destroy the natural flow of the liturgy. The silence is observed by

all. The cantor and musicians do not use this time to prepare for the psalm or gospel acclamation.

76. Immediately after the responsorial psalm, another lector comes to the ambo to proclaim the second reading, following the same pattern used for the first reading.

## Responsorial Psalm

77. The psalm is both part of the response of the assembly to the first reading and a proclamation of the word of God. It is for this reason that the cantor or psalmist proclaims the psalm from the lectern. In this respect both cantor and readers are ministers of the word.

78. The first response of the community to God's Word is silent prayer and reflection. Then the community verbalizes its response in the psalm and its refrain. It may be led by the cantor (psalmist) who sings the verses of the psalm or canticle. The refrain is always selected so that it can be sung easily by the entire community. The psalmist sings the refrain once, then it is repeated by the community. After each verse of the psalm the refrain is sung by all. The psalmist leads the responsorial psalm from the ambo.

79. The entire psalm may also be sung by the whole assembly. In this case the refrain is omitted.[2]

80. If it is difficult for the assembly to sing a new refrain each Sunday, a common refrain or seasonal psalm may be used, and repeated during the Sundays of the liturgical season. Nevertheless, the common refrain or the seasonal psalm should be selected so that it is an appropriate response to the first reading and is consistent with the thought of the reading. A variety of common refrains and seasonal psalms are provided in the *Catholic Book of Worship*.

81. The psalm is never replaced by a metrical hymn or by a song based on a psalm text. Since it is part of the word of God, fidelity to the scriptural text must be observed.

82. Ideally the psalm and its refrain should be sung. If this is not possible, the refrain may be sung and the verses are read preferably by a person other than the lector. The psalm should never be introduced with the phrase, "The response to the psalm is . . ."

## Gospel Acclamation

83. Following the period of silence, the assembly stands and the gospel acclamation is sung. The gospel acclamation is sung in the usual manner by the congregation, led by a cantor who intones it and sings the verse of the acclamation. The acclamation *Alleluia* or the lenten acclamation may be sung alone or a number of times. If the acclamation is not sung, the verse is omitted. During the season of Lent, the *Alleluia* is replaced by *Praise to you, Lord, King of eternal glory!* or another of the lenten acclamations found in the Lectionary and in the *Catholic Book of Worship*.

84. The cantor does not come to the ambo to lead and sing the acclamation, but does so from another appropriate place.

## Gospel

85. Meanwhile a third reader, but not the leader of prayer or the preacher (homily reader), comes to the ambo. If candles have not been placed by the lectern, ministers carrying candles stand on each side of the ambo for the proclamation of the gospel.

86. The reading of the word of God is a ministerial function and not a presidential role; therefore, it is not appropriate for the person who presides to read the gospel, even if that person is to preach or read the homily.

87. As the minister of the gospel, a deacon, even if he is presiding, should proclaim the gospel. However, if another deacon is present, he should proclaim the gospel even if he is not to give the homily.

88. When the gospel is proclaimed by a lay reader, the greeting *The Lord be with you* is not used, but the reading begins immediately with *A reading from the holy gospel according to* . . . The signs of the cross and the conclusion of the gospel are made as usual.

89. The Lectionary may be incensed as usual, before the proclamation of the gospel.

90. At the end of the gospel the *Alleluia* or another acclamation may be sung. After the response of the assembly the reader lifts the Lectionary and kisses it. However, the book is not raised at the acclamation *The gospel of the Lord*. The community is acclaiming the proclaimed gospel and not the Lectionary, itself.

91. Then the community sits, and the ministers return to their places.

## Homily or Reflection

92. A person authorized by the bishop to preach then gives the homily or reflection on the readings. If no one is authorized, another person, but not the person who has read the first or second reading or the gospel, reads the homily prepared for the day by the pastor or the diocese. Following the principle that no one exercises two ministries at a liturgy, those who have proclaimed the scriptures do not preach. The reflection may be given by the leader of prayer. The homily or reflection is given from the ambo.

93. Following the homily or reflection, a brief period of silent reflection is observed so that the community may further reflect on the Word of God. All remain seated.

94. If there is no homily or reflection, then a longer period of silence is observed.

95. If catechumens or the elect are present in the assembly, they are normally dismissed after the homily.

---

[2]   *Introduction to the Lectionary*, no. 20.

## Profession of Faith

96. The profession of faith, in addition to calling to mind the truths of the faith as a response to the word proclaimed in the assembly, is an affirmation of the faith in the Lord that binds the community together as one and unites them to the universal Church.

97. Either the Nicene Creed or the Apostles' Creed may be used. An optional introduction is provided. The Apostles' Creed in question form and the baptismal profession of faith are provided for use on Easter Sunday.

## General Intercessions

98. After the profession of faith the leader of prayer immediately invites the assembly to pray for the needs of the Church and the world. The invitation to prayer is addressed to the community and not to God. The invitation should be brief and to the point. It is not a summary of the readings or a homily, but an invitation to prayer.

99. In the general intercessions the community exercises its priestly role of interceding for the good of the Church and all humanity and the salvation of the world. The structure of the prayer follows the pattern of liturgical prayers:

a) an *invitation to prayer* which is addressed to the community by the leader of prayer;

b) the *prayer of the assembly*, expressed in silence and/or in a verbal refrain. The prayer of the assembly is assisted by the announcing of intentions by another minister;

c) the *collection* of the prayers of the people into a single prayer by the leader;

d) the *assent* of the community expressed in the acclamation: *Amen.*

100. Ideally a person other than one of the readers should announce the intentions from the ambo.

101. The petitions should be in simple sentence form and not too complex or long. The petitions should be universal in scope, reflecting the needs not only of the local community, but also of the universal Church and the world. Generally, the sequence of petitions is to be:

a) for the needs of the Church;

b) for civic authorities, the salvation of the world, or the pressing needs of the world;

c) for those suffering and oppressed;

d) for the local community.

102. In the absence of the celebration of the eucharist, it is recommended that there be a petition for vocations to the priesthood.

103. The petitions are statements of intercession, and not reasons for praise and thanksgiving. They should not be moralistic or didactic, but express the concerns of the people of God in a direct manner.

104. The prayer of the faithful is a litanic prayer, and as such may be more effective when sung. Suggestions and music, contained in the *Catholic Book of Worship*, are recommended. When the intercessions are sung, the singing is led by a cantor from the stand or from the ambo (lectern).

105. Model invitations and petitions are offered in the Ritual.

## Proclamation of Praise

106. The proclamation of praise gives thanks for all that God has done, especially for the word of God that was proclaimed in the assembly and for the greatest of all gifts, the eternal and saving Word, Jesus Christ. The purpose of the prayer of praise in the *Sunday Celebration of the Word* is to be a response to the Word of God heard in the readings and in the lives of the people of God. Thus the content of the proclamation of praise is directly related to the proclaimed Word and the saving activity of God in Christ. Inappropriate are references to the eucharist, which is not celebrated, nor should mention be made to holy communion, which may or may not be distributed.

107. The proclamation of praise may take several forms: a prayer, a litany, a song, a psalm or canticle.

108. The leader of prayer leads the proclamation of praise by inviting the assembly to join in the praise of God. An important element is the participation of the assembly by singing the whole song or psalm or canticle or by means of the acclamations, which assist the assembly in making the prayer or litany or psalm its own. Therefore, a cantor may assist, either to sing the unchanging introduction or invitation to the acclamation of the community, or to sing the acclamation the first time.

109. In order to be effective the acclamation must be short, unchanging and sung. Acclamations from the eucharistic prayers should not be used. Suggestions are offered in the Ritual.

110. The prayers, invocations, hymns and acclamations should always be addressed to God the Father.

111. The proclamation of praise is the concluding prayer of the general intercessions. It is a part of the liturgy of the word and is a response to the sacred readings. The Roman pattern of liturgical prayer includes praise-thanksgiving and petition-supplication. In this way, praise and thanksgiving pervade the community's supplication.

112. The *prayer of praise* is the title selected for this prayer in order to avoid confusion between the prayer of praise and the eucharistic prayer of the Mass which is the great prayer of thanksgiving. The prayers of praise, for the most part, are drawn from or based on sacred scripture. The prayers should not follow the form or style of a eucharistic prayer. A deliberate attempt has been made in the prayers to use a similar formula in order to facilitate the acclamation of the assembly.

113. The *litany of praise* offers a unique challenge for it demands a short invocation and response without a spoken or musical introduction or lead-in. Thus the inflection of the leader's voice is important to provide the proper invitation for the community's response. One method is for a cantor to use a sung introduction. As in other forms of the litany, it is better when the invocations as well as the response are sung. However, the use of this form of praise

is new and there is little musical repertoire or experience in its use. Hopefully, music may be written in the future.

114. The *song of praise* is an appropriate song of praise addressed to God the Father. Careful selection is required to ensure that the song is one of praise, is sufficiently long to establish an atmosphere of praise, is appropriate to the celebration in terms of its content and theme, and is not a eucharistic hymn. Some suggestions are provided in the Ritual.

115. A *psalm or canticle of praise* may be chosen. The psalm is sung in the same manner as a responsorial psalm. The gospel canticle used at morning or evening prayer is not recommended, as these have a unique relationship to the liturgy of the hours. The Ritual offers some suggestions for the selection of the psalm or canticle.

### The Lord's Prayer

116. The Lord's Prayer concludes the proclamation of praise when a communion service does not follow the liturgy of the word. Two versions of the Lord's Prayer are provided, each with their own distinctive introduction. In the *Sunday Celebration of the Word and Hours*, the doxology F*or the kingdom . . .* is always used.

### Sign of Peace

117. The purpose of the sign of peace is to express the love, unity and reconciliation that Christ has bestowed on the community of faith. By it the members of the community recognize the presence of Christ in each other and in the community assembled in love. It expresses in a visible way the unity of the body of Christ which was manifested in the prayer of the community.

118. The rite is meant to be brief, yet cordial. It is not a hierarchial greeting that is passed on from the leader of prayer downward to the other members of the community, but a sincere greeting to those near by. It is not necessary for the leader to share personally the sign of peace with all the members of the community.

119. It is inappropriate that a song or music prolong this rite, or overshadow its meaning.

## CONCLUDING RITE

### Announcements

120. Brief announcements, if any, may be made at this time by the leader of prayer or by a another member of the assembly. The temptation to read or repeat announcements contained in the parish bulletin should be avoided. The announcements should be so brief and to the point that it will not be necessary to invite the congregation to be seated.

121. The purpose of the announcements is to communicate any unexpected or recent events in a manner that will build up the faith of the community.

122. The announcements should not be made from the ambo, as this is reserved for the proclamation of the Word of God.

### Collection

123. Following the announcements or the sign of peace, a collection for the needs of the poor and the Church may be taken up.

124. It is not appropriate that a congregational hymn be sung; however, instrumental music may be played, or the choir may sing a liturgical selection. Hymns with eucharistic or offering themes should never be used.

125. The collection should avoid the appearance of the presentation of gifts as at Mass. The collection may be brought forward by the collectors and placed in a suitable place, but not on or near the altar. Neither should it be received by the leader of prayer. No other objects, such as candles, should be brought to the altar at this time or accompany the collection.

### Blessing

126. The blessing takes the form of the simple blessing. A lay person omits the greeting *The Lord be with you.* The blessing *May the almighty and merciful God . . ."* always employs the first person object *us*, rather than the second person *you*, which is used by a deacon or priest.

127. At the appropriate time during the blessing, the leader and the community sign themselves with the sign of the cross.

128. When other liturgical rites follow immediately, the blessing and the dismissal are omitted.

### Dismissal

129. The dismissal is more than the end of the celebration. It is the commissioning and sending forth of the community to proclaim the mighty deeds of the Lord in their daily lives. In this sense, it is the continuation of the Christian life celebrated in God's Word.

## COMMUNION RITE

130. The Ritual for *Sunday Celebration of the Word and Hours* adds the rite of the distribution of communion outside the Mass only to the Liturgy of the Word. It is not recommended that the distribution of communion be added to the Liturgy of the Hours.

131. A communion service should be held only when eucharistic bread (hosts) can be brought from a neighbouring parish the same day as the *Sunday Celebration of the Word*, at the longest the day before, or the pastor can leave consecrated bread from an earlier Mass, recently celebrated in the community, in order that there may be some connection between the receiving of communion and the celebration of the Eucharist from which communion proceeds.

132. When hosts are consecrated so long in advance of their use by the community that the link between the celebration of the eucharist is unclear, a communion service should not be joined to the *Sunday Celebration of the Word.*

133. The practice of celebrating the eucharist exclusively to provide communion for a *Sunday Celebration of the Word* is to be discouraged.

134. When the communion rite is included as part of the Celebration of the Word, a brief interval of silence is observed after the proclamation of praise and the sign of peace while the altar is prepared and the reserved Sacrament is brought to the altar.

135. The Blessed Sacrament, if it is brought from another church or celebration, is placed in the tabernacle or another suitable place, either in the sacristy or another place clearly distinct from the altar or ambo area.

### Preparation of the Altar

136. After the sign of peace the leader of prayer is seated. Ministers prepare the altar by placing the ritual and a corporal on it. Candles at or near the altar may be lighted or placed near the altar. Candles may also be brought from the tabernacle when the reserved Blessed Sacrament is brought to the altar.

### Bringing of the Blessed Sacrament to the Altar

137. After the altar has been prepared by the ministers, as many communion ministers as needed go to the tabernacle, or the place where the Blessed Sacrament has been properly reserved, genuflect before it and remove the ciborium or vessel containing the eucharistic bread. They transfer the eucharistic bread to as many vessels as are needed for communion. Then these are brought to the altar.

138. The procession is done with dignity and simplicity. The ministers may be accompanied by servers bearing candles. These may be placed on or near the altar; or if there already are candles at the altar, the processional candles are returned to the credence table. Incense and the processional cross are not used, nor is music or a hymn appropriate.

139. At the altar, the communion ministers place the vessels on the corporal and genuflect.

140. The other ministers of communion approach the altar at this time and take their places at the side of the altar or behind it with those who brought the eucharistic bread to the altar. It is inappropriate for ministers of communion to wash their hands before or during the communion rite.

141. The leader of prayer or the communion minister who is to lead the communion rite stands alone at the altar facing the assembly.

### Lord's Prayer

142. After the preparations at the altar have been completed, the minister introduces the Lord's Prayer and invites the community to prayer.

143. Two versions of the Lord's Prayer are provided, each with their own distinctive introduction. In the *Sunday Celebration of the Word*, the doxology *For the kingdom* . . . is always used.

144. The Lord's Prayer may be sung or recited.

### Invitation to Communion

145. The breaking of bread does not take place, nor is the *Lamb of God* sung or recited.

146. After genuflecting, the minister takes a host from the vessel, raises it slightly and recites one of the prescribed formulae.

147. The minister receives communion and then gives communion to the other communion ministers. The communion ministers then go to their stations and give communion in the usual manner. The ministers share in communion before going to the communion stations, since communion is a public act of covenant sealing. Moreover, the ministers must first receive what they themselves are going to give.

### Reposition of the Blessed Sacrament

148. After communion, the communion ministers return the eucharistic bread to the tabernacle. If servers carried candles to the altar, they may accompany the minister(s) to the tabernacle with their candles. In any case, candles are removed from or near the altar; they may be placed near the cross or at the side table.

149. Any empty communion vessels not returned to the tabernacle should be removed from the altar to a side table, and may be reverently purified after the celebration.

150. The ministers then return to their places.

### Period of Silence

151. A period of silent prayer then follows communion. While a psalm or hymn of praise is permitted, it is preferable to respect the silent prayer of the community.

### Prayer after Communion

152. The communion rite concludes with the prayer after communion, which follows immediately, before any announcements. Since it is a part of the communion rite, it is led by the minister who conducted the communion rite. The communion minister stands at the altar; the leader of prayer stands either at the altar or at the usual place of the leader of prayer.

153. The community stands, and the minister invites the community to pray. After a brief period of silence, the minister continues with the prayer after communion. The prayer is taken from the Proper of the Season. At the end the people give their assent by the acclamation *Amen.*

154. If the communion minister leads the prayer, then after the prayer the communion minister returns to his or her place.

155. The prayer after communion is not a prayer of thanksgiving but is a prayer asking that the effects of communion may be fruitful in the lives of the members of the community.

156. The concluding rites follow as usual.

# PART THREE

# LITURGY OF HOURS

## Introduction

157. Morning and Evening Prayer are the two forms that are presented from the Liturgy of the Hours. At Morning or Evening Prayer it is not normal to insert the three readings of the Sundays or to add a communion service.

## Ministers

158. In addition to the leader of prayer, the following ministers are needed to assist at the celebration of the Liturgy of the Hours.

   a) a lector to proclaim the reading;

   b) a cantor/psalmist to sing the verses of the psalm and the intentions;

   c) a leader of song to lead the assembly in the singing of the hymn and the canticle;

   d) servers to assist with the holy water and/or incense if either of these is used, to hold the Ritual for the leader of prayer.

   f) ministers of hospitality;

   g) a commentator, if used.

## Preparations

159. The Ritual is placed in the sanctuary near the place from which the leader of prayer will preside.

160. The Lectionary may be carried in procession by the lector, otherwise it is placed on the ambo before the celebration begins.

161. Hymnals and other participation aids should be placed at the chairs of the ministers.

162. During Morning and Evening Prayer incense may be used during the singing of the gospel canticle to incense the altar and the assembly. At Evening Prayer incense may be used to incense the candle during the celebration of light and/or during the evening psalm (Psalm 141) as well as during the singing of the gospel canticle. At Morning Prayer holy water may be used to sprinkle the assembly during the morning psalm (Psalm 63).

163. Candles may used by the assembly at Evening Prayer during the celebration of light.

## INTRODUCTORY RITE

### Gathering of the Community

164. As usual, the celebration begins with the gathering of the assembly, who, by cordially greeting one another, express the fellowship of the Spirit and the love of God that binds all into the one body of Christ. The members of the community may also be welcomed and assisted by ministers of hospitality.

165. The presidential chair remains empty. A lay leader of prayer sits in another place, either among the assembly or another place in the sanctuary. A deacon sits at a special chair placed to the right of the presidential chair.

166. The ministers may take their places without any liturgical form of entrance.

167. The leader of prayer takes his or her place with the community. When the time comes to begin the celebration the leader of prayer goes to the place from which he or she will preside. As in any liturgy of the church, the altar and the ambo (lectern) are inappropriate places from which to preside.

168. A server normally holds the Ritual for the leader of prayer whenever the ritual book is needed. Less preferable is the use of a stand to hold the Ritual as it places a barrier between the leader and the community. The use of several stands is aesthetically unpleasing and diminishes the uniqueness of the ambo (lectern), especially if there is a stand for the leader of song as well as for the leader of prayer.

169. At Evening Prayer the lights of the church are dimmed in advance. The community, except the ministers who will take part in the procession, take their places without any liturgical form of entrance. The members of the community are given candles as they enter the church.

## Introductory Remarks

170. The introductory remarks serve to prepare the community to join in the celebration and, if necessary, to inform any members who were not aware that the Eucharist would not be celebrated. This is especially appropriate when a *Sunday Celebration of the Word and Hours* is not regularly celebrated. It also functions to remind the congregation that this celebration is a true liturgy of the Church and is celebrated in union with the diocesan bishop, the pastor of the community and the universal church.

171. The introductory remarks may be given before the celebration begins or after the invitation to prayer. The texts provided for the introductory remarks are optional and may be adapted to the local circumstances and needs. The addition of lengthy explanations or remarks hinders the community from focusing on the presence of Christ in their midst, overshadows the more important elements of the introductory rite and reduces the effectiveness of the rite. Additional remarks that need to be made may be announced by a commentator before the celebration begins. These should concern the celebration.

172. The introductory remarks are not intended to welcome the assembly to the celebration. The welcoming of the assembly properly belongs to the gathering of the community and to the ministers of hospitality. It is inappropriate for the leader of prayer (lay or ordained) to presume to welcome the assembly. However it may be appro-

priate for the leader to welcome special visitors in the name of the assembly to a particular celebration.

173. The introductory remarks may be made by the leader of prayer or by another minister.

**Procession**

174. At Morning Prayer the ministers may take their places without any liturgical form of entrance. If there is to be an entrance procession, then when the community has assembled, a server carrying the thurible into which incense has just been placed leads the procession, followed by a minister carrying a vessel of holy water, if it is used during the morning psalm, a reader carrying the Lectionary and the leader of prayer. When the procession reaches the sanctuary, the Lectionary is placed upon the lectern. The ministers carrying the incense and vessel of water place these in an appropriate place until they are needed.

175. At Evening Prayer when the community has assembled, the procession begins in silence. The assembly stands. The procession is led by a server carrying the thurible into which incense has just been placed, then a minister carrying a large lighted candle, a cantor who sings the thanksgiving for the light, a reader carrying the Lectionary and the leader of prayer. When the procession reaches the sanctuary, the candle is put in a prominent place, and the Lectionary is placed upon the lectern.

176. It is not appropriate to sing a hymn at this time. Instrumental music may accompany the procession, otherwise the ministers enter in silence.

177. The Lectionary is the only book carried in the procession. The Ritual is placed near the place from which the leader of prayer will preside; it is never carried in procession.

**Invitation to Prayer**

178. At Morning Prayer the leader of prayer goes to the place from which he or she will preside, and sings or says the invitation to prayer according to the forms given in the Ritual. All trace the sign of the cross on their lips, while the leader of prayer sings or says the introductory verse. The leader of prayer remains standing at the place from which he or she presides for the morning hymn and morning psalm.

179. At Evening Prayer, the leader of prayer stands near the candle or goes to the place from which he or she will preside, and sings or says the opening verse, according to one of the forms provided. Music is given in *Catholic Book of Worship*. The leader of prayer may remain near the candle for the evening thanksgiving before going to the place of presiding for the hymn and the evening psalm.

180. A server holds the Ritual for the leader of prayer.

**Thanksgiving for the Light At Evening Prayer**

181. On Sundays and Solemnities it is fitting to begin evening prayer with a celebration of light (lucernarium). The candles of the people and the candles on or near the altar, or near the lectern or cross are lighted. The leader of prayer or a cantor invites the assembly to give thanks to God, and sings the prayer of thanksgiving for the light.

182. At the conclusion of the thanksgiving (or after the hymn), the people may extinguish their candles.

183. When the celebration of Light does not take place, the alternate invitation to prayer may be used.

**Hymn**

184. The hymn begins at once and is sung by the whole assembly. It may be led by a cantor or by the choir. Suitable hymns are suggested in the Ritual and in the index of the *Catholic Book of Worship*.

185. The community remains standing for the hymn. The leader of prayer remains standing near the place from which he or she is leading the celebration.

186. During the evening hymn, or afterward if candles are used, the lights of the church may be turned on gradually. During the hymn the candle may be incensed.

## PSALMODY

187. A psalm may be sung or recited in various ways: the whole psalm may be sung or recited by all; the verses may be alternated between the choir or cantor and the rest of the assembly; the verses may be alternated between one side of the assembly and the other; it may be sung responsorially, with the cantor singing the verses and the whole assembly singing the refrain after each verse.

188. If the psalm is sung, the cantor leads the psalm from the lectern.

189. If necessary, the psalm may be recited, with one section of the community alternating with the other.

**Morning or Evening Psalm**

190. After the hymn the morning or evening psalm is sung by the assembly. For this psalm the assembly usually remains standing, especially if incense or holy water is to be used.

191. At Morning prayer, if Psalm 63 is used, the assembly may be sprinkled with holy water during the singing of the psalm.

192. During the singing of the evening psalm (Psalm 141), it is appropriate that incense be placed in the thurible or in a brazier which has been placed in the midst of the assembly. It is also possible to incense the assembly during the singing of the psalm as a sign of respect for Christ's presence among those gathered in his name. In this case a server brings the thurible to the leader of prayer, who puts in it some incense. The server first incenses the leader of prayer, then goes throughout the assembly to incense the whole community.

193. A period of silence follows the psalm.

**Psalm Prayer**

194. If desired, a psalm prayer may follow the psalm. The psalm prayer is primarily a prayer of praise which sums up the praise of the assembly expressed in the psalm. Prayers of petition are inappropriate at this time.

195. If a psalm prayer is desired, the leader of prayer then stands at the place from which he or she presides.

196. The leader of prayer may introduce the period of silent reflection by saying: "Let us pray," or it may be omitted. After the period of silence the leader of prayer, with hands extended, sings or says one of the prayers contained in the Ritual. The prayers may be adapted or composed for the occasion.

197. The structure of liturgical prayer is complex and involves both the assembly and the leader of prayer, together with silent and verbal prayer.

    a) *Invitation:* The prayer may begin with an invitation to the assembly to pray.

    b) *Prayer of the assembly:* The most important element of the prayer is the silent prayer of the assembly. Therefore, the leader of prayer must respect the silence that is part of the rite.

    c) *Collect:* After the silent prayer of the community, the leader, exercising a ministry of unity, gathers the prayers of the community into one in a proclaimed prayer that is addressed to God the Father, through his Son, Jesus Christ, in the power of the Holy Spirit. The conclusion of the prayer is an important Trinitarian expression of divine activity and the mystery of our salvation; therefore, it should be prayed with conviction and deliberateness.

    d) *Assent:* The final element of the prayer is the assent expressed by the assembly in the acclamation *Amen.*

**Second Psalm**

198. After a brief pause, a second psalm is sung. A psalm suited to the liturgical season is particularly appropriate.

199. The community sits for the second psalm.

200. A period of silence follows the psalm.

201. If desired a psalm prayer may follow the psalm.

**Canticle or Psalm of Praise**

202. If desired a canticle of praise or a psalm of praise may be sung. A period of silence follows, but a psalm prayer is not prayed. All stand for the canticle or psalm of praise.

## WORD OF GOD
**Reading**

203. After the psalm or canticle the cantor leaves the ambo, and the community sits.

204. The reading may be chosen from the First or Second Reading from the Sunday Lectionary. It is recommended that the second reading should be read on the Sundays of Advent, Christmas, Lent, and Easter, and on Solemnities (e.g. Pentecost, Body and Blood of Christ, All Saints, Christmas, etc.). The gospel is never chosen as a reading since the gospel canticle serves this function.

205. The lector should sit near the ambo, either in the assembly or adjacent to it, so that it is not necessary to cross the church or sanctuary on the way to the ambo or cause unnecessary delays in the liturgy of the word. The reader approaches the ambo without any bows or signs of reverence. The only exception may be passing in front of the altar on the way to the ambo. In this case a slight bow is made to the altar.

206. The reading should always be proclaimed from the Lectionary and not from sheets of paper, missalettes or booklets. The use of the Lectionary is a sign of respect for the Word of God and emphasizes its importance and permanence in the life of the assembly.

207. As all are seated, and the reader approaches the ambo, opens the Lectionary and locates the proper reading. The lector should pause momentarily, in order to give the congregation sufficient time to get "settled" to listen to the Word of God. When all is quiet, the lector begins the reading without making any reference to chapter and verse, or the summary of the reading.

208. At the end of the reading, the lector pauses momentarily, and announces the acclamation: *The word of the Lord.* The lector does not hold up the Lectionary. The assembly is acclaiming the spoken Word of God, not the book itself.

209. A period of silence is observed after the reading. The lector remains at the ambo for the time of reflective silence, and leaves only as the leader of prayer or the person who gives the homily or reflection stands and comes to the ambo. The period of silence is an obligatory part of the celebration, since the word that has been proclaimed must be received in the heart. It should be of sufficient length to allow for genuine reflection, yet not so long as to destroy the natural flow of the liturgy. This silence is observed by all.

**Homily or Reflection**

210. A person authorized by the bishop to preach may then give a reflection on the reading. If no one is so authorized, a person other than the reader reads the homily for the day provided by the diocese or by the pastor. This may be done by the leader of prayer.

211. The reflection or homily is given from the ambo (lectern).

212. Following the reflection, the person who gives it returns to his or her seat.

213. After the homily, there follows a period of silence so that the community may further reflect on God's Word.

214. If there is no homily, there is a period of silent reflection.

## PRAISE AND INTERCESSION

215. The proclamation of praise gives thanks for all that God has done, especially for the word of God that was proclaimed in the assembly and for the greatest of all gifts, the eternal and saving Word, Jesus Christ. The purpose of the gospel canticle of praise in the *Sunday Celebration of the Hours* is to be a response to the Word of God heard in the reading and in the lives of the people of God. Thus the content of the proclamation of praise is directly related to the proclaimed Word and the saving activity of God in Christ.

### Gospel Canticle

216. The gospel canticle is sung as a hymn of praise. The canticle is to be sung by the whole community together, or with the community singing alternating verses with the choir, or with one side of the community alternating with the other.

217. The leader of prayer may introduce the gospel canticle using one of the forms provided.

218. At Morning Prayer, the Canticle of Zachariah *(Benedictus)* or the Hymn of Praise *(Gloria)* may be used. If the *Benedictus* is used, all may make the sign of the Cross at the beginning.

219. At Evening prayer, the Canticle of Mary *(Magnificat)* or the Canticle of Simeon *(Nunc dimittis)* may be sung. The Canticle of Simeon is especially appropriate at a celebration which takes place in the late evening. All may make the sign of the cross at the beginning.

220. The recommended forms of the canticles are found in the *Catholic Book of Worship.* Other forms of the canticle may be used, but they are always sung.

221. During the singing of the canticle, the altar may be incensed as a symbol of Christ, through whom our prayers are raised to God. Incense may be placed in a thurible or in a suitable insulated bowl (brazier).

222. If a brazier is used, then it is placed in front of the altar in the midst of the assembly. At the beginning of the gospel canticle, incense is placed on the charcoal by a minister.

223. If a thurible is used, then, when the canticle begins, a server brings the thurible to the leader of prayer, who places some incense in it. The leader of prayer or the server then goes to the altar, and walks slowly around it while incensing it. The people and the leader of prayer may be incensed after the incensation of the altar as a sign of respect for the presence of Christ among those gathered in his name.

### Intercessions

224. After the canticle the leader of prayer immediately invites the assembly to pray for the needs of the Church and the world. The invitation to prayer is addressed to the community and not to God. The invitation should be brief and to the point. It is not an summary of the readings or a homily, but an invitation to prayer.

225. In the general intercessions the community exercises its priestly role of interceding for the good of the Church and all humanity and the salvation of the world. The structure of the prayer follows the pattern of liturgical prayers:

a) an *invitation to prayer* which is addressed to the community by the leader of prayer;

b) the *prayer of the assembly,* expressed in silence and/or in a verbal refrain. The prayer of the assembly is assisted by the announcing of intentions by another minister;

c) the *collection* of the prayers of the people into a single prayer by the leader;

d) the *assent* of the community expressed in the acclamation: *Amen.*

226. Ideally a person other than the reader should announce the intentions from the ambo.

227. The petitions should be in simple sentence form and not too complex or long. The petitions should be universal in scope, reflecting the needs not only of the local community, but also of the universal Church and the world. Generally, the sequence of petitions is to be:

a) for the needs of the Church;

b) for civic authorities, the salvation of the world, or the pressing needs of society;

c) for those suffering and oppressed;

d) for the local community.

In the absence of the celebration of the eucharist, it is recommended that there be a petition for vocations to the priesthood.

228. The petitions are statements of intercession, and not reasons for praise and thanksgiving. They should not be moralistic or didactic, but express the concerns of the people of God in a direct manner.

229. The prayer of the faithful is a litanic prayer, and as such may be more effective when sung. Suggestions and music, contained in the *Catholic Book of Worship,* are recommended. When the intercessions are sung, the singing is led by a cantor from the ambo (lectern).

230. Model invitations and concluding prayers are offered in the Ritual.

231. The Lord's Prayer concludes the general intercessions. The Lord's Prayer may follow the concluding prayer of the intercessions or be used in place of the concluding prayer. Two versions of the Lord's Prayer are provided, each with their own distinctive introduction. In the *Sunday Celebration of the Word and Hours.* The doxology *For the kingdom . . .* is not used when a prayer follows the Lord's Prayer.

## CONCLUDING RITE

### Announcements

232. Brief announcements, if any, may be made at this time by the leader of prayer or a another member of the

assembly. The temptation to read or repeat announcements contained in the parish bulletin should be avoided. The announcements should be brief. If the collection follows the announcements, the assembly may be invited to be seated.

233. The purpose of the announcements is to communicate any unexpected or recent events in a manner that will build up the faith of the community.

234. The announcements should not be made from the ambo, as this is reserved for the proclamation of the Word of God.

### Collection

235. Following the Lord's Prayer and the announcements, a collection may be taken up for the needs of the Church and the poor.

236. This is not an appropriate time for a congregational hymn, but instrumental music may be used, or the choir may sing a selection. Hymns with eucharistic or offering themes are not to be chosen.

237. The collection begins without any introduction.

238. The collection may be brought forward by the collectors, and placed in a suitable place, but not on or near the altar; neither should it be received by the leader of prayer.

### Blessing

239. The blessing takes the form of the simple blessing. Formulas are provided in the Ritual.

240. A lay person omits the greeting *The Lord be with you.* The words *May the almighty and merciful God . . .* always employs the first person object *us*, rather than the second person *you*, which is used by a deacon or priest.

241. At the appropriate time during the blessing, the leader and the community sign themselves with the sign of the cross.

242. When other liturgical rites follow immediately, the blessing and the dismissal are omitted.

### Sign of Peace

243. Following the blessing, the leader of prayer invites the members of the assembly to exchange a sign of peace.

244. The leader of prayer exchanges a sign of peace with those nearby. Members of the community exchange the sign of peace and leave informally, as do the leader of prayer and other ministers.

245. As the community is leaving, music may be played or the choir may sing a suitable selection, but a congregational hymn is inappropriate.

# PART FOUR
# LITURGICAL MUSIC

## Importance of Singing and Music

246. Singing is an essential and integral part of any liturgical celebration; it is a sign of love and joy[3] and an expression of the heart as well as the mind. A text is always made more significant when it is sung. The assembly singing appropriate acclamations, responses and hymns is considered normative for a gathering of the Church for the purposes of worshipping God in ritual prayer.[4]

247. Music, both instrumental and choral, can also create an environment of prayer and meditation. Music can move and inspire. The songs and refrains of the liturgy express our response to a loving Creator who sustains and continues the work of redemption in the coming of Jesus into our lives. Singing in our culture is often an activity reserved for special occasions. The celebration of our unique relationship to God through Jesus should be the highlight of the week.

248. Music has practical applications as well. The hymns and acclamations accompany processions or ritual actions: the gathering of the community with the entrance of the ministers, the procession of the Lectionary, the procession to receive communion and the assembly's going forth to live the good news. Music is functional, but it also expresses the involvement of the assembly in what is happening, and opens up the meaning the rites. In other words, song helps to unite the physical event to the spiritual significance: song makes the rites incarnational.

## The Assembly and Liturgical Action

249. Singing by the assembly is one way that the community expresses its faith and participates fully in the liturgical action. Never should the ministers of music so dominate the celebration that the assembly is reduced to spectators or listeners. Liturgy should not resemble a concert.

250. Whatever can be said about music at the Eucharist is true also at a Sunday Celebration of the Word and at Morning or Evening Prayer. Music has the capacity to serve as a vehicle of God's self-revelation.[5] The music ministry has an important role in these celebrations. A cantor, a leader of song, instrumentalists, and a choir (if there is normally a choir present at Sunday liturgies) should each do their part in facilitating the prayer of the assembly.

## Ministry of Music

251. Every liturgy is a celebration of the whole Church community; therefore, there are many important ministries needed for its fruitful celebration. One of these is the presence of musicians who are willing to serve the assembly by leading the community in the worship of God and assisting them to sing the songs and acclamations.

252. Musicians who lead the singing at a liturgical celebration are servants of the community; their role is to facilitate the sung prayer of the assembly, the primary agent in the common expression of faith and worship.

253. The *General Instruction of the Roman Missal* speaks of the unique function of the choir or musicians (no. 63). First of all it is, and must be seen to be, a part of the assembled people of God. It is the task of the choir "to encourage the active participation of the people in the singing." (no. 63. See also Congregation of Rites, Instruction, *Musicam sacram*, no. 19). The *Instruction* also speaks of another function of the choir: to sing the parts proper to it. There are at least two distinctions to be made: music that belongs to the assembly as a whole (with the choir and/or cantor leading), and music which belongs to the choir or cantor.

254. The role of the psalmist in a *Sunday Celebration of the Word* is, first of all, to lead the assembly's response to the first reading, the responsorial psalm, and to sing the verses of the psalm.

255. The role of the leader of song is to facilitate the sung prayer the assembly. The song leader may be the same person as the psalmist. The song leader's verbal invitation to the people to sing, a friendly and welcoming manner (but dignified out of reverence for Christ's presence in the assembly), and the modelling of energetic singing can do much to encourage the people to sing.

256. The organist and other instrumentalists also have a ministry to the prayer of the community. The music ministry also participates in the welcoming of members of the Body of Christ. By playing appropriate music before the liturgy, they can do much to create an atmosphere that is welcoming and prayerful. Instrumental music can be played when the communion song is finished while the procession to communion continues. During the collection reflective music may be played and is more appropriate than a song. Instrumental music can be played when the assembly has been dismissed, giving expression to joy of the celebration just experienced by the worshipping community.

---

[3]  *General Instruction of the Roman Missal*, no. 19.

[4]  Second Vatican Council, *Constitution on the Sacred Liturgy*, no. 30.

[5]  "The Milwaukee Symposia for Church Companies – A Ten-Year Report." no. 13.

## Selection of Liturgical Music

257. Pastoral sensitivity is necessary in attending to the songs and the words of hymns for use in all worship. The words should reflect the nature of the community assembled and the ritual action, should help the assembly express their faith in God or should help to connect the liturgical action to the meaning of the rite. In other words, music, melody and words, must be servants of the liturgy. They must raise the community to an increased level of participation that is both spiritual and incarnational. There may be many old favourites that, while they are excellent pieces of music, are no longer appropriate for use at the eucharist and at the liturgy of the word and rite of communion. There is a distinction between religious and liturgical music.

258. The singing of four hymns during Mass was a temporary measure introduced to accommodate singing in the language of the people without disrupting the structure of the Latin Mass. The singing of only four hymns does not reflect the fact that there were other more important, sung elements of the Latin Mass. Singing should surround the more important parts of the celebration: in the eucharist these are the response to the word of God and the acclamations for the gospel and the eucharistic prayer; in the Sunday Celebration of the Word the important parts are the response to the word of God and the acclamations for the gospel and the proclamation of praise. Present guidelines abandon the practice of singing only four hymns, and emphasize singing those parts which express and affirm our faith in God's word and activity in the assembly. These are the primary sung elements of the word and praise.

## Music in the Liturgy of the Word

259. At a Sunday Celebration of the Word the processional song, the refrain for the responsorial psalm, the gospel acclamation, the acclamation during the proclamation of praise, and the communion song should be sung by the assembly, and these parts should have priority when music for the liturgy is chosen. It is recommended that the selection of music be done together with those who will preside at the liturgy, so that all concerned will know what choices have been made, especially in regard to the prayer of praise. Team work is essential for a good celebration of any liturgy.

260. By its nature, a liturgy of the word contains a lot of words. Therefore, there is a danger that it can lose its vitality. When the Liturgy of the Word is reduced to the spoken word, this reduction imposes a severe handicap to the celebration: an injustice that the liturgy cannot carry. Lack of variety in the celebration and lack of activity on the part of the congregation leads to an uninspired celebration of the word. The Liturgy of the Word is meant to be a dialogue of speaking and singing, listening and responding. The assembly's song adds a vitality and variety to the Word of God. The sung refrain allows a more engaging response on the part of the assembly, and the singing of the psalm by the cantor allows a meditative proclamation of the word of God.

## Processional Songs

261. The processional songs include hymns or acclamations sung during the entrance, enthronement of the Word and communion processions. The purpose of each song is to give a sense of unity to the many members, to unfold the meaning of the rite and to be an expression of the faith of the community. This song must be familiar to the community so that it might be effective.

262. The purpose of the gathering song is to form community; to "intensify the unity of the gathered people, lead their thoughts to the mystery . . ." that is being celebrated (*GIRM*, 25). Thus the opening song seeks to bring an awareness to those assembled that they are a unified community with a common purpose. The song may also provide the first expression of the feast or season being celebrated. This song, therefore, should be familiar to the community so that all can participate, at least in the refrain; it also may reflect the celebration, which is often most evident in the gospel, and expresses a sense of the community gathered to celebrate thanksgiving and praise to God. This song must be chosen in light of the song to be selected for the procession and enthronement of the Word of God. It is recommended that a shorter piece of music be used for the gathering rite in order to highlight the procession of the word.

263. The song during the procession and enthronement of the Lectionary serves to highlight the importance of the Word of God within the assembly, expresses the nature of this celebration as one of the proclamation of the word and allows the community to express it faith in the presence of Christ in the Word. The hymn or acclamation must be chosen in reference to the gathering song. Two hymns placed in close proximity could overburdened the assembly and obscure the importance of the Word. The song may be a hymn or an acclamation; it should be joyful and allow the assembly a lively expression of its faith.

264. The communion song fosters unity by helping all to reflect on the meaning of the act of communion. Not only is the communicant in union with Christ, but with the whole body of Christ, represented by those gathered around, who journey together to the kingdom of God. The hymns chosen at this time should not speak of adoration, but the act and meaning of communion. The song during the communion procession should also be familiar so that the assembly can participate fully. If a hymn without a refrain is used, the words should be so familiar that people can sing it without carrying a book. The form that serves best is one with a refrain, which can be sung easily by memory. The verses can be sung either by a cantor, the choir or sections of the choir alternating. The text should either reflect the ritual action or speak of unity and service.

## Psalms

265. The psalm in the liturgy of the word, along with the silence following the reading, is the assembly's response to God's Word. As such, the refrain is not the response to the psalm, but the response to the preceding lesson. The psalm as a whole is a proclamation of God's Word which

helps the community to reflect on the reading. The true nature of the liturgy of the word as a dialogue between God and the assembly is made more evident.

266. In the traditional manner of singing the responsorial psalm,[6] the psalmist or cantor sings the refrain and the assembly repeats it; the cantor then sings the verses and the assembly sings the response or refrain after each verse. The psalm is either the one given in the Lectionary for the particular Sunday or feast, or a seasonal psalm found in the *Catholic Book of Worship*. The *Catholic Book of Worship* contains a number of seasonal psalms at the beginning of the section of psalms for each liturgical season. With a limited repertoire, even a small community could learn nine or ten psalms and refrains which could be used throughout the liturgical year. It is important to choose a refrain or psalm that is connected with the theme of the individual reading, and that the alternate text be similar in meaning to the proper psalm (*GIRM*, 36). Since the psalm itself is a response to God's word, the psalm and refrain must fit the context of the reading. If the words of the psalm allow it, the *Alleluia*, sung two or three times, is a suitable refrain that may be sung even if the verses are recited. The *Alleluia* could be used throughout the Easter Season, as indicated in the Lectionary and hymnal.

267. If the psalm cannot be sung, an alternative practice is to sing a seasonal refrain, and a minister other than the first or second reader of the scriptures proclaims the verses of the psalm of the Sunday (with some instrumental background music, if possible). At the very least, the person who leads the response to the Word of the God should be different from the person who proclaimed the Word.

**Acclamations**

268. Acclamations are "shouts of joy which arise from the whole assembly as forceful and meaningful assents to God's Word and Action. They are important because they make some of the most significant moments of the [Liturgy] . . . stand out."[7] In the Sunday Celebration of the Word these acclamations are the gospel acclamation and the acclamation to the proclamation of praise. These should be the first parts chosen for singing and sung even if nothing else can be sung.

269. The gospel acclamation consists of two parts: the acclamation and the scriptural verse. The cantor first sings the acclamation then leads the assembly in the acclamation; next the cantor sings the verse, followed by the acclamation which is sung by cantor and assembly. The acclamation is the *Alleluia* which may be sung any number of times, usually two or three. In Lent the *Alleluia* is never sung but is replaced by *Praise to you, Lord, King of eternal glory* or its equivalent. It is possible to sing the acclamation only and omit the verse. However, if the

acclamation is not sung, the verse is omitted completely. In brief the *Alleluia* is either sung or it is omitted.

270. The response to the general intersessions may also be sung, using a suitable acclamation that is well known.

271. Once the proclamation of praise has been chosen from the selection provided, an appropriate acclamation may be selected. The acclamation chosen should be familiar to the assembly. A cantor may sing the acclamation first and then invite the assembly to repeat it. In any case, a brief rehearsal of the acclamation before the liturgy starts is recommended, especially if the assembly does not sing it frequently. A song of praise may be chosen in place of the prayer of praise. The song of praise should be addressed to God, and should be a song that the assembly knows.

**Silence**

272. Of concern to musicians should be the periods of silence that follow the readings and homily.[8] This most-overlooked directive often turns the Liturgy of the Word into a speed race, one that perpetuates the attitude that the Word of God is unimportant and something to be done, rather than a means of communication between God the assembly. The first response of the assembly after hearing the word of God is silent reflection, before the psalm is sung.

**Other Occasions for Music**

273. As in the celebration of the Eucharist, music sung by the choir or cantor or instrumental music is more appropriate to accompany the collection and the recessional at the *Sunday Celebration of the Word or Hours*. These do not properly belong to the assembly and should be sung by the choir or cantor. At times instrumental music may be desirable. The pastoral decision of the liturgy committee should take into consideration the nature of the parish. Parishes in which the assembly loves to sing may choose to sing a congregational hymn at the recessional, especially at rich celebrations of greater solemnities. However, there should be sensitivity to the role of music to highlight the more important parts of the celebration. Singing at these parts of the celebration may diminish the emphasis placed on other parts of the liturgy.

**Music in the Liturgy of the Hours**

274. Morning and Evening Prayer utilizes a dynamic different from that of the Liturgy of the Word. The emphasis of the Liturgy of Hours is the praise of God and the intercession of a priestly people ascending from the gathered community to God. In this model the hymns and scriptures, (psalms, canticles and readings)

---

[6]  The *General Instruction on the Roman Missal*, no. 36, as well as the *Introduction to the Lectionary for Mass*, nos. 19-22, and the *Guidelines for Music in the Liturgy*, presume that the psalm will be sung.

[7]  *Music in Catholic Worship*, no 53, United States Catholic Conference.

[8]  The *General Instruction*, 23, states: "at the conclusion of a reading or the homily, all mediate briefly on what has been heard . . ."

---

are vehicles for the praise or eliciting praise. The general intercessions concluded by the Lord's Prayer form the supplication of the second part of the liturgy. In choosing music for the hours, planners should be careful that the selection of music reflects and maintains this balance of praise and intercession.

275. In the Liturgy of the Hours, the psalms and canticles express the praise of the community. As in a liturgy of the word, the psalm may be sung in various ways: the whole psalm may be sung by all; the verses may be alternated between the choir or cantor and the rest of the assembly; the verses may be alternated between one side of the assembly and the other; the psalm may be sung responsorially, with the cantor singing the verses and the whole assembly singing the refrain after each verse.

276. Psalms chosen in the Liturgy of the Hours should be predominately psalms of praise. A second psalm, penitential in nature, may be used in Lent.

277. On most occasions, to show the importance of the intercessory character of the hours, the petitions, or at least the response of the assembly, should be sung.

# PROPER OF SEASONS

### INTRODUCTORY RITES
### AND
### OPENING PRAYERS

# SEASON OF ADVENT

1.    In the course of the year, the Church unfolds the whole mystery of Christ from the incarnation and nativity to the Ascension, Pentecost, and the expectation of the blessed hope of the coming of the Lord.[1] The season of Advent, at the conclusion of the calendar year and the beginning of the Church's year, embraces both ends of this cycle. Advent begins with Evening Prayer I of the First Sunday of Advent and ends on 24 December, before Evening Prayer I of Christmas.

2.    In some parts of the Church where baptism was once celebrated at Epiphany, the forty days prior to it were devoted to ascetical preparation, and Advent took on several of the liturgical features of Lent. Now, however, "it is no longer considered a penitential season but a time of joyful expectation."[2]

3.    Advent has a twofold character. It is the season to prepare for Christmas, when Christ's first coming is remembered, and it is the "season when that remembrance directs the mind and heart to await Christ's Second Coming at the end of time. For these two reasons, the season of Advent is thus a period for devout and joyful expectation."[3]

4.    This twofold character is reflected in the two stages of Advent, each with its own special focus. From the first Sunday to 16 December, the liturgy expresses the eschatological expectation of Advent, the watchfulness of God's people looking forward to the time when Christ will come "again in glorious majesty," and "we shall at last possess in its fullness the promise for which we dare to hope."[4] From 17 December until Christmas eve, the texts proper to each day prepare us more directly to celebrate the Lord's birth, "our hearts filled with wonder and praise."[5]

5.    Advent is not simply a preparation to commemorate the historical event of Christmas nor primarily an expectation of the parousia, but is rather an anticipation or a beginning of the celebration of the integral mystery of the incarnation, the advent and the epiphany of the Son of God in flesh and in majesty. The Christian community lives in an "interim" time between two historical events: the coming of Christ in the flesh and his coming in glory at the end of time. The Church is called to be strong in faith "as we wait in joyful hope for the coming of our Saviour, Jesus Christ."[6]

\* The use of violet in Advent suggests a state of unfulfilled readiness and should no longer be regarded as an expression of penitence. It serves to set off the joyful white of Christmas with greater dramatic effect.

\* For the same reason, music in Advent may be more restrained, for example, in the use of the organ and other instruments. The *Gloria* is not used as the opening rite in Advent, not because it is a penitential season, but so that the hymn of the angels may resound with greater freshness on Christmas night.

\* In all three years of the lectionary cycle, the focus of each Sunday is clearly identifiable: on the first Sunday, the return of the Lord; on the second, John the Baptist's call to conversion; on the third, the relationship of John to Jesus; on the fourth, Mary and the events immediately preceding Christ's birth.

6.    Advent, as a period of expectation and preparation, is closely related to, yet distinct from, the feast of Christmas for which it prepares. This can create a certain tension in those places where the weeks before Christmas are exploited for commercial purposes or where social celebrations of the feast are anticipated in schools and places of work.

\* Popular devotions should respect the nature and character of Advent and should be consistent with the themes presented in the *Lectionary for Mass* and the Sacramentary volume of the Missal. Songs, carols, and devotions which focus on the nativity itself are out of place in Advent, especially before 17 December.

\* Where they are the custom, the Advent wreath and the Jesse tree, which help to sustain an expectant orientation toward Christmas, can assist the liturgical celebration and may be associated with the celebration of Mass.

\* Vigils, services of light, and celebrations of reconciliation may be very effective in fostering a sense of watchfulness and prayer and in disposing the community to a more fruitful participation in the celebrations of Advent.

---

[1]    See Vatican Council II, Constitution on the Liturgy *Sacrosanctum Concilium*, 4 December 1963, art. 102; see Congregation of Rites, General Norms for the Liturgical Year and Calendar, 21 March 1969 (hereafter, GNLYC), no. 17.

[2]    See Congregation of Rites, *The Roman Calendar: Text and Commentary*, English ed., 1975, p. 24.

[3]    GNLYC, no. 39.

[4]    Preface, Advent I.

[5]    Preface, Advent II; see GNLYC, no. 42; see The Roman Missal, *Lectionary for Mass*, 2nd English ed., 1981, Introduction, no. 94.

[6]    Order of Mass, Communion Rite; see Titus 2:13.

---

[Optional Rite]

# FIRST SUNDAY OF ADVENT

## Prayer over the Advent Wreath

When the Prayer over the Advent Wreath is not used, see Introductory Rites, page 6.

PREPARATION: The Advent Wreath is meant to be a visual reminder of the joy and expectation of this season and a means of uniting the observance of Advent in the home to the parish gathering; therefore, the rites surrounding the Wreath should not become primary or unduly extended so as to distract from the gathering of the assembly or the celebration of the word. Since the lighted candle is the sign of Christ, the first candle of the Wreath should always be lighted before the celebration begins. This rite is not repeated on the following Sundays of Advent; rather the candles of the Wreath are lighted before each celebration, and the Introductory Rites begin as usual.

### SIGN OF THE CROSS

All make the sign of the cross, as the leader of prayer says:

In the name of the Father, and of the Son,
✠ and of the Holy Spirit.

All respond: **Amen.**

### GREETING

The leader of prayer says:

Blessed be Jesus Christ
who was, who is, and who is to come.
Bless the Father and the Son and the Holy Spirit.

or

Blessed be the God of hope,
who has filled us with joy and peace by the Spirit,
that we may abound in hope
at the coming of our Lord Jesus Christ.
Bless the Father and the Son and the Holy Spirit.

All respond: **Blessed be God for ever.**

### PRAYER OF PRAISE OVER THE ADVENT WREATH

INVITATION: After the greeting, the leader of prayer invites the people to pray, using the following or similar words.

My brothers and sisters,
as we wait in joyful hope
for the coming of our Lord Jesus Christ in glory,
let us pray that God will make us witnesses of the Light of love,
who has taken on our humanity
to bring salvation to all people.

Lord God,
our Source of hope and Fountain of love,
you gather all peoples and nations
to be one in your kingdom of light and peace.

On this day that we celebrate Jesus' victory over sin and death,
we look forward to his return
when we will share the vision of your glory.
We thank you for this wreath,
the evergreen sign of your faithful love.
Dispel the darkness of sin,
that the light and joy of Jesus may shine in this waiting world.

We ask this through Jesus Christ our Lord.

All respond: **Amen.**

LITANY OF PRAISE: Then the leader of prayer, or another minister or a cantor, sings or says one of the following forms of invocation or other similar invocations to Christ..

The minister sings or says:

Lord Jesus, you came among us as the Light of the world:
Lord, have mercy.

All respond: **Lord, have mercy.**

The minister sings or says:

Christ Jesus, you fill your Church with the Spirit of hope and love:
Christ, have mercy.

All respond: **Christ, have mercy.**

The minister sings or says:

Lord Jesus, you will come in glory
to gather us into your Father's kingdom:
Lord, have mercy.

All respond: **Lord, have mercy.**

The opening prayer then follows (see pages 8-9).

# SUNDAYS OF ADVENT

## Introductory Rites

### SIGN OF THE CROSS

All make the sign of the cross, as the leader of prayer says:

In the name of the Father, and of the Son,
✠ and of the Holy Spirit.

All respond: Amen.

### GREETING

The leader of prayer says:

Blessed be Jesus Christ
who was, who is, and who is to come.
Bless the Father and the Son and the Holy Spirit.

or

Blessed be the God of hope,
who has filled us with joy and peace by the Spirit,
that we may abound in hope
at the coming of our Lord Jesus Christ.
Bless the Father and the Son and the Holy Spirit.

All respond: Blessed be God for ever.

### OPENING RITE

Only one of the options for the opening rite is chosen on any Sunday. The following is suggested for the Season of Advent. The *Gloria* is not used during Advent.

#### I.    LITANY OF PRAISE

INVITATION: After the greeting, the leader of prayer invites the people to praise Christ, using the following formularies or similar words.

Rich in mercy is our Saviour and great in kindness.
Praise the Lord Jesus Christ.

INVOCATIONS TO CHRIST: After a brief pause, the leader of prayer, or another minister or a cantor, sings or says one of the following forms of invocation or other similar invocations to Christ.

#### A

The minister sings or says:

Lord Jesus, you are the dawn of our salvation:
Lord, have mercy.

All respond: Lord, have mercy.

Christ Jesus, you came among us in human flesh:
Christ, have mercy.

All respond Christ, have mercy.

The minister sings or says:

Lord Jesus, you will come in glory at the end of time:
Lord, have mercy.

All respond: Lord, have mercy.

### B

The minister sings or says:

Lord Jesus, you came among us as the Light of the world:
Lord, have mercy.

All respond: Lord, have mercy.

The minister sings or says:

Christ Jesus, you fill your Church with the Spirit of hope and love:
Christ, have mercy.

All respond: Christ, have mercy.

The minister sings or says:

Lord Jesus, you will come in glory
to gather us into your Father's kingdom:
Lord, have mercy.

All respond: Lord, have mercy.

### C

The minister sings or says:

O Radiant Dawn, splendour of eternal light, coming in justice:
Lord, have mercy.

All respond: Lord, have mercy.

The minister sings or says:

O King of all nations, source of your Church's unity and faith, coming in love:
Christ, have mercy.

All respond: Christ, have mercy.

The minister sings or says:

O Emmanuel, God's presence among us, coming in power:
Lord, have mercy.

All respond: Lord, have mercy.

The opening prayer then follows (see pages 8-15).

# FIRST SUNDAY OF ADVENT

## OPENING PRAYER

Let us pray.

A period of silent prayer follows.

Almighty God,
strengthen the resolve of your faithful people
to prepare for the coming of your Christ
by works of justice and mercy,
so that when we go forth to meet him
he may call us to sit at his right hand
and possess the kingdom of heaven.

We ask this through our Lord Jesus Christ, your Son,
who lives and reigns with you in the unity of the Holy Spirit,
God for ever and ever.

## ALTERNATIVE OPENING PRAYER

### YEAR A

God of majesty and power,
amid the clamour of our violence
your Word of truth resounds;
upon a world made dark by sin
the Sun of Justice casts his dawning rays.

Keep your household watchful
and aware of the hour in which we live.
Hasten the advent of that day
when the sounds of war will be for ever stilled,
the darkness of evil scattered,
and all your children gathered into one.

We ask this through him whose coming is certain,
whose day draws near:
your Son, our Lord Jesus Christ,
who lives and reigns with you in the unity of the Holy Spirit,
God for ever and ever.

## YEAR B

Rend the heavens and come down,
O God of all the ages!
Rouse us from sleep,
deliver us from our heedless ways,
and form us into a watchful people,
that, at the advent of your Son,
he may find us doing what is right,
mindful of all you command.

Grant this through him whose coming is certain,
whose day draws near:
your Son, our Lord Jesus Christ,
who lives and reigns with you in the unity of the Holy Spirit,
God for ever and ever.

## YEAR C

God our Saviour,
you utter a word of promise and hope
and hasten the day of justice and freedom,
yet we live in a world forgetful of your word,
our watchfulness dulled by the cares of life.

Keep us alert.
Make us attentive to your word,
ready to look on your Son
when he comes with power and great glory.
Make us holy and blameless,
ready to stand secure
when the day of his coming shakes the world with terror.

We ask this through him whose coming is certain,
whose day draws near:
your Son, our Lord Jesus Christ,
who lives and reigns with you in the unity of the Holy Spirit,
God for ever and ever.

# SECOND SUNDAY OF ADVENT

## OPENING PRAYER

Let us pray.

Almighty and merciful God,
do not let our earthly concerns
keep us from hastening to meet your Son,
but teach us that heavenly wisdom
which makes us his true companions.

Grant this through our Lord Jesus Christ, your Son,
who lives and reigns with you in the unity of the Holy Spirit,
God for ever and ever.

## ALTERNATIVE OPENING PRAYER

### YEAR A

Your kingdom is at hand,
O God of justice and peace;
you made John the Baptist its herald
to announce the coming of your Christ,
who baptizes with the Holy Spirit and with fire.

Give us a spirit of repentance
to make us worthy of the kingdom.
Let complacency yield to conviction,
that in our day justice will flourish
and conflict give way
to the peace you bestow in Christ.

Grant this through him whose coming is certain,
whose day draws near:
your Son, our Lord Jesus Christ,
who lives and reigns with you in the unity of the Holy Spirit,
God for ever and ever.

## YEAR B

With tender comfort and transforming power
you come into our midst,
O God of mercy and might.

Make ready a way in the wilderness,
clear a straight path in our hearts,
and form us into a repentant people,
that the advent of your Son
may find us watchful and eager for the glory he reveals.

We ask this through him whose coming is certain,
whose day draws near:
your Son, our Lord Jesus Christ,
who lives and reigns with you in the unity of the Holy Spirit,
God for ever and ever.

## YEAR C

God of our salvation,
you straighten the winding ways of our hearts
and smooth the paths made rough by sin.

Make our conduct blameless,
keep our hearts watchful in holiness,
and bring to perfection the good you have begun in us.

We ask this through him whose coming is certain,
whose day draws near:
your Son, our Lord Jesus Christ,
who lives and reigns with you in the unity of the Holy Spirit,
God for ever and ever.

# THIRD SUNDAY OF ADVENT

## OPENING PRAYER

Let us pray.

A period of silent prayer follows.

Gracious God,
your people look forward in hope
to the festival of our Saviour's birth.

Give us the strength to reach that happy day of salvation,
and to celebrate it with hearts full of joy.

We ask this through our Lord Jesus Christ, your Son,
who lives and reigns with you in the unity of the Holy Spirit,
God for ever and ever.

## ALTERNATIVE OPENING PRAYER

### YEAR A

God of glory and compassion,
at your touch the wilderness blossoms,
broken lives are made whole,
and fearful hearts grow strong in faith.

Open our eyes to your presence
and awaken our hearts to sing your praise.
To all who long for your Son's return
grant perseverance and patience,
that we may announce in word and deed
the good news of the kingdom.

We ask this through him whose coming is certain,
whose day draws near:
your Son, our Lord Jesus Christ,
who lives and reigns with you in the unity of the Holy Spirit,
God for ever and ever.

## YEAR B

O God, most high and most near,
you send glad tidings to the lowly,
you hide not your face from the poor;
those who dwell in darkness you call into the light.

Take away our blindness,
remove the hardness of our hearts,
and form us into a humble people,
that, at the advent of your Son,
we may recognize him in our midst
and find joy in his saving presence.

We ask this through him whose coming is certain,
whose day draws near:
your Son, our Lord Jesus Christ,
who lives and reigns with you in the unity of the Holy Spirit,
God for ever and ever.

## YEAR C

Almighty God,
you sent your Son into a world
where the wheat must be winnowed from chaff
and wickedness clings even to what is good.

Let the fire of your Spirit
purge us of greed and deceit,
so that, purified, we may find our peace in you
and you may delight in us.

Grant this through him whose coming is certain,
whose day draws near:
your Son, our Lord Jesus Christ,
who lives and reigns with you in the unity of the Holy Spirit,
God for ever and ever.

# FOURTH SUNDAY OF ADVENT

## OPENING PRAYER

Let us pray.

A period of silent prayer follows.

Pour forth, O Lord, your grace into our hearts:
once through the message of an angel
you revealed to us the incarnation of Christ your Son;
now through his passion and cross
lead us to the glory of his resurrection.

We ask this through our Lord Jesus Christ, your Son,
who lives and reigns with you in the unity of the Holy Spirit,
God for ever and ever.

## ALTERNATIVE OPENING PRAYER

### YEAR A

Eternal God,
in the psalms of David,
in the words of the prophets,
in the dream of Joseph
your promise is spoken.
At last, in the womb of the Virgin Mary,
your Word takes flesh.

Teach us to welcome Jesus, the promised Emmanuel,
and to preach the good news of his coming,
that every age may know him
as the source of redemption and grace.

Grant this through him whose coming is certain,
whose day draws near:
your Son, our Lord Jesus Christ,
who lives and reigns with you in the unity of the Holy Spirit,
God for ever and ever.

## YEAR B

Here in our midst, O God of mystery,
you disclose the secret hidden for countless ages.
For you we wait; for you we listen.

Upon hearing your voice
may we, like Mary, embrace your will
and become a dwelling fit for your Word.

Grant this through him whose coming is certain,
whose day draws near:
your Son, our Lord Jesus Christ,
who lives and reigns with you in the unity of the Holy Spirit,
God for ever and ever.

## YEAR C

Who are we, Lord God,
that you should come to us?
Yet you have visited your people
and redeemed us in your Son.

As we prepare to celebrate his birth,
make our hearts leap for joy at the sound of your Word,
and move us by your Spirit to bless your wonderful works.

We ask this through him whose coming is certain,
whose day draws near:
your Son, our Lord Jesus Christ,
who lives and reigns with you in the unity of the Holy Spirit,
God for ever and ever.

# SEASON OF CHRISTMAS

1.   The season of Christmas begins with Evening Prayer I of Christmas and concludes with the feast of the Baptism of the Lord, that is, the Sunday after Epiphany or after 6 January. This season celebrates the birth of Christ and his early manifestations, and the Church considers it second only to the annual celebration of the Easter mystery.[1]

2.   In the earliest centuries, the Church had but one feast, the weekly and yearly celebration of the paschal mystery. Soon the Church began to celebrate the birth and manifestation of Christ, the sun of justice (see Malachi 4:2) and light of the world (see John 8:12). This feast coincided with the winter solstice. Since the days of Saint Leo the Great, the texts of the season have expressed the Church's understanding of Christmas as more than the simple commemoration of a historical event. It is rather the celebration of a mystery, not a separate mystery independent of the paschal mystery, but the beginnings of that mystery of salvation. From the first moments of his human existence, Christ was achieving humanity's redemption. The Christ who was to die and rise for us is recognized as the incarnate Son of God: "Today a new day dawns, the day of our redemption, prepared by God from ages past, the beginning of our never ending gladness."[2]

3.   A high point of the Christmas celebration is the reading of Saint John's prologue, which proclaims that "the Word was made flesh and lived among us" (John 1:14). All the readings and prayers lead up to, or echo, this conviction, proclaimed by the great councils of Nicaea, Ephesus, and Chalcedon and celebrated in the Christmas liturgy as the "holy exchange," whereby "we come to share in the divinity of Christ, who humbled himself to share in our humanity."[3]

4.   The Church celebrates the one true light, the light that banishes darkness.[4]

   *   The Christmas image of light, of night giving way to day, is reinforced by the sequence of the scriptural texts of each celebration. Texts are provided for celebrations in the evening (vigil), at midnight, at dawn, and during the day. The texts of these several celebrations are meant to be used at the actual time of day indicated by the titles of the celebrations.

   *   The *Gloria* is inspired by the song of the angels at the birth of Christ (see Luke 2:14). On Christmas night it is heard for the first time since the beginning of Advent. On this occasion above all others it should be sung by the whole assembly with joy and festive fervour.

   *   Symbols of the triumph of light over darkness and of life over death, for example, in some places candlelight and evergreens, are traditionally used to decorate the church and assist devotion.

   *   The rich images of new light and new life provide many creative possibilities for decorating the church in harmony with the local culture and traditions. The symbol of light recalls the Christian celebration of Easter and helps to link the incarnation with the paschal mystery of salvation. The symbol will be expressed differently in the northern hemisphere, where Christmas occurs at the winter solstice, and the southern hemisphere, where it coincides with the height of summer.

   *   The manger scene can be of great assistance to all in recalling the story and the circumstances of Jesus' birth in history and in rekindling a sense of wonder and simplicity. By its design or location, however, it should not displace or overshadow the signs of the Lord's real presence and activity in word and sacrament, in the assembly and in its ministers.

5.   Christmas has its own octave, during which the feasts of Saint Stephen (26 December), Saint John (27 December), and the Holy Innocents (28 December) are celebrated. These saints are seen as having a particular relation to the Christmas mystery and were traditionally honoured as "companions of Christ." The Sunday occurring within the octave is celebrated as the feast of the Holy Family.[5]

6.   The octave day itself, 1 January, is observed as the Solemnity of Mary, Mother of God, and like the Fourth Sunday of Advent it highlights the role of the Blessed Virgin Mary in the incarnation and manifestation of the Lord. It also recalls the conferral of the name of Jesus.[6] In some places people seek God's blessing for the year that begins on this day.

7.   In the Eastern Churches the solemnity of the Epiphany was the original feast of Christ's birth. When adopted by the West, it became a celebration of the revelation of God's eternal plan of salvation in Christ, manifested as "the light to enlighten all nations" and represented traditionally in the story of

---

[1]   See Congregation of Rites, General Norms for the Liturgical Year and Calendar, 21 March 1969 (hereafter, GNLYC), nos. 32 and 33.

[2]   The *Liturgy of the Hours*, Christmas, office of readings, responsory.

[3]   Christmas, Mass at Midnight, prayer over the gifts; Order of Mass, Preparation of the Gifts.

[4]   See Christmas, Mass at Midnight, opening prayer; see Fifth Day in the Octave of Christmas, opening prayer.

[5]   See GNLYC, no. 35.

[6]   Ibid.

the Magi.[7] From early times it was associated also with a commemoration of the Lord's baptism when he was anointed as Messiah and revealed as God's Son.

* The Epiphany is celebrated on 6 January or, wherever it is not observed as a day of obligation, on the Sunday falling between 2 and 8 January.[8]

* The custom of keeping Christmas decorations until Epiphany has been celebrated helps to show that Christmas and Epiphany are but two aspects of the same feast. It would be even more appropriate to extend this custom through the celebration of the Baptism of the Lord, the close of the season of Christmas.

8. The Baptism of the Lord is now celebrated separately on the Sunday after 6 January.[9] (In those places where the Epiphany is transferred to the Sunday falling on 7 or 8 January, the Baptism of the Lord is celebrated on the following Monday.[10]) The Baptism of the Lord brings to a close the Christmas season and recalls the opening of Jesus' public mission and ministry. The voice from the cloud acknowledging Christ as the beloved Son of God ushers the Church into Ordinary Time and its weekly proclamation of the life and teaching of the Lord.

---

[8] See GNLYC, no. 37.

[9] See GNLYC, no. 38.

[10] Congregation for Sacraments and Divine Worship, Decree *Celebratio Baptismatis Domini* on the celebration of the Baptism of the Lord, 7 October 1977.

# SUNDAYS OF CHRISTMAS
## Introductory Rites

### SIGN OF THE CROSS

All make the sign of the cross, as the leader of prayer says:

In the name of the Father, and of the Son,
✠ and of the Holy Spirit.

All respond: Amen.

### GREETING

The leader of prayer says:

Blessed be God,
who has shown his love in his Son, Jesus Christ,
for the salvation of all people.
Bless the Father and the Son and the Holy Spirit.

or

Blessed be God the Father,
for the mystery hidden from all eternity,
now revealed in Christ to all nations.
Bless the Father and the Son and the Holy Spirit.

or

Blessed be God,
who has spoken through his Son,
born for us of the Virgin Mary by the power of the Holy Spirit.
Bless the Father and the Son and the Holy Spirit.

or

Blessed be Christ, made visible in the flesh,
seen by the angels,
and proclaimed among the nations.
Bless the Father and the Son and the Holy Spirit.

All respond: Blessed be God for ever.

# Opening Rite

Only one of the options for the opening rite is chosen on any Sunday. The following are suggested for the Season of Christmas.

## I.  HYMN OF PRAISE (*GLORIA*)

INVITATION: After the greeting, the leader of prayer invites the people to praise God, using one of the following formularies or similar words.

With people everywhere, let us glorify our God in joyful song:

or

With all the voices of heaven,
let us sing praise and honour and glory to God:

GLORIA: The hymn of praise is then sung.

The opening prayer then follows (see pages 20-31).

or

## II.  LITANY OF PRAISE

INVITATION: After the greeting, the leader of prayer invites the people to praise Christ, using one of the following formularies or similar words.

Before listening to the words of our salvation,
let us praise the Lord Jesus Christ.

or

The risen Saviour was born for our salvation;
let us call out for Christ's mercy.

or

As we celebrate the mystery of God with us,
let us remember that our Saviour is rich in mercy and great in kindness.
Praise the Lord Jesus Christ.

INVOCATIONS TO CHRIST: After a brief pause, the leader of prayer, or another minister or a cantor, sings or says the following forms of invocation or other similar invocations to Christ.

The minister sings or says:

Eternal Word, you have scattered the darkness of sin and death:
Lord, have mercy.

All respond: Lord, have mercy.

The minister sings or says:

Word made flesh, you have made us children of God most high:
Christ, have mercy.

All respond: Christ, have mercy.

The minister sings or says:

Incarnate Son, you have united heaven and earth in God's peace.
Lord, have mercy.

All respond: Lord, have mercy.

The opening prayer then follows (see pages 20-31).

# THE BIRTH OF THE LORD

## Vigil

### OPENING PRAYER

Let us pray.

A period of silent prayer follows.

Eternal God,
every year you gladden our hearts
by renewing our hope of redemption;
grant that we who accept your Son as our Redeemer
may face him with confidence when he comes as our judge,
who lives and reigns with you in the unity of the Holy Spirit,
God for ever and ever.

### ALTERNATIVE OPENING PRAYER

#### YEARS A, B, C

God of Abraham and Sarah,
of David and his descendants,

unwearied is your love for us
and steadfast your covenant;
wonderful beyond words
is your gift of the Saviour,
born of the Virgin Mary.

Count us among the people in whom you delight,
and by this night's marriage of earth and heaven
draw all generations into the embrace of your love.

We ask this through Jesus Christ, your Word made flesh,
who lives and reigns with you in the unity of the Holy Spirit,
in the splendour of eternal light,
God for ever and ever.

# THE BIRTH OF THE LORD
## during the Night

### OPENING PRAYER

Let us pray.

A period of silent prayer follows.

God our Creator,
who made this most holy night radiant
with the splendour of the one true light,
grant in your mercy
that, as we celebrate on earth the mystery of that light,
we may also rejoice in its fullness in heaven.

We ask this through our Lord Jesus Christ, your Son,
who lives and reigns with you in the unity of the Holy Spirit,
God for ever and ever.

### ALTERNATIVE OPENING PRAYER

#### YEARS A, B, C

Good and gracious God,
on this holy night you gave us your Son,
the Lord of the universe, wrapped in swaddling clothes,
the Saviour of all, lying in a manger.

On this holy night
draw us into the mystery of your love.
Join our voices with the heavenly host,
that we may sing your glory on high.
Give us a place among the shepherds,
that we may find the one for whom we have waited,
Jesus Christ, your Word made flesh,
who lives and reigns with you in the unity of the Holy Spirit,
in the splendour of eternal light,
God for ever and ever.

# THE BIRTH OF THE LORD
## at Dawn

### OPENING PRAYER

Let us pray.

A period of silent prayer follows.

God of splendour,
at the birth of your incarnate Word
we are bathed in new radiance;
grant that the light which shines in our hearts through faith
may also show forth in our actions.

We ask this through our Lord Jesus Christ, your Son,
who lives and reigns with you in the unity of the Holy Spirit,
God for ever and ever.

### ALTERNATIVE OPENING PRAYER

**YEARS A, B, C**

Today, O God of light,
your loving kindness dawns,
your tender compassion shines upon us,
for in our Saviour, born of human flesh,
you reveal your gracious gift
of our birth to life eternal.

Fill us with wonder on this holy day:
let us treasure in our hearts
what we have been told,
that our lives may proclaim
your great and gentle mercy.

We ask this through Jesus Christ, your Word made flesh,
who lives and reigns with you in the unity of the Holy Spirit,
in the splendour of eternal light,
God for ever and ever.

# THE BIRTH OF THE LORD
## during the Day

## OPENING PRAYER

Let us pray.

A period of silent prayer follows.

O God,
you wonderfully created human nature
and even more wonderfully restored its dignity.
Give us the grace to share in the divinity of Christ,
who humbled himself to share in our humanity.

We ask this through our Lord Jesus Christ, your Son,
who lives and reigns with you in the unity of the Holy Spirit,
God for ever and ever.

## ALTERNATIVE OPENING PRAYER

### YEARS A, B, C

We praise you, gracious God,
for the glad tidings of peace,
the good news of salvation:
your Word became flesh,
and we have seen his glory.

Let the radiance of that glory
enlighten the lives
of those who celebrate his birth.
Reveal to all the world
the light no darkness can extinguish,
our Lord Jesus Christ,
who lives and reigns with you in the unity of the Holy Spirit,
in the splendour of eternal light,
God for ever and ever.

# THE HOLY FAMILY

## Sunday within the Octave of the Birth of the Lord

### (Or, if the Birth of the Lord falls on Sunday, 30 December)

This feast was established as part of the Christmas season in 1921 following promotion of the cult in the 19th century; it was linked to the octave of Christmas in 1969. The holy family of Jesus, Mary, and Joseph, itself subject to the difficulties and social pressures of its time, is offered as a model for Christian family life today.

## OPENING PRAYER

Let us pray.

A period of silent prayer follows.

God of blessings,
in the Holy Family you give us the model
of a household drawn together in love.
Grant that we may follow their example
and be welcomed with joy into your home in heaven.

We ask this through our Lord Jesus Christ, your Son,
who lives and reigns with you in the unity of the Holy Spirit,
God for ever and ever.

## ALTERNATIVE OPENING PRAYER

### YEAR A

Loving God,
guardian of our homes,
when you entrusted your Son
to the care of Mary and Joseph,
you did not spare them the pains
that touch the life of every family.

Teach us to rely on your word,
that in our trials as in our joys
we may be clothed in gentleness and patience
and united in love.
Make us ever thankful
for the blessings you give us
through Jesus Christ, your Word made flesh,
who lives and reigns with you in the unity of the Holy Spirit,
in the splendour of eternal light,
God for ever and ever.

## YEAR B

O God,
you cradle us at the beginning of life
and embrace us at our journey's end,
for you love us as your own.

Bind our families together
and deepen our faith,
that, like the Holy Family of Nazareth,
we may grow in wisdom,
obedient to your word.

We ask this through Jesus Christ, your Word made flesh,
who lives and reigns with you in the unity of the Holy Spirit,
in the splendour of eternal light,
God for ever and ever.


## YEAR C

As your sons and daughters, O loving God,
we come before you in thanksgiving,
called and united by your eternal Word.

Teach us to ponder the mystery of Nazareth,
that we may always find in you
the source of our strength
and the unity of our families.

We ask this through Jesus Christ, your Word made flesh,
who lives and reigns with you in the unity of the Holy Spirit,
in the splendour of eternal light,
God for ever and ever.

# 1 JANUARY
# MARY, MOTHER OF GOD

The Virgin Mary was already venerated as Mother of God when, in 431, the Council of Ephesus acclaimed her *Theotokos* (God-bearer). Her role in the mystery of the incarnation was celebrated on this day in Rome in the 7th century but was soon eclipsed by other feasts of Mary. Restored to the liturgical calendar in 1931, and to this day in 1969, the feast celebrates from a Marian perspective the Word made flesh, and so enriches the observance of the octave of Christmas and provides a solemn beginning to the New Year.

## OPENING PRAYER

Let us pray.

A period of silent prayer follows.

O God,
through the fruitful virginity of blessed Mary
you offered to the human race
the treasures of eternal salvation.

Let us experience the power of her prayers,
for through her we have received the author of life, your Son,
who lives and reigns with you in the unity of the Holy Spirit,
God for ever and ever.

## ALTERNATIVE OPENING PRAYER

### YEARS A, B, C

Most high God,
you come near to us this Christmas season
in the child born of the Virgin Mary.
In the depths of darkness, she gave birth to light;
in the depths of silence, she brought forth the Word.

Grant that we who ponder these things in our hearts
may recognize in her child
our Lord and Saviour, Jesus Christ,
who lives and reigns with you in the unity of the Holy Spirit,
in the splendour of eternal light,
God for ever and ever.

# SECOND SUNDAY OF CHRISTMAS

(In Canada this Sunday is always replaced by Epiphany.)

## OPENING PRAYER

Let us pray.

*A period of silent prayer follows.*

All-powerful and ever-living God,
glory of those who believe in you,
fill the world with your splendour
and show every nation the radiance of your light.

We ask this through our Lord Jesus Christ, your Son,
who lives and reigns with you in the unity of the Holy Spirit,
God for ever and ever.

## ALTERNATIVE OPENING PRAYER

### YEARS A, B, C

God most high,
your only Son embraced the weakness of our flesh
to give us the power to become your children;
your eternal Word chose to dwell among us,
that we might live in your presence.

Grant us a spirit of wisdom
to know how rich is the glory you have made our own,
and how great the hope to which we are called
in Jesus Christ, your Word made flesh,
who lives and reigns with you in the unity of the Holy Spirit,
in the splendour of eternal light,
God for ever and ever.

## 6 JANUARY
# THE EPIPHANY OF THE LORD

Epiphany is the earliest Christmas feast, originating in the East in the 3rd century and passing to the West in the 4th. A celebration of the divine "manifestation" or "coming," in the East it commemorates the baptism of the Lord and in the West the visit of the Magi. These wise men represent all peoples on earth, to whom the mystery of the incarnation is now revealed.

## OPENING PRAYER

Let us pray.

A period of silent prayer follows.

God of mystery,
on this day you revealed your only Son to the nations
by the guidance of a star.
We know you now by faith;
lead us into that presence
where we shall behold your glory face to face.

We ask this through our Lord Jesus Christ, your Son,
who lives and reigns with you in the unity of the Holy Spirit,
God for ever and ever.

## ALTERNATIVE OPENING PRAYER

### YEARS A, B, C

Lord God of the nations,
we have seen the star of your glory
rising in splendour.
The radiance of your incarnate Word
pierces the darkness that covers the earth
and signals the dawn of peace and justice.

Make radiant the lives of your people
with that same brightness,
and beckon all the nations
to walk as one in your light.

We ask this through Jesus Christ, your Word made flesh,
who lives and reigns with you in the unity of the Holy Spirit,
in the splendour of eternal light,
God for ever and ever.

# THE BAPTISM OF THE LORD

(If Epiphany falls on 7 or 8 January, the Baptism of the Lord
is transferred to the following Monday, 8 or 9 January.)

Drawing from the Eastern tradition of Epiphany, the West has remembered the baptism of the
Lord on the octave of the Epiphany since the 8th century. The feast was formally introduced into
the Roman calendar in 1960 and is now celebrated on the Sunday after the Epiphany as the conclusion to the season of Christmas. It commemorates the revelation of Jesus as God's beloved Son,
the Christ, anointed by the Spirit.

## OPENING PRAYER

Let us pray.

A period of silent prayer follows.

Almighty and eternal God,
when Christ was baptized in the River Jordan,
the Holy Spirit came upon him
and your voice declared him your beloved Son.

Keep all who are reborn of water and the Spirit
as children of adoption in whom you are well pleased.

We ask this through our Lord Jesus Christ, your Son,
who lives and reigns with you in the unity of the Holy Spirit,
God for ever and ever.

or

O God,
your only-begotten Son has appeared in human flesh;
grant that he, whose outward form is like our own,
may reshape us inwardly by his grace.

We ask this through our Lord Jesus Christ, your Son,
who lives and reigns with you in the unity of the Holy Spirit,
God for ever and ever.

## ALTERNATIVE OPENING PRAYER

### YEAR A

God of the covenant,
you anointed your beloved Son
with the power of the Holy Spirit,
to be light for the nations
and release for captives.

Grant that we who are born again
of water and the Spirit
may proclaim with our lips the good news of his peace
and show forth in our lives the victory of his justice.

We make our prayer through Jesus Christ, your Word made flesh,
who lives and reigns with you in the unity of the Holy Spirit,
in the splendour of eternal light,
God for ever and ever.

### YEAR B

God of salvation,
in the river Jordan you bathed your Son Jesus in glory
and revealed him as your obedient servant.

In spirit and in power
rend the heavens and come down to us.
Strengthen us to acknowledge your Christ,
that we who are reborn in his likeness
may walk with him the path of obedience.

Grant this through Jesus Christ, your Word made flesh,
who lives and reigns with you in the unity of the Holy Spirit,
in the splendour of eternal light,
God for ever and ever.

## YEAR C

Open the heavens,
almighty Father,
and pour out your Spirit
upon your people gathered in prayer.

Renew the power of our baptismal cleansing
and fill us with zeal for good deeds.
Let us hear your voice once again,
that we may recognize in your beloved Son
our hope of inheriting eternal life.

Grant this through Jesus Christ, your Word made flesh,
who lives and reigns with you in the unity of the Holy Spirit,
in the splendour of eternal light,
God for ever and ever.

# SEASON OF LENT

1.    Lent is the season in which we "prepare joyfully for the mystery of Easter with minds and hearts renewed."[1] In Lent, the community of faith is blessed with a spirit of loving reverence for God and of willing service to neighbour. The season of Lent begins on Ash Wednesday and concludes before the Evening Mass of the Lord's Supper on Holy Thursday.[2]

## Baptismal and Penitential Themes

2.    The liturgy of Lent is marked by two closely related themes, the baptismal and the penitential.[3] It is a time of purification and enlightenment for the elect, those preparing to receive the sacraments of Easter initiation. In this they are helped by the local Church, the whole community of the faithful who recall their own baptism and prepare for its renewal. Both the elect and the local community join together in a spirit of repentance and conversion of heart, making Lent a time of spiritual recollection for the whole Church as it prepares for the celebration of Easter.[4]

3.    Therefore Lent is a time for more intense prayer and reflection and for particular attention to the word of God.[5] This takes place above all in the Sunday eucharist. Lenten penance is not "only inward and individual but also outward and social."[6] Prayer, fasting, almsgiving, and other works of charity are the traditional ways of deepening conversion to Christ.

4.    The celebration of the Rite of Election or Enrollment of Names usually coincides with the beginning of Lent. By means of this rite, the candidates for initiation are accepted for their final preparation for the sacraments of initiation. The Church's acceptance of the candidates is founded on the election by God, in whose name the Church acts. As a pledge of fidelity, they inscribe their names in the book containing the list of those who have been chosen for initiation.[7]

   * Sponsors and godparents, as well as catechists, priests, and deacons have particular responsibilities toward the elect. They show the elect how to practice the gospel in personal and social life, sustain them in moments of hesitancy or anxiety, guide them, and bear witness on their behalf before the whole community.[8]

   * The presence of the elect in the midst of the community and their gracious dismissal from the eucharistic assembly during Lent are strong symbols of the baptismal character of the season. The celebration of the scrutinies during the parish Sunday eucharist not only heals and strengthens the elect, but helps all the faithful to deepen their own conversion.

   * The scrutinies always take place within the celebration of the eucharist and are celebrated on the Third, Fourth, and Fifth Sundays of Lent. When this is not possible, they are celebrated on other Sundays of Lent or even convenient days during the week.[9]

   * As the season of Lent leads the elect to the sacraments of initiation, so it leads the faithful to celebrate the sacrament of penance, which restores them from sin to baptismal innocence and reconciles them to God and the Church. Opportunities for communal and individual forms of reconciliation should be provided, especially toward the end of Lent.[10]

   * Because Lent is a time of preparation for the Easter sacraments, parents and godparents of infants to be baptized are also to receive appropriate formation so that the infants can be baptized on Easter Sunday, either at the Vigil or at one of the Masses during the day, or on one of the Sundays of Easter,[11] when the eucharist can be celebrated.[12]

   * A homily is recommended at weekday Masses during Lent; intercession for the elect and for sinners is especially appropriate in this season; and the Eucharistic Prayers for Masses of Reconciliation may be especially suitable[13] when the eucharist can be celebrated.

   * Music should reflect the more sober mood of Lent and thus provide a contrast with the festive music of the Easter season which follows. The

---

[1]    Preface, Lent I.

[2]    See Congregation of Rites, General Norms for the Liturgical Year and Calendar, 21 March 1969 (hereafter, GNLYC), no. 28.

[3]    See Vatican Council II, Constitution on the Liturgy Sacrosanctum Concilium, 4 December 1963 (hereafter, SC), art. 109.

[4]    See Roman Ritual, *Rite of Christian Initiation of Adults* (hereafter, RCIA), Introduction, no. 9; see RCIA, no. 125.

[5]    See SC, art. 109.

[6]    SC, art. 110.

[7]    See RCIA, nos. 105 and 106.

[8]    See RCIA, Introduction, no. 11.

[9]    See RCIA, no. 133.

[10]    See Roman Ritual, *Rite of Penance*, Introduction, no. 13.

[11]    See Roman Ritual, *Rite of Baptism for Children*, Introduction, no. 9.

[12]    The sacraments of initiation for adults and infants are not celebrated at a Sunday Celebration of the Word. See Part Four of the Formation Notes entitled *Special Occasions*, nos. 107, 108, 114 and 115, on pages 41-42, and on page 63 of this Ritual.

[13]    See General Instruction of the Roman Missal (hereafter, GIRM), no. 42; see SC, art. 109.

---

*Gloria* is not used as the opening rite at Mass and the *Alleluia* is replaced by other gospel acclamations.[14]

* The use of violet vestments and the simplicity of decoration in the church reflect the penitential nature of this season.[15] In those places where the conference of bishops has decided that the custom be maintained of covering crosses and images in the church during the last two weeks of Lent, the crosses are uncovered after the Good Friday liturgy, and other images before the Easter Vigil.

* Penitential services, the Liturgy of the Hours, and devotions such as the Stations of the Cross can play a part in stirring up a spirit of repentance during the season of Lent.

### The Role of the Bishop

5.     The celebration of the Easter mystery is the high point of the Church's year and is accomplished with the utmost solemnity. The intimately related seasons of Lent and Easter are therefore an eminently suitable time for the bishop as chief shepherd of the diocese to gather the flock of God's people for special liturgical celebrations. Thus it becomes clear that initiation, reconciliation, and healing are essentially ecclesial acts.[16]

* As the focal point of the church's concern for the catechumens, admission to election belongs to the bishop. The presiding celebrant for the rite is the bishop himself or one who acts as his delegate.[17]

* Following the ancient custom of the Church of Rome, the bishop is strongly encouraged to gather the faithful on Sundays or on other days during Lent, in the principal parish churches or places of pilgrimage in the diocese, to celebrate the liturgy with them.

* Toward the end of Lent, the bishop gathers the diocese to bless the oils for its ministry to catechumens and the sick and to consecrate the chrism used in the sacraments of Easter initiation and holy orders. Although presbyters may bless oil before anointing catechumens in the initiation of adults and, in case of necessity, before anointing the sick, use of the oil blessed by the bishop expresses more strongly the ministry of the whole local Church. The bishop may take this opportunity to instruct the presbyters about the reverent use and safe custody of the holy oils.[18]

### The Days of Lent

6.     The season of Lent leads to the Easter Triduum, which begins with the evening Mass of the Lord's Supper on Holy Thursday and ends with evening prayer on Easter Sunday. The final days of Lent together with the Easter Triduum make up Holy Week. Beginning on Passion Sunday (Palm Sunday) with Jesus' messianic entry into Jerusalem, Holy Week recalls the passion and resurrection of Christ.[19]

* The Sundays of Lent, Ash Wednesday, and the weekdays of Holy Week take precedence over all feasts and solemnities; only feasts and solemnities take precedence over the weekdays of Lent.[20]

7.     Ash Wednesday, a day of fast and abstinence, sets the tone for Lent through the call to turn away from sin and to be faithful to the gospel.

8.     The Sundays of Lent each have a special character drawn from the gospel of the day. On the first Sunday, the Church remembers how the Lord is led into the wilderness for forty days where he is tempted, and on the second, how Christ is transfigured on the mountain. On the next three Sundays, three great Johannine passages of major importance for Christian initiation are read: the Samaritan woman at the well, the man born blind, and the raising of Lazarus. While alternatives are given for years B and C, these gospels from year A may always be used with the other readings from year A, especially where the elect are preparing for Easter. Finally, on the last Sunday of Lent, the account of the Lord's passion is proclaimed from one of the synoptic gospels.[21]

9.     The first readings for the Sundays of Lent present the main elements of the history of salvation from its beginning until the promise of the new covenant. The readings from the letters of the apostles have been selected to complement the gospel and the first readings and, as far as possible, to make a connection between them.[22]

* The opening prayers and prefaces for the Sundays of Lent serve to reinforce the power of the readings for these Sundays. The scrutinies, which are celebrated on the third, fourth, and fifth Sundays of Lent, draw from and build upon the gospel reading in particular for each of these Sundays. The penitential rite is particularly appropriate as an opening rite for the celebration of the eucharist or word in Lent.

---

[14]     See GNLYC, no. 28; see GIRM, nos. 31 and 37.

[15]     See GIRM, no. 308.

[16]     See RCIA, Introduction, no. 12.

[17]     See RCIA, no. 108.

[18]     See The Roman Pontifical, *Rite of the Blessing of Oils and Consecrating the Chrism*, Introduction, nos. 1, 6-9.

[19]     See GNLYC, nos. 19 and 31.

[20]     See GNLYC, nos. 5 and 16.

[21]     See The Roman Missal, *Lectionary for Mass*, 2nd English ed., 1981, Introduction, no. 97.

[22]     Ibid.

# ASH WEDNESDAY
## Introductory Rites

The Introductory Rites for the Sundays of Lent are found on page 42.

## SIGN OF THE CROSS

All make the sign of the cross, as the leader of prayer says:

In the name of the Father, and of the Son,
✠ and of the Holy Spirit.

All respond: **Amen.**

## GREETING

The leader of prayer says:

Blessed be God,
who has reconciled us through Christ
and calls us to new life by his grace.
Bless the Father and the Son and the Holy Spirit.

or

Blessed be Jesus Christ,
who has shown the greatness of his love,
by dying for us while we were still sinners.
Bless the Father and the Son and the Holy Spirit.

or

Blessed be Christ Jesus,
who bore our sins in his body on the cross,
that we might die to sin and live to righteousness.
Bless the Father and the Son and the Holy Spirit.

All respond: **Blessed be God for ever.**

The opening rite is omitted.

## OPENING PRAYER

Let us pray.

Grant us, Lord, the grace
to begin this time of Christian service with a holy fast,
that, as we struggle against the spirit of evil,
we may be strengthened by the practice of self-discipline.

We ask this through our Lord Jesus Christ, your Son,
who lives and reigns with you in the unity of the Holy Spirit,
God for ever and ever.

## ALTERNATIVE OPENING PRAYER

Gracious and merciful God,
you look with love upon a sinful people
and desire only their return to you.

We beg of you the grace to live this holy season,
to persevere in prayer, fasting, and almsgiving.
By the discipline of Lent
purify our hearts of all pretension,
bring us back to you,
and make the whole Church ready
to celebrate the mysteries of Easter.

Grant this through Christ, our liberator from sin,
who lives and reigns with you in the unity of the Holy Spirit,
holy and mighty God for ever and ever.

LITURGY OF THE WORD: The readings follow as usual.

## PRAYER OVER THE ASHES

INVITATION: After the Gospel and Reflection the leader of prayer addresses the people in these
or similar words:

Dear friends,
let us implore God our Father
to renew us in spirit
as these ashes are placed on our heads
as a sign of repentance.

PRAYER: All pause for silent prayer, then the leader of prayer says the collect:

Lord,
you do not wish sinners to die
but to turn to you and live.
In your goodness hear our prayer:
pour out your blessing on these ashes,
which we place on our heads to remind us
that we are dust and unto dust we shall return.

Grant that by our faithful observance of Lent
we may gain pardon for our sins
and newness of life
in the image of your risen Son.
We ask this through Jesus Christ our Lord.

The ashes may be sprinkled with holy water in silence.

If the leader of prayer is a deacon, the following is used:

INVITATION: After the Gospel and Reflection the deacon addresses the people in these or similar words:

Dear friends,
let us implore God our Father
to bless and sanctify these ashes,
which we place on our heads as a sign of repentance.

PRAYER: All pause for silent prayer, then the deacon says the collect:

Lord God,
you are moved by humility
and grant pardon to those who repent.

Listen to our prayers
and pour out ✠ your blessing
on those who are marked by these ashes,
that, observing the season of Lent,
they may come with hearts made clean
to celebrate the paschal mystery of your Son.
We ask this through Jesus Christ our Lord.

or

Lord,
you do not wish sinners to die
but to turn to you and live.
In your goodness hear our prayer:
pour out your blessing on these ashes,
which we place on our heads to remind us
that we are dust and unto dust we shall return.

Grant that by our faithful observance of Lent
we may gain pardon for our sins
and newness of life
in the image of your risen Son.

We ask this through Jesus Christ our Lord.

The ashes may be sprinkled with holy water in silence.

## DISTRIBUTION OF ASHES

Then the leader of prayer, and if necessary other ministers, place ashes on those who come forward, saying to each:

Turn away from sin and be faithful to the gospel.

or

Remember, mortal, you are dust
and to dust you will return.

After the giving of ashes, the ministers wash their hands.

GENERAL INTERCESSIONS: The celebration continues with the general intercessions.

[Optional Rite]

# FIRST SUNDAY IN LENT

## Lenten Procession

*When the procession does not take place, see Introductory Rites, page 42.*

This procession may take place at any or all celebrations of the Sunday Eucharist even when the Rite of Election does not take place. Two forms are provided.

### Form A

The assembly and ministers gather in some place distinct from the church to which the procession will move. When all have assembled, the leader of prayer makes the sign of the cross and greets the assembly as usual.

### Form B

When the community cannot gather in a place distinct from the church, the Introductory Rites may begin at the entrance of the assembly. The ministers gather at the back of the church, and the people turn and face the leader of prayer. In this case the celebration begins as set out below. The litany of saints replaces the gathering hymn, and the ministers enter during the singing of the litany.

## SIGN OF THE CROSS

All make the sign of the cross, as the leader of prayer says:

In the name of the Father, and of the Son,
✠ and of the Holy Spirit.

All respond: Amen.

## GREETING

The leader of prayer says:

Blessed be God
who has reconciled us through Christ
and calls us to new life by his grace.
Bless the Father and the Son and the Holy Spirit.

All respond: Blessed be God for ever.

My brothers and sisters,
the great festival of our salvation is approaching
and so we begin the days of preparation and renewal
to celebrate the Easter sacraments of Christ's death and resurrection.
Today, throughout the whole Church,
the elect are called to the saving waters of new life.
With joy we accompany them on the journey of salvation
to the mysteries of Christ's life–giving love.

Entrusting them to the care of the Blessed Virgin Mary and all the saints,
we call upon the mercy of the Lord,
that together we may come to the joys of Easter.

In union with all the saints,
let us go forth, acclaiming the mercy of our God.

PROCESSION: The litany of saints is sung as the procession moves to the church. If incense is used, grains of incense are placed in the thurible, and the minister carrying the censer goes first, followed by those carrying the cross and candles, the leader of prayer and the assembly. A reader carries the Lectionary in the procession and waits at the ambo with the Lectionary for the Enthronement of the Word after the opening prayer. The opening rite is omitted.

When the procession reaches the altar, the ministers venerate it and take their places. The Lectionary may be enthroned and incensed as usual, although the liturgy of the word begins without the Procession of the Word of God.

## OPENING PRAYER

Let us pray.

A period of silent prayer follows.

Grant us, almighty God,
that through this yearly observance of Lent
we may enter more deeply into the mystery of Christ
and draw upon its power in the conduct of our lives.

We ask this through our Lord Jesus Christ, your Son,
who lives and reigns with you in the unity of the Holy Spirit,
God for ever and ever.

# ALTERNATIVE OPENING PRAYER

## YEAR A

Lord our God,
in every age you call a people
to hear your word
and to do your will.

Renew us in these Lenten days:
washed clean of sin,
sealed with the Spirit,
and sustained by your living bread,
may we remain true to our calling
and, with the elect, serve you alone.

Grant this through Christ, our liberator from sin,
who lives and reigns with you in the unity of the Holy Spirit,
holy and mighty God for ever and ever.

## YEAR B

God of the covenant,
as the forty days of deluge
swept away the world's corruption
and watered new beginnings
of righteousness and life,
so in the saving flood of baptism
your people are washed clean and born again.

Throughout these forty days, we beg you,
unseal for us the wellspring of your grace,
cleanse our hearts of all that is not holy,
and cause your gift of new life to flourish once again.

Grant this through Christ, our liberator from sin,
who lives and reigns with you in the unity of the Holy Spirit,
holy and mighty God for ever and ever.

## YEAR C

Lord our God,
you alone do we worship,
only your word gives life.

Sustain your Church on its Lenten journey.
When we walk through the desert of temptation,
strengthen us to renounce the power of evil.
When our faith is tested by doubt,
illumine our hearts with Easter's bright promise.

We ask this through Christ, our deliverance and hope,
who lives and reigns with you in the unity of the Holy Spirit,
holy and mighty God for ever and ever.

# SUNDAYS IN LENT
## Introductory Rites

### SIGN OF THE CROSS

All make the sign of the cross, as the leader of prayer says:

In the name of the Father, and of the Son,
✠ and of the Holy Spirit.

All respond: Amen.

### GREETING

The leader of prayer says:

Blessed be God,
who has reconciled us through Christ
and calls us to new life by his grace.
Bless the Father and the Son and the Holy Spirit.

or

Blessed be Jesus Christ,
who has shown the greatness of his love,
by dying for us while we were still sinners.
Bless the Father and the Son and the Holy Spirit.

or

Blessed be Christ Jesus,
who bore our sins in his body on the cross,
that we might die to sin and live to righteousness.
Bless the Father and the Son and the Holy Spirit.

or

Blessed be God,
who has given us life by glorifying his Son Jesus Christ
upon the altar of the cross.
Bless the Father and the Son and the Holy Spirit.

or

Blessed be Christ Jesus,
who bore our sins in his body on the cross,
that we might die to sin and live to righteousness.
Bless the Father and the Son and the Holy Spirit.

All respond: Blessed be God for ever.

# Opening Rite

Only one of the options for the opening rite is chosen on any Sunday. The following are suggested for the Season of Lent. The *Gloria* is not used during Lent.

## I. PENITENTIAL RITE

INVITATION TO REPENTANCE: After the greeting, the leader of prayer invites the people to acknowledge their sins in silence and to repent of them, using one of the following formularies or similar words.

As we prepare to listen to the Word of God,
we confess that we are sinners
and ask the Lord for pardon and strength

or

Gathered together in Christ,
let us ask forgiveness with confidence,
for God is full of gentleness and compassion.

or

My brothers and sisters,
let us acknowledge our sinfulness,
that we may receive God's word with faith.

CONFESSION OF SIN: After a period of silence one of the following forms is used.

All say:

I confess to almighty God
and to you, my brothers and sisters,
that I have sinned through my own fault,

All strike their breast as a sign of sorrow.

in my thoughts and in my words,
in what I have done,
and in what I have failed to do;
and I ask blessed Mary, ever virgin,
all the angels and saints,
and you, my brothers and sisters,
to pray for me to the Lord our God.

CONCLUSION: The leader of prayer says:

May almighty God have mercy on us,
forgive us our sins,
and bring us to everlasting life.

All respond: Amen.

The opening prayer then follows (see pages 46-56).

or

## II. LORD, HAVE MERCY (KYRIE)

INVITATION: After the greeting, the leader of prayer invites the people to acclaim Christ, using one of the following formularies or similar words.

You are called by God to rejoice in the embrace of mercy.
Acclaim Christ our Saviour.

or

God is making all things new.
Acclaim Christ, the first fruits of the new creation.

or

You are called by God out of darkness,
into the dawn of radiant light.
Acclaim Christ, the sun of justice.

INVOCATIONS TO CHRIST: One of the following forms of invocation of praise and petition to Christ the Lord is sung.

| A | B |
|---|---|
| Lord, have mercy. | Kyrie, eleison. |
| Christ, have mercy. | Christe, eleison. |
| Lord, have mercy. | Kyrie, eleison. |

The opening prayer then follows (see pages 46-56).

or

## III. LITANY OF PRAISE

INVITATION: After the greeting, the leader of prayer invites the people to praise Christ, using one of the following formularies or similar words.

Before listening to the word,
let us praise the Lord Jesus Christ.

or

Praise the risen Saviour
and call out for Christ's mercy.

or

Rich in mercy is our Saviour and great in kindness.
Praise the Lord Jesus Christ.

INVOCATIONS TO CHRIST: After a brief pause, the leader of prayer, or another minister or a cantor, sings or says one of the following forms of invocation or other similar invocations to Christ.

# A

The minister sings or says:

Loving Saviour, you died to bring us new life:
Lord, have mercy.

All respond: Lord, have mercy.

The minister sings or says:

Faithful Servant, you cleanse us from sin:
Christ, have mercy.

All respond: Christ, have mercy.

The minister sings or says:

Merciful Redeemer, you humbled yourself for our salvation:
Lord, have mercy.

All respond: Lord, have mercy.

# B

The minister sings or says:

Lord Jesus, you came to reconcile us
to one another and to the Father:
Lord, have mercy.

All respond: Lord, have mercy.

The minister sings or says:

Christ Jesus, you heal the wounds of sin and division:
Christ, have mercy.

All respond: Christ, have mercy.

The minister sings or says:

Lord Jesus, you raise us to new life in the Spirit:
Lord, have mercy.

All respond: Lord, have mercy.

The opening prayer then follows (see pages 46-56).

# FIRST SUNDAY IN LENT

## OPENING PRAYER

Let us pray.

A period of silent prayer follows.

Grant us, almighty God,
that through this yearly observance of Lent
we may enter more deeply into the mystery of Christ
and draw upon its power in the conduct of our lives.
We ask this through our Lord Jesus Christ, your Son,
who lives and reigns with you in the unity of the Holy Spirit,
God for ever and ever.

## ALTERNATIVE OPENING PRAYER

### YEAR A

Lord our God,
in every age you call a people
to hear your word
and to do your will.
Renew us in these Lenten days:
washed clean of sin,
sealed with the Spirit
and sustained by your living bread,
may we remain true to our calling
and, with the elect, serve you alone.
Grant this through Christ, our liberator from sin,
who lives and reigns with you in the unity of the Holy Spirit,
holy and mighty God for ever and ever.

## YEAR B

God of the covenant,
as the forty days of deluge
swept away the world's corruption
and watered new beginnings
of righteousness and life,
so in the saving flood of baptism
your people are washed clean and born again.

Throughout these forty days, we beg you,
unseal for us the wellspring of your grace,
cleanse our hearts of all that is not holy,
and cause your gift of new life to flourish once again.

Grant this through Christ, our liberator from sin,
who lives and reigns with you in the unity of the Holy Spirit,
holy and mighty God for ever and ever.


## YEAR C

Lord our God,
you alone do we worship,
only your word gives life.

Sustain your Church on its Lenten journey.
When we walk through the desert of temptation,
strengthen us to renounce the power of evil.
When our faith is tested by doubt,
illumine our hearts with Easter's bright promise.

We ask this through Christ, our deliverance and hope,
who lives and reigns with you in the unity of the Holy Spirit,
holy and mighty God for ever and ever.

# SECOND SUNDAY IN LENT

## OPENING PRAYER

Let us pray.

A period of silent prayer follows.

O God,
who commanded us to listen to your beloved Son,
nourish us inwardly with your word of life
and purify the eyes of our spirit,
that we may rejoice in the sight of your glory.

We ask this through our Lord Jesus Christ, your Son,
who lives and reigns with you in the unity of the Holy Spirit,
God for ever and ever.

## ALTERNATIVE OPENING PRAYER

### YEAR A

Holy God,
from the dazzling cloud
you revealed Jesus in glory
as your beloved Son.

During these forty days
enlighten your Church with the bright glory of your presence.
Inspire us by your word,
and so transform us into the image of the risen Lord,
who lives and reigns with you in the unity of the Holy Spirit,
holy and mighty God for ever and ever.

## YEAR B

Ever-faithful God,
you were well pleased with Abraham's obedience
and you accepted the sacrifice of your Son,
who gave himself up for the sake of us all.

Train us by Christ's teaching
and school us in his obedience,
that as we walk his way of sacrifice
we may come to share in your glory.

We ask this through Christ, our deliverance and hope,
who lives and reigns with you in the unity of the Holy Spirit,
holy and mighty God for ever and ever.

## YEAR C

God of the covenant,
your presence fills us with awe,
your word gives us unshakable hope.

Fix in our hearts
the image of your Son in glory,
that, sustained on the path of discipleship,
we may pass over with him to newness of life.

Grant this through Christ, our deliverance and hope,
who lives and reigns with you in the unity of the Holy Spirit,
holy and mighty God for ever and ever.

# THIRD SUNDAY IN LENT

## (Sunday of the First Scrutiny)

See page 56

## OPENING PRAYER

Let us pray.

A period of silent prayer follows.

O God, source of all mercy and goodness,
in almsgiving, fasting, and prayer
you have shown us a remedy for sin.
Listen with love as we confess our weakness,
and, when we are bowed down by the knowledge of our guilt,
lift up our hearts with the assurance of your mercy.

We ask this through our Lord Jesus Christ, your Son,
who lives and reigns with you in the unity of the Holy Spirit,
God for ever and ever.

## ALTERNATIVE OPENING PRAYER

### YEAR A

O God, living and true,
look upon your people,
whose dry and stony hearts are parched with thirst.

Unseal the living water of your Spirit;
let it become within us an ever-flowing spring,
leaping up to eternal life.
Thus may we worship you in spirit and in truth
through Christ, our deliverance and hope,
who lives and reigns with you in the unity of the Holy Spirit,
holy and mighty God for ever and ever.

## YEAR B

Holy God,
the folly of the cross
mocks our human wisdom,
and the weakness of the crucified
puts worldly power to shame.

Banish from our hearts
every pretence of might and of knowledge,
that by the power flowing from Christ's resurrection
your people may be raised up from the death of sin
and fashioned into a living temple of your glory.

Grant this through Christ, our liberator from sin,
who lives and reigns with you in the unity of the Holy Spirit,
holy and mighty God for ever and ever.

## YEAR C

God of salvation,
we stand before you on holy ground,
for your name is glorified
and your mercy revealed
wherever your mighty deeds are remembered.

Since you are holy and forbearing,
turn us from every rash and shallow judgment
to seek the ways of repentance.

We ask this through Christ, our deliverance and hope,
who lives and reigns with you in the unity of the Holy Spirit,
holy and mighty God for ever and ever.

# FOURTH SUNDAY IN LENT

## (Sunday of the Second Scrutiny)

See page 56

## OPENING PRAYER

Let us pray.

A period of silent prayer follows.

In a wonderful manner, Lord God,
you reconcile humankind to yourself
through your only Son, the eternal Word.
Grant that your Christian people
may press on toward the Easter sacraments
with lively faith and ready hearts.

We ask this through our Lord Jesus Christ, your Son,
who lives and reigns with you in the unity of the Holy Spirit,
God for ever and ever.

## ALTERNATIVE OPENING PRAYER

### YEAR A

God our Creator,
show forth your mighty works
in the midst of your people.

Enlighten your Church,
that we may know your Son
as the true light of the world
and through our worship confess him
as Christ and Lord,
who lives and reigns with you in the unity of the Holy Spirit,
holy and mighty God for ever and ever.

## YEAR B

O God, rich in mercy,
you so loved the world
that when we were dead in our sins,
you sent your only Son for our deliverance.

Lifted up from the earth,
he is light and life;
exalted upon the cross,
he is truth and salvation.

Raise us up with Christ
and make us rich in good works,
that we may walk as children of light
toward the paschal feast of heaven.

We ask this through Christ, our deliverance and hope,
who lives and reigns with you in the unity of the Holy Spirit,
holy and mighty God for ever and ever.

## YEAR C

God of compassion,
you await the sinner's return
and spread a feast to welcome home the lost.
Save us from the temptations
that lead away from you,
and draw us back by the constancy of your love,
that we may take our place in your household
and gladly share our inheritance with others.

Grant this through Christ, our liberator from sin,
who lives and reigns with you in the unity of the Holy Spirit,
holy and mighty God for ever and ever.

# FIFTH SUNDAY IN LENT
## (Sunday of the Third Scrutiny)
See page 56

## OPENING PRAYER

Let us pray.

A period of silent prayer follows.

Come to our aid, Lord God,
that we may walk courageously in that love
of which your Son gave proof
when he handed himself over to death
out of love for the world.

We ask this through our Lord Jesus Christ, your Son,
who lives and reigns with you in the unity of the Holy Spirit,
God for ever and ever.

## ALTERNATIVE OPENING PRAYER

### YEAR A

Merciful God,
you showed your glory to our fallen race
by sending your Son
to confound the powers of death.

Call us forth from sin's dark tomb.
Break the bonds which hold us,
that we may believe and proclaim Christ,
the cause of our freedom
and the source of life,
who lives and reigns with you in the unity of the Holy Spirit,
holy and mighty God for ever and ever.

## YEAR B

In our hearts, O God,
you have written a covenant of grace,
sealed by the obedience of Jesus your Son.

Raise us up with Christ,
the grain fallen to earth
that yields a harvest of everlasting life.
Bring us to glorify your name
by following faithfully where he has led.

We ask this through Christ, our deliverance and hope,
who lives and reigns with you in the unity of the Holy Spirit,
holy and mighty God for ever and ever.

## YEAR C

God of power,
God of mercy,
you bring forth springs in the wasteland
and turn despair into hope.

Look not upon the sins of our past,
but lift from our hearts
the failures that weigh us down,
that we may find refreshment and life
in Christ, our liberator from sin,
who lives and reigns with you in the unity of the Holy Spirit,
holy and mighty God for ever and ever.

# CHRISTIAN INITIATION

## First Scrutiny

**OPENING PRAYER**

Grant, all–provident God,
that our elect may grow in wisdom and reverence
as they prepare to confess your name.
Through your grace
restore them to that first innocence
which was lost by the sin of Adam and Eve.
We ask this through our Lord Jesus Christ, your Son,
who lives and reigns with you in the unity of the Holy Spirit,
God for ever and ever.

## Second Scrutiny

**OPENING PRAYER**

Almighty and eternal God,
fill your Church with the joy of the Spirit,
that these elect, born once of earthly parents,
may be born again to the new life of your kingdom.
We ask this through our Lord Jesus Christ, your Son,
who lives and reigns with you in the unity of the Holy Spirit,
God for ever and ever.

## Third Scrutiny

**OPENING PRAYER**

O God, source of all life,
that our elect,
who have been grounded in the mysteries of faith,
may receive new life at the font of baptism
and be numbered among the members of your Church.
We ask this through our Lord Jesus Christ, your Son,
who lives and reigns with you in the unity of the Holy Spirit,
God for ever and ever.

# PASSION SUNDAY
## Pastoral Notes

75.     The celebration of Passion Sunday may be observed in the following manner.

76.     The community may celebrate Christ's entry into Jerusalem to accomplish his paschal mystery by a procession (first form) or solemn entrance (second form). The simple entrance (third form) does not fit the order of the *Sunday Celebration of the Word* and is not used. The essence of the procession or solemn entrance is that the whole community (or those who wish) join in the procession. When the community cannot join in the procession, the commemoration of the Lord's entry into Jerusalem is not celebrated and the celebration begins in the usual way.

77.     The community assembles in a suitable place distinct from the church (first form) or, if the procession cannot be held outside the church, the community gathers in front of the church doors or inside the church in a place distinct from the sanctuary (second form). In all cases all members of the assembly hold palm branches. The leader of prayer, ministers carrying the processional cross, which is suitably decorated, and candles and incense, if it is used, and the other ministers gather with the community.

78.     The leader of prayer addresses the people, using the introductory remarks given for Passion Sunday, then continues with the sign of the cross and the liturgical greeting. Next follows the invitation to the celebration of the entry into Jerusalem. The blessing of the branches does not take place unless a deacon presides, therefore the lay leader of prayer uses the second form of the prayer provided in the sacramentary or the first form provided in the ritual.

79.     A gospel reader then comes forward to proclaim the gospel, the account of the Lord's entry into Jerusalem. The ministers with the candles stand on each side of the reading stand for the proclamation of the gospel. Incense may be placed in the censer and the Lectionary is incensed before the reading.

80.     After the gospel, the leader invites the community to join in the procession. The procession proceeds to the church or to the sanctuary, or around the church to the sanctuary. The minister with incense leads, followed by the cross-bearer accompanied by ministers carrying lighted candles, then a lector carrying the Lectionary. The community, including the leader and the other ministers, follow. A hymn in honour of Christ the King, such as *All Glory, Laud and Honour*, is sung during the procession.

81.     The assembly takes its place in the church and the procession is concluded with a prayer led by the leader of prayer. Since the prayer is an integral part of the procession and concludes it, no other elements should intervene. The opening (preparatory) rite is omitted.

82.     The ministers carrying the cross, candles and incense, and the Lectionary enter the sanctuary as usual and place the cross and candles in their places. The enthronement of the Word of God is not held after the opening prayer. The lector places the Lectionary on the ambo immediately upon arriving at the lectern and then stands near-by for the prayer. The first reading follows immediately after the opening prayer.

83.     The passion narrative may be read in parts as usual. The gospel reader, and not the leader of prayer, takes the part of the narrator. The leader of prayer may take the part of Christ.

84.     If a song of praise is chosen for the proclamation of praise, the hymn should be addressed to God the Father and not to Christ.

# PASSION SUNDAY
## Commemoration of the Lord's Entrance into Jerusalem

*The community assembles in some other place distinct from the church to which the procession will move. A suitable song or acclamation may be sung as the assembly and ministers gather. Then the leader of prayer makes the sign of the cross and greets the assembly, as usual.*

## SIGN OF THE CROSS

All make the sign of the cross, as the leader of prayer says:

**In the name of the Father, and of the Son,
✠ and of the Holy Spirit.**

All respond: **Amen.**

## GREETING

The leader of prayer says:

**Blessed be God,
who has given us life by glorifying his Son Jesus Christ
upon the altar of the cross.
Bless the Father and the Son and the Holy Spirit.**

or

**Blessed be Christ Jesus,
who bore our sins in his body on the cross,
that we might die to sin and live to righteousness.
Bless the Father and the Son and the Holy Spirit.**

All respond: **Blessed be God for ever.**

INTRODUCTORY REMARKS: Then the leader gives a brief introduction, using these or similar words:

**Dear friends in Christ,
since the beginning of Lent we have been preparing,
by works of charity and self–sacrifice,
to celebrate the Lord's paschal mystery.
Today we come together to begin this solemn celebration
in union with the whole Church throughout the world.
Jesus entered in triumph into his own city, Jerusalem,
to complete his work:
to suffer, to die, and to rise again.**

**With lively faith and devotion,
let us recall this entry, which began his saving work**

and follow him in his footsteps.
United with him in his suffering on the cross,
may we share his resurrection and new life.

INVITATION: The leader of prayer says:

Let us pray.

PRAYER: After a brief pause, the leader of prayer says the following prayer, with hands extended:

Merciful God,
increase the faith of those who place their hope in you,
and listen kindly to our prayers,
that we who carry these branches (palms) today
in honour of Christ, the triumphant King,
may live in him to bear abundant fruit,
for he lives and reigns for ever and ever.

All respond: **Amen.**

If the leader of prayer is a deacon, he may say the following:

Almighty and eternal God,
bless ✠ these branches (palms) and make them holy;
and grant that we who joyfully accompany Christ the King today
may by his grace arrive one day
in the new and eternal Jerusalm,
where he lives and reigns for ever and ever.

All respond: **Amen.**

GOSPEL: Then the account of the Lord's entrance is proclaimed from one of the four gospels by the gospel reader from the Lectionary. Incense, if used, and the signs of the cross are made as usual.

REFLECTION: After the gospel a brief homily or reflection may be given.

PROCESSION: If incense is used, grains of incense are placed in the thurible. Then the leader says:

| A | B |
|---|---|
| Acclaiming Jesus, | Let us go forth in peace, |
| like the people of Jerusalem, | All respond: **In the name of Christ.** |
| let us go forth in peace. | |

PROCESSIONAL SONG: A processional song is sung as the procession moves to the church. If incense is used, a minister carrying the censer goes first, followed by those carrying the cross and candles, the leader of prayer and the assembly. A reader carries the Lectionary in the procession and places it at the ambo. The procession and enthronement of the Lectionary is omitted after the opening prayer. The opening rite is also omitted.

When the procession reaches the altar, the ministers venerate it and take their places. The leader of prayer goes to the place from which he or she will preside for the opening prayer.

## Opening Prayer

The leader of prayer says:

Let us pray.

A period of silent prayer follows.

Almighty and eternal God,
when you sent our Saviour into the world,
you gave us all an example to follow:
in humble obedience he took upon himself a body like ours
and gave himself up to death on the cross.
In your mercy, grant us the grace
to learn from the example of his passion
and to share in the glory of his resurrection.

We ask this through Christ, our deliverance and hope,
who lives and reigns with you in the unity of the Holy Spirit,
God for ever and ever.

## Alternate Opening Prayer

### YEARS A, B, C

O God of eternal glory,
you anointed Jesus your servant
to bear our sins,
to encourage the weary,
to raise up and restore the fallen.

Keep before our eyes
the splendour of the paschal mystery of Christ
and, by our sharing in the passion and resurrection,
seal our lives with the victorious sign
of his obedience and exaltation.

We ask this through Christ, our liberator from sin,
who lives with you in the unity of the Holy Spirit,
holy and mighty God for ever and ever.

LITURGY OF THE WORD: The readings begin without the Procession of the Word of God.

# EASTER TRIDUUM
## Pastoral Notes

85.　　The Easter or Paschal Triduum is the centre or heart of the liturgical year and the life of the Church. The Paschal Triduum is to the liturgical year what Sunday is to the week. "The Easter Triduum begins with the evening Mass of the Lord's Supper, reaches its high point in the Easter Vigil, and closes with evening prayer on Easter Sunday."[23]

86.　　The central mystery of faith that is celebrated is the life-giving death and resurrection of the Lord Jesus Christ. Thus the Easter Triduum is one great feast and should not be seen as three separate days or celebrations. Each celebration highlights one dimension of the Paschal Mystery within the larger context of the mystery of our salvation and the ongoing saving reality of God's action in the world. Therefore, all three celebrations of the Triduum must be celebrated, or the Triduum is not celebrated at all. Moreover, all three elements of the Triduum must be celebrated by the same community. A community cannot celebrate some parts of the Triduum and not others. The integrity of the Triduum must be respected.

87.　　The celebration of the death and resurrection of Jesus links the Easter Triduum in a unique manner to the celebration of initiation and to the eucharist. The assembling of a Christian community deprived of celebrating the eucharist and initiation removes the heart of the liturgy of the Triduum. Through no fault of its own, the community attempts to observe the paschal mystery without celebrating those sacramental rites which embody the paschal mystery: initiation and eucharist.

88.　　It is for this reason that if at all possible, several communities should assemble as a larger community to celebrate the Triduum.[24]

### Evening Vigil the Lord's Death

89.　　Most of the elements in this celebration centre on the eucharist: the solemn celebration of the eucharist itself, communion under both kinds directly from the eucharist, the solemn transfer of the eucharist to a chapel of adoration, and prayer before the reserved sacrament. According to the Church's ancient tradition, and to emphasize the unity that springs from the eucharist, the only Mass that can be celebrated, other than the diocesan chrism Mass, is the evening Mass of the Lord's Supper.

90.　　When it is impossible for the eucharist to be celebrated, and the community is unable to celebrate with another community, it may gather to celebrate evening prayer in a more solemn form. The celebration of the liturgy of the word on Holy Thursday presents special difficulties, since the prayers and readings presume the context of the eucharist and the union of the community in celebrating the self-offering of Jesus in the sacred meal and sacrifice of the eucharist. Since the celebration on this night commemorates the institution of the eucharist and its saving reality, any celebration without the eucharist must be well planned and prepared. Any and every attempt to imitate the rites of the evening Mass of the Lord's Supper must be avoided.

91.　　Since the prayers and readings of the eucharist refer to the Church's participation in the action of the eucharist, which is the mystery of the Lord's death and resurrection, their use outside Mass is problematic and is not recommended. The celebration of evening prayer may be the best way to begin the celebration of the Triduum. The reading and prayer from the Liturgy of Hours is recommended.

92.　　On Holy Thursday, communion outside the eucharist may be given only to the sick and dying. On this night the tabernacle of the church should be empty and communion should not be given outside Mass. Therefore, the eucharist should not be reserved beforehand for distribution at any celebration.

93.　　Although the Blessed Sacrament is not reserved for the adoration of the community when the eucharist is not celebrated, the community can gather to pray and observe a vigil and begin the paschal fast. If desired, appropriate readings may be proclaimed and psalms and hymns be sung for an extended period of time in the form of night prayer or a vigil.

94.　　Since the washing of feet is dependent upon the presence of the community's leader and the leader's relationship of service to the community, the washing of feet is not an appropriate gesture in all circumstances. Bringing gifts to church for the poor or the collecting of the community's contribution to the Share Lent campaign may express the Church's concern for and service to others.

### Proclamation of the Lord's Death

95.　　At first thought, it seems that the celebration of the Passion of the Lord may be an ideal celebration for a community without a priest since it is a celebration of the word with holy communion. However, the distribution of holy communion on this day is tied to the celebration of the eucharist on the preceding evening. In the absence of a priest and the celebration of the evening Mass of the Lord's Supper, there is no reserved sacrament to receive. While it may be possible to receive consecrated hosts from another

---

[23]　*General Norms for the Liturgical Year and the Calendar*, 19.

[24]　See *Eucharisticum mysterium*, nos. 26 and 27; and Congregation for Divine Worship, Circular Letter *Paschalis solemnitas*, 16 January 1988, nos. 43 and 94.

parish, communion from another community cannot unite the community to a eucharistic celebration it did not celebrate. Since the Triduum is one celebration, the unity of the great feast would be fragmented. If the evening Mass of the Lord's Supper was not celebrated within the community, the distribution of communion at the Celebration of the Lord's Passion is not to take place even if a priest presides.

96.    In this case, the order of the celebration of the Lord's Passion would consist of two parts: the liturgy of the word and the veneration of the cross. The prayer after communion would be omitted and the liturgy would close with the prayer over the people. A prayer of praise would not be used.

**Evening Vigil of the Lord's Rising**

97.    In accord with ancient tradition, this night is one of vigil for the Lord, consisting of prayer, readings and psalms. The entire vigil takes place at night. It begins after dark and concludes before daybreak.[25] The form of this ancient service is essentially the celebration of hours called a vigil, and not a liturgy of the word.

98.    The purpose of the vigil is to celebrate the resurrection of the Lord in the sacraments of initiation: baptism, confirmation and eucharist. A problem arises in planning this celebration when the community cannot celebrate initiation: some parts of the vigil are not appropriate to a celebration of the word.

99.    The blessing of the fire and candle is omitted, but the community may gather in darkness to light a large candle and join in a procession to the church, carrying lighted tapers, in other words, to celebrate a form of the celebration of the light which is a part of evening prayer. The proclamation of Easter (*Exsultet*) and the liturgy of the word take place as usual.

100.    The celebration of initiation cannot take place since the process of initiation cannot be completed without the celebration of confirmation and the eucharist.

101.    As on Holy Thursday evening, the reception of communion is so tied to the celebration of the eucharist, that communion should not be distributed outside of Mass. [See *Roman Missal* (*RM*) Canadian edition, pages 218 and 244].

102.    The renewal of baptismal promises may take place, but since water for baptism was not blessed, the sprinkling rite is omitted, since all holy water was removed from the church at the beginning of the Triduum. It would not be appropriate to use "old" water to express the "new" beginning of life in Christ on this most holy night.

103.    The proclamation of praise may be used. A special form of the prayer of praise is provided in the Ritual.

**Day of the Lord's Rising**

104.    A *Sunday Celebration of the Word* may be celebrated on Easter Sunday, however, communion should be distributed only if consecrated hosts can be brought to the church from the celebration of the Easter Vigil or an Easter Sunday Mass in a neighbouring parish.

105.    The renewal of baptismal promises replaces the creed, but the sprinkling of the assembly is done only if water from the Easter Vigil can be used. The form of the baptismal creed is provided in the Ritual.

106.    A form of the prayer of praise for Easter is provided in the Ritual.

**Sacraments of Initiation of Adults and Children**

107.    The sacraments of initiation for adults and children of catechetical age are always celebrated in the context of the eucharist,[26] with the celebration of the eucharist as the climax of initiation; therefore, baptism and confirmation cannot be celebrated in the context of a *Sunday Celebration of the Word and Hours*.

**Baptism of Infants**

108.    The baptism of infants is normally not celebrated in the absence of an ordained minister. If a community is without an ordained minister for a prolonged period of time and the bishop appoints an administrator or moderator for the parish and/or authorizes that person to perform the baptism of infants, the celebration of baptism of infants may take place within a liturgy of the word.

109.    The rite outlined in the *Rite of Baptism for Children* is followed, using the "Rite of Baptism by a Catechist When No Priest or Deacon Is Available." The preparatory rites of the celebration are omitted and the reception of the child or children takes place at the entrance of the church.

110.    If the opening prayer is prayed at the entrance of the church, the ministers carrying the censer, processional cross, candles and Lectionary may lead the family, sponsors and others in procession to the front of the church, where the family and friends of the child take their place. The enthronement of the word may take place as usual.

111.    If the opening prayer takes place after the procession, the lector remains at the ambo. After the opening prayer, the Lectionary is placed on the ambo and the enthronement may take place as usual, or the enthronement of the Lectionary may be omitted.

112.    The rite of baptism takes place after the homily or reflection, as outlined in the *Ritual of Baptism for Children*. The prayer over the water takes the place of the proclamation of praise, and therefore the proclamation of praise is not repeated. The intercessions and profession of faith are part of the rite of baptism and

---

[25]    Congregation for Divine Worship, *Paschalis solemnitas*, nos. 3, 77, and *Roman Missal*, Canadian Edition, page 245.

[26]    *Code of Canon Law*, nos. 866 and 883; RCIA, nos. 14, 198, 208; RCIC, nos. 280-284; *Rite of Confirmation*, no 7b.

are not repeated. After the rite of baptism the *Sunday Celebration of the Word* continues with the sign of peace.

113.    If a communion service is held, the rite outlined in the Ritual for Baptism or in the Ritual for Sunday Celebrations of the Word is followed. When the Rite in the Ritual for Baptism is followed, a communion minister may conduct the communion service in place of the leader of prayer or a catechist.

### Reception of Baptized Persons into Full Communion

114.    The reception of baptized persons into full communion with the Catholic Church never takes place outside Mass, since the act of full communion can only take place by celebrating the eucharist. In addition, since the sacrament of confirmation cannot be celebrated without a priest, the rite of reception is delayed.

### First Communion of Children

115.    The reception of communion for the first time refers not just to the act of receiving communion, but to the act of fully participating in the celebration of the eucharist, which includes the act of joining the assembly in presenting gifts of bread and wine, giving thanks to God in the great prayer of the church, breaking bread, and receiving communion. For this reason, the first communion of children baptized as infants cannot be celebrated outside the Mass, except as Viaticum, in the danger of death.

# VIGIL OF THE PASSION
## Celebration of Evening Prayer

See page 289

## READING

One of the following readings may be chosen for evening prayer: Zechariah 12.10-11; 13.6-7 or Hebrews 10.12-23 or Ephesians 2.13-18.

## PRAYER FOR EVENING PRAYER

With hands extended, the leader of prayer says:

Father,
for your glory and our salvation
you appointed Jesus Christ eternal High Priest.

May the people he gained for you by his blood
come to share in the power
of his cross and resurrection
by celebrating his memorial
in the new and eternal covenant.

We ask this through Jesus Christ our Lord,
who lives and reigns with you in the unity of the Holy Spirit,
God for ever and ever.

All respond: **Amen.**

# HOLY SATURDAY

On Holy Saturday the Church waits at the tomb of Jesus, meditating on his suffering and death and looking forward to the holy night of the Easter Vigil. This day is characterized by fasting, waiting, and alertness in prayer.

# EASTER SUNDAY

See the Introductory Rites on page 67.

## OPENING PRAYER

Let us pray.

A period of silent prayer follows.

On this most holy day, Lord God,
through the triumph of your only-begotten Son
you have shattered the gates of death
and opened the way to everlasting life.

Grant we beseech you,
that we who celebrate the festival of the Lord's resurrection,
may rise to a new and glorious life
through the quickening power of your Spirit.

We ask this through Christ, our deliverance and hope,
who lives and reigns with you in the unity of the Holy Spirit,
God for ever and ever.

## ALTERNATE OPENING PRAYER

YEARS A, B, C

God of undying life,
by your mighty hand
you raised up Jesus from the grave
and appointed him judge of the living and the dead.

Bestow upon those baptized into his death
the power flowing from his resurrection,
that we may proclaim near and far
the pardon and peace you give us.

Grant this through our Lord Jesus Christ, firstborn from the dead,
who lives with you now and always in the unity of the Holy Spirit
God for ever and ever.

Or in the late afternoon or evening:

O God, worker of wonders,
you made this day for joy and gladness.
Let the risen Lord abide with us this evening,
opening the Scriptures to us
and revealing their meaning.

Set our hearts aflame and open our eyes,
that we may see in his sufferings
all that the prophets spoke
and recognize him in our midst
the Christ now entered into glory, firstborn from the dead,
who lives with you now and always in the unity of the Holy Spirit,
God for ever and ever.

# SEASON OF EASTER

1. Easter Sunday is both the third day of the Triduum and the first day of the season of Easter. The first eight days of the season, the octave of Easter, are celebrated as solemnities of the Lord. The Sundays of Easter take precedence over all other solemnities and feasts. The Ascension is celebrated on the fortieth day after Easter, or, if the conference of bishops so decides, it is observed on the Seventh Sunday of Easter. The fiftieth and last day is the feast of Pentecost. These fifty days are an unbroken celebration of the victory of the risen Lord; they are celebrated as one feast day, sometimes called "the great Sunday."[1]

2. Throughout this festive season, *Alleluias* are sung and the Easter candle stands in the midst of the assembly. Christ is risen, reigns glorious with the Father, and is present through the gift of the Spirit. This is the Easter mystery that is celebrated in the symbolic period of fifty days.

* The Acts of the Apostles and the Gospel of John are at the heart of the liturgy of the word throughout the fifty days of Easter. The Gospel of John offers the community of faith an opportunity to deepen its understanding of the central place that Christ's dying and rising, the paschal mystery, occupies in its life. The Acts of the Apostles shows how the Church derives its entire life from this mystery and its ultimate fruit, the gift of the Holy Spirit.[2] The prayers for the season of Easter serve to reinforce the paschal character of the Scripture readings for the season. The solemn Easter dismissal with its *Alleluias* is used during the octave of Easter and on Pentecost Sunday.

* Special attention is given to the mystagogical catechesis of those initiated at the Easter Vigil. This is a time for the community and the neophytes together to deepen their grasp of the paschal mystery and to make it part of their lives. For the neophytes in particular, a fuller and more effective understanding of the mysteries comes through meditation on the gospel message they have learned and above all through their new and personal experience of the sacraments they have received. The community of faith helps them and prays for them and, in turn, is inspired by their fervour. The neophytes, their godparents, and those who have assisted them in their preparation for baptism

have a special place reserved for them in the Sunday assemblies during the season of Easter.[3]

* The whole season is a suitable time for Christian initiation. Special attention could be given to the celebration of infant baptism. In particular, it is the best time to celebrate the confirmation of children baptized as infants and their first reception of Eucharist.[4]

* During the fifty days of this season, the Easter candle, suitably decorated and lighted, has a prominent place in the sanctuary. The baptismal font remains an important symbol during the fifty days. The sprinkling with water from the font is a most suitable opening rite. At the end of the season of Easter, the Easter candle is kept with honour in the baptistery. The candles of the newly baptized are lighted from it. The Easter candle may also be used near the coffin in funeral Masses as a sign of the Lord's resurrection.

* White vestments are worn throughout the season of Easter. Red vestments are worn on the feast of Pentecost, the last day of the Easter festival. The powerful gift of the Spirit has been celebrated by the community without ceasing since the baptisms and confirmations at the Easter Vigil. This gift of the Spirit and the feast of Pentecost fulfill the Easter promise and bring the Easter mystery to its completion. In addition to the lighted paschal candle, other ritual elements serve to emphasize the unity of the first and last days of the Easter season: for example, the dismissal with Easter *Alleluias* is used for Pentecost and a sequence, in addition to the *Alleluia*, is sung on both days.

* The eve of Pentecost is a good occasion for an extended vigil, possibly arranged by combining evening prayer with the Mass of the vigil. The Old Testament readings indicated in the *Lectionary for Mass* may be used for this. While its character is not baptismal, as is the Easter Vigil, this vigil may provide a suitable way of closing the period of post-baptismal catechesis. For all the faithful, it is a waiting for the ultimate completion of the paschal mystery when the Spirit will unite the peoples and nations on earth to proclaim the glory of God with one voice and one song.[5]

---

[1]   See Congregation of Rites, General Norms for the Liturgical Year and Calendar, 21 March 1969, nos. 5, 22-25.

[2]   See The Roman Missal, *Lectionary for Mass*, 2nd English ed., 1981, Introduction, no. 74.

[3]   See Roman *Ritual, Rite of Christian Initiation of Adults*, nos. 234-241.

[4]   In the absence of an ordained minister the sacraments of initiation are not celebrated. See Section Four of the Pastoral Notes for Sunday Celebration of the Word, nos. 107-115 on page 00 of this Ritual.

[5]   See General Instruction of the Liturgy of the Hours, no. 71; see Congregation for Divine Worship, Circular Letter *Paschalis solemnitas* to presidents of the conferences of bishops and presidents of national liturgical committees, on the preparation and celebration of the Easter Triduum, 16 January 1988, no. 107.

# SUNDAYS OF EASTER
## Introductory Rites

### SIGN OF THE CROSS

All make the sign of the cross, as the leader of prayer says:

In the name of the Father, and of the Son,
✠ and of the Holy Spirit.

All respond: **Amen.**

### GREETING

The leader of prayer says:

Blessed be the God of life,
who broke the bonds of death by raising Jesus from the dead
through the power of the Holy Spirit.
Bless the Father and the Son and the Holy Spirit.

or

Blessed be God who has given us the victory
through our Lord Jesus Christ.
Bless the Father and the Son and the Holy Spirit.

or

Blessed be the God and Father of our Lord Jesus Christ,
who in his great mercy has given us a new birth
by raising Jesus Christ from the dead.
Bless the Father and the Son and the Holy Spirit.

or

Blessed be Christ Jesus who died for our sins
and rose again for our life.
Bless the Father and the Son and the Holy Spirit.

or

Blessed be Jesus Christ, the faithful witness,
the firstborn from the dead,
who has redeemed us
and made us a kingdom of priests for our God.
Bless the Father and the Son and the Holy Spirit.

All respond: **Blessed be God for ever.**

# Opening Rite

Only one of the options for the opening rite is chosen on any Sunday. The following are suggested for the Season of Easter.

## I. SPRINKLING OF HOLY WATER

INVITATION TO PRAYER: After the greeting, a server brings a vessel of water, which was previously blessed, or not. Then the leader of prayer invites the people to pray, using one of the formularies or similar words.

My brothers and sisters in Jesus Christ,
let us praise God our Father,
who called us in baptism to be his people.

or

Brothers and sisters,
let us invoke and bless the name of God the all-holy,
that this water may be for us a sign of the new life in Christ
which in baptism we have all received.

ACCLAMATIONS OVER THE WATER: After a brief period of silence the leader of prayer, or another minister or a cantor, sings or says:

O Lamb of God,
by your sacrifice upon the cross
you have made fountains of living water spring up for us.

All sing: **Alleluia.** (Two or three times)

The minister says or sings:

O risen Christ,
by the cleansing word of the Father's love
you have restored the holiness of the church.

All sing: **Alleluia.** (Two or three times)

The minister says or sings:

O firstborn from the dead,
by the gift of the Spirit in the waters of baptism
you have made us the first fruits of a new humanity.

All sing: **Alleluia.** (Two or three times)

PRAYER:* With hands extended, the leader of prayer concludes:

Almighty God,
in the sacred signs of our faith,
you renew the wonders of creation and redemption.

We give you thanks for this water
and we pray that all who have been born again in baptism
may be heralds of the paschal mystery,
forever renewed in your church

We ask this through Christ our Lord.

All respond: **Amen.**

---

\*   Translation of an excerpt from the Missale Romano (1983 ed.) Copyright © Peter J. Scagnelli. All rights reserved. Used with permission.

SPRINKLING: Taking the sprinkler the leader of prayer moves through the church to sprinkle the assembly. If the church is large, other ministers may assist in the sprinkling by moving through the church, in addition to the leader.

Meanwhile an appropriate psalm, acclamation or song is sung.

The opening prayer then follows (see pages 71-86).

or

## II. LITANY OF PRAISE

INVITATION: After the greeting, the leader of prayer invites the people to praise Christ, using one of the following formularies or similar words.

Before listening to the word,
let us praise the Lord Jesus Christ
who has raised us to new life.

or

Praise the risen Saviour who is exalted at the right hand of God,
let us call out for Christ's mercy.

or

As we celebrate the mystery of our new life with Christ,
let us remember that our Saviour is rich in mercy and great in kindness.
Praise the Lord Jesus Christ.

INVOCATIONS TO CHRIST: After a brief pause, the leader of prayer, or another minister or a cantor, sings or says one of the following forms of invocation or other similar invocations to Christ.

### A

The minister sings or says:

Risen Lord, by your blood you have redeemed us from slavery to sin:
Lord, have mercy.

All respond: Lord, have mercy.

The minister sings or says:

Lord of life, by your rising you have claimed us as God's own people:
Christ, have mercy.

All respond: Christ, have mercy.

The minister sings or says:

Paschal Lamb, by baptism you have raised us to new life in the Spirit:
Lord, have mercy.

All respond: Lord, have mercy.

The opening prayer then follows (see pages 71-86).

### B

The minister sings or says:

Lord Jesus, you have called us out of darkness
into your own marvellous light:
Lord, have mercy.

All respond: Lord, have mercy.

➤

*The minister sings or says:*

Christ Jesus, you have clothed us with holiness and love:
Christ, have mercy.

*All respond:* Christ, have mercy.

*The minister sings or says:*

Lord Jesus, you have made us a new creation in the Spirit:
Lord, have mercy.

*All respond:* Lord, have mercy.

## C

*The minister sings or says:*

Lord Jesus, you are the firstborn from the dead,
showing us the way to the Father:
Lord, have mercy.

*All respond:* Lord, have mercy.

*The minister sings or says:*

Lord Jesus, you are the faithful witness,
giving us the consolation of the truth:
Christ, have mercy.

*All respond:* Christ, have mercy.

*The minister sings or says:*

Lord Jesus, you are the Good Shepherd,
leading us into everlasting life:
Lord, have mercy.

*All respond:* Lord, have mercy.

## D

*The minister sings or says:*

By your resurrection you have made us into the kingdom of God:
Lord, have mercy.

*All respond:* Lord, have mercy.

*The minister sings or says:*

By your ascension you have raised us to new life:
Christ, have mercy.

*All respond:* Christ, have mercy.

*The minister sings or says:*

By your Spirit you have made us temples of your glory:
Lord, have mercy.

*All respond:* Lord, have mercy.

*The opening prayer then follows (see pages 71-86).*

# SECOND SUNDAY OF EASTER

## OPENING PRAYER

Let us pray.

A period of silent prayer follows.

God of everlasting mercy,
each year when the feast of Easter returns
you enliven the faith of your holy people.

Increase in us the grace you have already bestowed,
that we may understand more fully
in whose font we have been washed,
in whose Spirit we have been reborn,
and in whose blood we have found redemption.

We ask this through our Lord Jesus Christ, your Son,
who lives and reigns with you in the unity of the Holy Spirit,
God for ever and ever.

## ALTERNATIVE OPENING PRAYER

### YEARS A, B, C

God of life,
source of all faith,
through the waters of baptism
you have raised us up in Jesus
and given us life that endures.

Day by day refine our faith,
that we who have not seen the Christ
may truly confess him as our Lord and God,
and share the blessedness of those who believe.

Grant this through Jesus Christ, the resurrection and the life,
who lives and reigns with you in the unity of the Holy Spirit,
God for ever and ever.

# THIRD SUNDAY OF EASTER

## Opening Prayer

Let us pray.

A period of silent prayer follows.

Let your people for ever exult, O God,
let the joy of their youth be renewed,
that we who now rejoice to be your adopted children
may look forward with certain hope
to the day of resurrection.

Grant this through our Lord Jesus Christ, your Son,
who lives and reigns with you in the unity of the Holy Spirit,
God for ever and ever.

## Alternative Opening Prayer

### YEAR A

O God of mystery,
out of death you delivered Christ Jesus,
and he walked in hidden glory with his disciples.

Stir up our faith,
that our hearts may burn within us
at the sound of his word,
and our eyes be opened to recognize him
in the breaking of the bread.

Grant this through Jesus Christ, the firstborn from the dead,
who lives and reigns with you now and always in the unity of the Holy Spirit,
God for ever and ever.

God of all the prophets,
you fulfilled your promise of old
that your Christ would suffer
and so rise to glory.

Open our minds to understand the Scriptures
and fill us with joyful wonder in the presence of the risen Christ,
that we may be his witnesses
to the farthest reaches of the earth.

We ask this through Jesus Christ, the firstborn from the dead,
who lives and reigns with you now and always in the unity of the Holy Spirit,
God for ever and ever.


## YEAR C

God of life,
in your risen Son
you reveal your abiding presence among us
and summon those reborn in baptism
to lives of worship and service.

Fill this assembly with reverence
as we come before you in prayer.
Grant us courage and zeal
in bearing witness before the world
to your Son, Jesus Christ, the firstborn from the dead,
who lives and reigns with you now and always in the unity of the Holy Spirit,
God for ever and ever.

# FOURTH SUNDAY OF EASTER

## OPENING PRAYER

Let us pray.

A period of silent prayer follows.

God of everlasting power,
guide us toward the joyful company of heaven,
so that your lowly flock may follow
where Christ, the great Shepherd, has gone before,
who lives and reigns with you in the unity of the Holy Spirit,
God for ever and ever.

## ALTERNATIVE OPENING PRAYER

### YEAR A

O God,
you never cease to call even those far away,
for it is your will
that all be drawn into one fold.

Attune our ears to the voice of the Good Shepherd,
who leads us always to you,
that we may find under your tender protection
life in all its fullness.

We ask this through Jesus Christ, the resurrection and the life,
who lives and reigns with you in the unity of the Holy Spirit,
God for ever and ever.

God of lasting love,
fulfill your plan of salvation
to gather into one fold
the peoples of the whole world.

Let everyone on earth
recognize your Christ as the Good Shepherd,
who freely lays down his life for all
to take it up again in power.

Grant this through Jesus Christ, the resurrection and the life,
who lives and reigns with you in the unity of the Holy Spirit,
God for ever and ever.

## YEAR C

Safe in your hand, O God,
is the flock you shepherd
through Jesus your Son.

Lead us always to the living waters
where you promise respite and refreshment,
that we may be counted among those
who know and follow you.

We ask this through Jesus Christ, the resurrection and the life,
who lives and reigns with you in the unity of the Holy Spirit,
God for ever and ever.

# FIFTH SUNDAY OF EASTER

## OPENING PRAYER

Let us pray.

A period of silent prayer follows.

God of unfailing mercy,
who redeemed us and adopted us as your children,
look upon us with tender love,
that we who believe in Christ
may enjoy true freedom
and enter our promised inheritance.

We ask this through our Lord Jesus Christ, your Son,
who lives and reigns with you in the unity of the Holy Spirit,
God for ever and ever.

## ALTERNATIVE OPENING PRAYER

### YEAR A

We have beheld your glory, O God,
in the face of Christ Jesus your Son.

Enliven our faith,
that through Christ we may put our trust in you.
Deepen our faith,
that in Christ we may serve you.
Complete our faith,
that one day we may live with you
in that place which Christ prepares for us,
where he lives with you now and always in the unity of the Holy Spirit,
God for ever and ever.

## YEAR B

O God,
you graft us onto Christ, the true vine,
and, with tireless care,
you nurture our growth in knowledge and reverence.

Tend the vineyard of your Church,
that in Christ each branch may bring forth
to the glory of your name
abundant fruits of faith and love.

Grant this through Jesus Christ, the resurrection and the life,
who lives and reigns with you in the unity of the Holy Spirit,
God for ever and ever.


## YEAR C

We behold your glory, O God,
in the love shown by your Son,
lifted up on the cross
and exalted on high.

Increase our love for one another,
that both in name and in truth
we may be disciples of the risen Lord Jesus,
and so reflect by our lives
the glory that is yours.

Grant this through Jesus Christ, the firstborn from the dead,
who lives and reigns with you now and always in the unity of the Holy Spirit,
God for ever and ever.

# SIXTH SUNDAY OF EASTER

## OPENING PRAYER

Let us pray.

A period of silent prayer follows.

Almighty God,
enable us to celebrate with fitting joy
these days of happiness,
that as we accompany the risen Lord in faith
we may express in our daily lives the joyful memory of Easter.

Grant this through our Lord Jesus Christ, your Son,
who lives and reigns with you in the unity of the Holy Spirit,
God for ever and ever.

## ALTERNATIVE OPENING PRAYER

### YEAR A

Faithful God,
who love us in Christ Jesus,
send your Spirit of truth to dwell within us,
that we may always reject what is false,
live by the commands of Christ,
and be true to the love you have shown us.

Grant this through Jesus Christ, the resurrection and the life,
who lives and reigns with you in the unity of the Holy Spirit,
God for ever and ever.

## YEAR B

God of all nations,
in the gift of your Son
you have embraced the world
with a love that takes away our sin
and bestows perfect joy.

Grant to all who have been reborn in baptism
fidelity in serving you
and generosity in loving one another.

We ask this through Jesus Christ, the firstborn from the dead,
who lives and reigns with you now and always in the unity of the Holy Spirit,
God for ever and ever.

## YEAR C

Great and loving Father,
your will for us in Jesus
is the peace the world cannot give;
your abiding gift
is the Advocate he promised.

Calm all troubled hearts,
dispel every fear.
Keep us steadfast in love
and faithful to your word,
that we may always be your dwelling place.

Grant this through Jesus Christ, the firstborn from the dead,
who lives and reigns with you now and always in the unity of the Holy Spirit,
God for ever and ever.

# THE ASCENSION OF THE LORD

The Ascension has always been an element in the joyful celebration of the fifty days from Easter Sunday to Pentecost but was singled out for commemoration on the fortieth day (see Acts 1:3) toward the end of the 4th century. The feast develops the glory of the resurrection by acclaiming the exaltation of Christ as Lord of heaven and earth. It serves to prepare the Church, toward the end of the season of Easter, for the coming of the Holy Spirit at Pentecost.

## OPENING PRAYER

Let us pray.

A period of silent prayer follows.

Almighty God,
make our hearts dance with joy and thanksgiving;
for in the ascension of Christ, your Son,
our human nature is raised above the heavens,
and where Christ the Head has gone before in glory
we, his Body, are called in hope.

We make our prayer through our Lord Jesus Christ, your Son,
who lives and reigns with you in the unity of the Holy Spirit,
God for ever and ever.

## ALTERNATIVE OPENING PRAYER

### YEAR A

God of majesty,
yours is the power that raised Christ from death,
yours the glory that exalted him to your right hand.

By the mystery of the Ascension,
sustain our hope
as we bear witness to our baptism.
By the perpetual outpouring of your Spirit,
confirm your Church
in its mission of salvation.

Grant this through Jesus Christ, the firstborn from the dead,
who lives and reigns with you now and always in the unity of the Holy Spirit,
God for ever and ever.

## YEAR B

God of power and might,
in the mystery of the Ascension
you have raised up and glorified your Son,
and exalted our humanity at your right hand.

Confirm the good news your Church proclaims,
so that when Christ returns in glory
all nations may be gathered into the kingdom,
where he lives and reigns with you now and always in the unity of the Holy Spirit,
God for ever and ever.

## YEAR C

God of majesty,
you led the Messiah
through suffering into risen life
and took him up to the glory of heaven.

Clothe us with the power
promised from on high,
and send us forth to the ends of the earth
as heralds of repentance
and witnesses of Jesus Christ, the firstborn from the dead,
who lives and reigns with you now and always the unity of the Holy Spirit,
God for ever and ever.

# SEVENTH SUNDAY OF EASTER

(In Canada, this Sunday is always replaced by the Ascension of the Lord.)

## OPENING PRAYER

Let us pray.

A period of silent prayer follows.

Lord God,
we firmly believe that Christ our Saviour
now reigns with you in majesty.
Open your ears to our prayer,
that we may also experience the truth of his promise
to remain with us always, even to the end of time.

We ask this through our Lord Jesus Christ, your Son,
who lives and reigns with you in the unity of the Holy Spirit,
God for ever and ever.

## ALTERNATIVE OPENING PRAYER

### YEAR A

God our Father,
glorify your Son
in the lives of the people called by his name.

Through no merit of ours, you have made us your own,
to be your witnesses on earth.
Keep us true to the name we bear,
that people everywhere may know
that you are the God and lover of us all.

We ask this through Jesus Christ, the resurrection and the life,
who lives and reigns with you in the unity of the Holy Spirit,
God for ever and ever.

## YEAR B

Father most holy,
look upon this people
whom you have sanctified by the dying and rising of your Son.

Keep us one in love
and consecrate us in your truth,
that the new life you have given us
may bring us to the fullness of joy.

Grant this through Jesus Christ, the firstborn from the dead,
who lives and reigns with you now and always in the unity of the Holy Spirit,
God for ever and ever.

## YEAR C

Father, righteous one,
your beloved Son prayed
that his disciples in every generation
might be one as you and he are one.

Look upon this assembly
gathered in his name.
Fulfill in us the prayer of Jesus
and crown our celebration of this paschal season
with your Spirit's gift of unity and love.

Grant this through Jesus Christ, the firstborn from the dead,
who lives and reigns with you now and always in the unity of the Holy Spirit,
God for ever and ever.

# PENTECOST SUNDAY
## Vigil

This, the "fiftieth day," concludes the season of Easter, the continuous single festival of the risen Christ. Pentecost, the Jewish feast of harvest, which also commemorates the giving of the Law of Moses, was the day when the Holy Spirit came upon the apostles (see Acts 2:1ff.); the event has been celebrated on this day at least since the 3rd century. The joy of Pentecost is that the risen Christ breathes upon the Church and says, "Receive the Holy Spirit" (John 20:22).

## OPENING PRAYER

Let us pray.

A period of silent prayer follows.

Almighty and ever-living God,
whose will it was
to encompass the paschal mystery within a season of fifty days,
grant that the people once scattered over the face of the earth
and divided by many tongues
may be gathered together by your heavenly Spirit
to confess your name with a single voice.

We ask this through our Lord Jesus Christ, your Son,
who lives and reigns with you in the unity of the Holy Spirit,
God for ever and ever.

or

God of power,
let the splendour of your glory come upon us,
and through the radiance of the Holy Spirit
let the brightness of Christ,
who is light from light,
shine in the hearts of those born again by grace.

Grant this through our Lord Jesus Christ, your Son,
who lives and reigns with you in the unity of the Holy Spirit,
God for ever and ever.

## ALTERNATIVE OPENING PRAYER

God of majesty and glory,
you bring us to the day
that crowns our joyful Easter feast.

Open for us the fountain of living waters
promised to the faithful,
that the outpouring of the Spirit
may reveal Christ's glory
and enlighten all who wait in hope
for the glorious day of redemption.

We ask this through Jesus Christ, the resurrection and the life,
who lives and reigns with you in the unity of the Holy Spirit,
God for ever and ever.

# PENTECOST SUNDAY
## during the Day

### OPENING PRAYER

Let us pray.

A period of silent prayer follows.

Lord God,
through the mystery of this holy feast
you sanctify your Church in every nation and people.

Pour out the gifts of your Spirit
across the face of the earth,
and in your merciful kindness
touch the hearts of all believers
as you touched those who first heard
the preaching of the gospel.

We ask this through our Lord Jesus Christ, your Son,
who lives and reigns with you in the unity of the Holy Spirit,
God for ever and ever.

### ALTERNATIVE OPENING PRAYER

#### YEARS A, B, C

Send down, O God, upon your people
the flame of your Holy Spirit,
and fill with the abundance of your sevenfold gift
the Church you brought forth
from your Son's pierced side.

May your life-giving Spirit
lend fire to our words
and strength to our witness.
Send us forth to the nations of the world
to proclaim with boldness your wondrous work
of raising Christ to your right hand.

We make our prayer through our Lord Jesus Christ, your Son,
who lives and reigns with you in the unity of the Holy Spirit,
God for ever and ever.

# ORDINARY TIME

1. The Church celebrates the mystery of Christ according to the rhythm of a yearly cycle whose climax is the Easter triduum. The seasons of Lent and Easter and, to a somewhat lesser extent, the seasons of Advent and Christmas are the most solemn times of the year. The yearly cycle is completed by the thirty-three or thirty-four weeks which comprise Ordinary Time.

2. Ordinary Time begins on the Monday after the Sunday following 6 January and continues until the Tuesday before Ash Wednesday inclusive. It begins again on the Monday after Pentecost and ends before Evening Prayer I of the First Sunday of Advent.[1]

* The numbering of Sundays in Ordinary Time is computed in this way: The first week in Ordinary Time follows the feast of the Baptism of the Lord. The other Sundays and weeks are numbered in order until the beginning of Lent. If there are thirty-four weeks in Ordinary Time, the numbering of the weeks resumes after Pentecost, even though the solemnities of the Holy Trinity and of the Body and Blood of Christ (transferred to the Sunday after Trinity Sunday where it is not observed as a holy day) will be celebrated on the first Sundays after the Easter season. If there are thirty-three weeks in Ordinary Time, the first week which would otherwise follow Pentecost is omitted.

* The transitions between seasons deserve special attention in order to enhance the rhythm of the liturgical year. After the feasts of the Epiphany and the Baptism of the Lord, the Sunday gospels concentrate on the beginnings of the Lord's preaching. As the liturgical year draws to a close and Advent approaches, eschatological themes predominate.[2] After the Easter season, the solemnities of the Holy Trinity and of the Body and Blood of Christ provide a kind of transition to Ordinary Time.

3. While the other liturgical seasons have their own distinctive character and celebrate a specific aspect of the mystery of Christ, the weeks of Ordinary Time – especially the Sunday – are devoted rather to the mystery of Christ in all its aspects.[3]

4. Ordinary Time enables the Church to appreciate more fully the ministry and message of Christ.

The *Lectionary for Mass* provides a semi-continuous reading of the Synoptic Gospels on the Sundays in Ordinary Time in such a way that, as the Lord's life and preaching unfold, the teaching proper to each of these gospels is presented.[4]

* For this reason the integrity of the Lectionary is respected, and the homily at the Sunday eucharist normally draws upon the Scriptures to open up for the assembly the mysteries of the faith and the guiding principles of the Christian life. In this way, the celebration of the mystery of Christ is connected with the everyday life and commitments of the Christian people who make up the assembly.[5]

* Thanks to the continuity of the scriptural texts used on Sundays, the liturgy sometimes commemorates a certain aspect of Christ's life and ministry over a period of several weeks, for example, the five weeks in year B of the Lectionary when the reading of chapter six of the Gospel of John is inserted into the cycle of Mark's Gospel.[6] It can be helpful in planning the Sunday liturgy to take notice of these elements of unity.

* Sensitive selection from among the variety of texts and alternative ritual elements can assist the assembly to celebrate the various aspects of the mystery of Christ. For instance, different forms of the opening rite may be chosen. The prayer formulary for each Sunday includes opening prayers inspired by the readings of the three-year lectionary cycle.

* General intercessions are ordinarily included by which the people of God exercise their priestly ministry of interceding for all humanity.[7]

5. When a solemnity, or a feast of the Lord, or the Commemoration of All the Faithful Departed falls on a Sunday in Ordinary Time, this celebration normally takes precedence over the Sunday liturgy. Some special feasts are normally celebrated on a Sunday in Ordinary Time (the Holy Trinity, Christ the King, and the Body and Blood of Christ where it is not observed as a holy day).[8]

6. By its nature, however, Sunday excludes the permanent assignment of any other celebration to

---

[1]   Congregation of Rites, General Norms for the Liturgical Year and Calendar, 21 March 1969 (hereafter, GNLYC), no. 44.

[2]   See The Roman Missal, *Lectionary for Mass*, 2nd English ed., 1981 (hereafter, LM), Introduction, no. 105.

[3]   See GNLYC, no. 43.

[4]   See LM, Introduction, no. 105.

[5]   See Vatican Council II, Constitution on the Liturgy *Sacrosanctum Concilium*, 4 December 1963 (hereafter, SC), art. 52; see General Instruction of the Roman Missal (hereafter, GIRM), nos. 41-42; see LM, Introduction, no. 25.

[6]   See LM, Introduction, no. 105.

[7]   See SC, art. 53; see GIRM, no. 45.

[8]   See GNLYC, nos. 58-59.

the day.[9] While on rare occasions it may be appropriate to celebrate a ritual, votive, or other special Mass on a Sunday in Ordinary Time, this should only occur when a serious need or pastoral advantage is present and at the direction of the local Ordinary or with his permission.[10]

* It may happen that special themes are proposed for the Sunday eucharist, for example, peace, Christian unity, vocations, the missions, Christian education, and social justice. These intentions may be referred to in the homily when appropriate to the prayers and readings of the day's liturgy. They may be expressed in the general intercessions, mentioned at the time for announcements, and reflected in the decoration of the church. But these observances do not change the liturgical calendar or displace the regular Sunday liturgy.

* Out of respect for the nature of the liturgy and in order to avoid the possibility of its being perceived as a means for promoting various worthwhile causes, it may be better to rely mostly on other means of education or exhortation concerning special themes. These could include the distribution of printed matter, the use of the church notice board or special displays, separate talks, discussions, films, and the like.

* The collection of money for one of these special intentions could likewise take place outside the liturgy, for example, as the people leave the church. If money gifts are to be received during the liturgy, they should be collected at the time of the preparation of the gifts.[11]

7.    Ordinary Time provides the Church with an opportunity to bring out more clearly the importance of Sunday as the first feast day of all, the weekly celebration of the paschal mystery.[12]

* Good quality in liturgical celebration should be maintained throughout Ordinary Time, as in all the seasons of the liturgical year. The planning and preparation of the liturgy should seek to develop consistent patterns for both ministers and the assembly as they fulfill their respective roles in the celebration of the eucharist. Such patterns can be achieved without the loss of appropriate variety in the choice of texts and ritual elements for particular celebrations. In this way liturgical ministers will be well prepared for their tasks, and the actions and objects used will have the strength and clarity of symbols that are effective.

* Vestments are green in colour for Sundays and weekdays.[13] Decorations may appropriately reflect the beauty of nature and the changes in the local natural environment.

---

[9]    See GNLYC, no. 6.

[10]    See GIRM, no. 332.

[11]    See GIRM, nos. 49 and 101.

[12]    See GNLYC, no. 4.

[13]    See GIRM, no. 308.

# SUNDAYS IN ORDINARY TIME
## Introductory Rites

## SIGN OF THE CROSS

All make the sign of the cross, as the leader of prayer says:

In the name of the Father, and of the Son,
✠ and of the Holy Spirit.

All respond: **Amen.**

## GREETING

The leader of prayer says:

Blessed be God, the Father of tenderness and compassion,
who is rich in kindness and faithfulness
and who keeps us in his love for all time.
Bless the Father and the Son and the Holy Spirit.

or

Blessed be God the Father, the Lord of heaven and earth,
who has revealed the mystery of his presence
to us his children.
Bless the Father and the Son and the Holy Spirit.

or

Blessed be Jesus Christ who died for our sins
and rose again for our life.
Bless the Father and the Son and the Holy Spirit.

or

Blessed be Jesus, who has made us one
to give glory to our God and Father
by the power of the Holy Spirit.
Bless the Father and the Son and the Holy Spirit.

or

Blessed be God in the Church
and in Christ Jesus for all generations,
who has strengthened us with power in the Spirit.
Bless the Father and the Son and the Holy Spirit.

or

Blessed be God, who has begun a good work in us
and who will bring it to completion
on the day of our Lord Jesus Christ.
Bless the Father and the Son and the Holy Spirit.

All respond: **Blessed be God for ever.**

## OPENING RITE

Only one of the options for the opening rite is chosen on any Sunday. The following is suggested for Ordinary Time.

### I. LITANY OF PRAISE

INVITATION: After the greeting, the leader of prayer invites the people to praise Christ, using one of the following formularies or similar words.

**Before listening to the word,**
**let us praise the Lord Jesus Christ.**

or

**Praise the risen Saviour;**
**call out for Christ's mercy.**

or

**Rich in mercy is our Saviour**
**and great in kindness.**
**Praise the Lord Jesus Christ.**

INVOCATIONS TO CHRIST: After a brief pause, the leader of prayer, or another minister or a cantor, sings or says one of the following forms of invocation or other similar invocations to Christ.

**A**

The minister sings or says:

**Lord Jesus, you were sent to heal the contrite:**
**Lord, have mercy.**

All respond: **Lord, have mercy.**

The minister sings or says:

**You came to call sinners:**
**Christ, have mercy.**

All respond: **Christ, have mercy.**

The minister sings or says:

**You plead for us at the right hand of the Father;**
**Lord, have mercy.**

All respond: **Lord, have mercy.**

**B**

The minister sings or says:

**Lord Jesus, you came to gather the nations**
**into the peace of God's kingdom:**
**Lord, have mercy.**

All respond: **Lord, have mercy.**

*The minister sings or says:*

You come in word and sacrament
to strengthen us in holiness:
Christ, have mercy.

   *All respond:* Christ, have mercy.

*The minister sings or says:*

You come in glory with salvation for your people:
Lord, have mercy.

   *All respond:* Lord, have mercy.

## C

*The minister sings or says:*

Lord Jesus, you are the mighty God and Prince of Peace:
Lord, have mercy.

   *All respond:* Lord, have mercy.

*The minister sings or says:*

You are the Son of God and Son of Mary:
Christ, have mercy.

   *All respond:* Christ, have mercy.

*The minister sings or says:*

You are Word made flesh and radiance of God's glory:
Lord, have mercy.

   *All respond:* Lord, have mercy.

## D

*The minister sings or says:*

Lord Jesus, you have shown us the way to the Father:
Lord, have mercy.

   *All respond:* Lord, have mercy.

*The minister sings or says:*

Lord Jesus, you have given us the consolation of the truth:
Christ, have mercy.

   *All respond:* Christ, have mercy.

*The minister sings or says:*

Lord Jesus, you are the Good Shepherd,
leading us into everlasting life:
Lord, have mercy.

   *All respond:* Lord, have mercy.

The opening prayer then follows (see pages 92-158).

# FIRST SUNDAY IN ORDINARY TIME
# THE BAPTISM OF THE LORD

See page 29-31

# FIRST WEEK IN ORDINARY TIME

## OPENING PRAYER

Let us pray.

A period of silent prayer follows.

Attend with kindness, Lord God,
to the cries of your people,
that we may see the things that ought to be done
and grow in the strength to do them.

We ask this through our Lord Jesus Christ, your Son,
who lives and reigns with you in the unity of the Holy Spirit,
God for ever and ever.

# SECOND SUNDAY IN ORDINARY TIME

## OPENING PRAYER

Let us pray.

A period of silent prayer follows.

Almighty God,
whose unfailing providence rules all things
both in heaven and on earth,
listen to the cry of your people
and guide in your peace the course of our days.

We ask this through our Lord Jesus Christ, your Son,
who lives and reigns with you in the unity of the Holy Spirit,
God for ever and ever.

# ALTERNATIVE OPENING PRAYER

## YEAR A

Merciful God,
you sent your Son, the spotless Lamb,
to take upon himself the sin of the world.

Make our lives holy,
that your Church may bear witness to your purpose
of reconciling all things in Christ,
who lives and reigns with you in the unity of the Holy Spirit,
God for ever and ever.

## YEAR B

From our earliest days, O God,
you call us by name.

Make our ears attentive to your voice,
our spirits eager to respond,
that, having heard you in Jesus your anointed one,
we may draw others to be his disciples.

We ask this through our Lord Jesus Christ, your Son,
who lives and reigns with you in the unity of the Holy Spirit,
God for ever and ever.

## YEAR C

God of wonders,
at Cana in Galilee
you revealed your glory in Jesus Christ
and summoned all humanity
to life in him.

Show to your people gathered on this day
your transforming power
and give us a foretaste
of the wine you keep
for the age to come.

We make our prayer through our Lord Jesus Christ, your Son,
who lives and reigns with you in the unity of the Holy Spirit,
God for ever and ever.

# THIRD SUNDAY IN ORDINARY TIME

## Opening Prayer

Let us pray.

A period of silent prayer follows.

Almighty and eternal God,
direct all our actions to accord with your holy will,
that our lives may be rich in good works
done in the name of your beloved Son,
who lives and reigns with you in the unity of the Holy Spirit,
God for ever and ever.

## Alternative Opening Prayer

### YEAR A

God of salvation,
the splendour of your glory
dispels the darkness of earth,
for in Christ we behold
the nearness of your kingdom.

Now make us quick to follow where he beckons,
eager to embrace the tasks of the gospel.

We ask this through our Lord Jesus Christ, your Son,
who lives and reigns with you in the unity of the Holy Spirit,
God for ever and ever.

## YEAR B

Your sovereign rule, O God,
draws near to us
in the person of Jesus your Son.
Your word summons us to faith;
your power transforms our lives.

Free us to follow in Christ's footsteps,
so that neither human loyalty
nor earthly attachment
may hold us back from answering your call.

We ask this through our Lord Jesus Christ, your Son,
who lives and reigns with you in the unity of the Holy Spirit,
God for ever and ever.

## YEAR C

Lord God,
whose compassion embraces all peoples,
whose law is wisdom, freedom, and joy for the poor,
fulfill in our midst your promise of favour,
that we may receive the gospel of salvation with faith
and, anointed by the Spirit, freely proclaim it.

Grant this through our Lord Jesus Christ, your Son,
who lives and reigns with you in the unity of the Holy Spirit,
God for ever and ever.

# FOURTH SUNDAY IN ORDINARY TIME

## OPENING PRAYER

Let us pray.

A period of silent prayer follows.

Teach us, Lord God,
to worship you with undivided hearts
and to cherish all people with true and faithful love.

We ask this through our Lord Jesus Christ, your Son,
who lives and reigns with you in the unity of the Holy Spirit,
God for ever and ever.

## ALTERNATIVE OPENING PRAYER

### YEAR A

O God,
teach us the hidden wisdom of the gospel,
so that we may hunger and thirst for holiness,
work tirelessly for peace,
and be counted among those
who seek first the blessedness of your kingdom.

We ask this through our Lord Jesus Christ, your Son,
who lives and reigns with you in the unity of the Holy Spirit,
God for ever and ever.

## YEAR B

Faithful God,
your Holy One, Jesus of Nazareth,
spoke the truth with authority,
and you confirmed his teaching by wondrous deeds.

Through his healing presence,
drive far from us all that is unholy,
so that by word and deed
we may proclaim him Messiah and Lord
and bear witness to your power to heal and save.

We ask this through our Lord Jesus Christ, your Son,
who lives and reigns with you in the unity of the Holy Spirit,
God for ever and ever.

## YEAR C

God of salvation,
in your prophet, Jesus the Christ,
you announce freedom
and summon us to conversion.

As we marvel at the grace and power of your word,
enlighten us to see the beauty of the gospel
and strengthen us to embrace its demands.

Grant this through our Lord Jesus Christ, your Son,
who lives and reigns with you in the unity of the Holy Spirit,
God for ever and ever.

# FIFTH SUNDAY IN ORDINARY TIME

## OPENING PRAYER

Let us pray.

A period of silent prayer follows.

Watch over your household, Lord, with unfailing care,
that we who rely solely on the hope of your grace
may always be sheltered by your protection.

We ask this through our Lord Jesus Christ, your Son,
who lives and reigns with you in the unity of the Holy Spirit,
God for ever and ever.

## ALTERNATIVE OPENING PRAYER

### YEAR A

Heavenly Father,
you have called your Church
to be the salt of the earth and the light of the world.

Give us vigorous faith and a love that is genuine,
so that all may see our works
and give you the glory.

We make our prayer through our Lord Jesus Christ, your Son,
who lives and reigns with you in the unity of the Holy Spirit,
God for ever and ever.

## YEAR B

Out of your power and compassion, O God,
you sent your Son into our afflicted world
to proclaim the day of salvation.

Heal the brokenhearted;
bind up our wounds.
Bring us health of body and spirit
and raise us to new life in your service.

We make our prayer through our Lord Jesus Christ, your Son,
who lives and reigns with you in the unity of the Holy Spirit
God for ever and ever.

## YEAR C

Most holy God,
the earth is filled with your glory,
and in your presence angels stand in awe.

Enlarge our vision,
that we may recognize your power at work in your Son
and join the apostles and prophets
as heralds of your saving word.

We ask this through our Lord Jesus Christ, your Son,
who lives and reigns with you in the unity of the Holy Spirit,
God for ever and ever.

# SIXTH SUNDAY IN ORDINARY TIME

## OPENING PRAYER

Let us pray.

*A period of silent prayer follows.*

O God,
you promise to remain with those
whose hearts are faithful and just.
By the gift of your grace
make our lives worthy of your abiding presence.

We ask this through our Lord Jesus Christ, your Son,
who lives and reigns with you in the unity of the Holy Spirit,
God for ever and ever.

## ALTERNATIVE OPENING PRAYER

### YEAR A

All-seeing God,
you alone judge rightly our inmost thoughts.

Teach us to observe your law from the heart
even as we keep it outwardly.
Purify our desires,
calm every anger,
and reconcile us to one another.
Then will our worship at your altar
render you perfect praise.

We make our prayer through our Lord Jesus Christ, your Son,
who lives and reigns with you in the unity of the Holy Spirit,
God for ever and ever.

We come before you, O God,
confident in Christ's victory over sickness and death.

Heal us again
from sin, which divides us,
and from prejudice, which isolates us.
Bring us to wholeness of life
through the pardon you grant your people.

We ask this through our Lord Jesus Christ, your Son,
who lives and reigns with you in the unity of the Holy Spirit,
God for ever and ever.

## YEAR C

O God,
who alone can satisfy our deepest hungers,
protect us from the lure of wealth and power;
move our hearts to seek first your kingdom,
that ours may be the security and joy
of those who place their trust in you.

We make our prayer through our Lord Jesus Christ, your Son,
who lives and reigns with you in the unity of the Holy Spirit,
God for ever and ever.

# SEVENTH SUNDAY IN ORDINARY TIME

## OPENING PRAYER

Let us pray.

A period of silent prayer follows.

Almighty God,
fix our hearts on what is right and true,
that we may please you always
by observing your will in both word and deed.

We ask this through our Lord Jesus Christ, your Son,
who lives and reigns with you in the unity of the Holy Spirit,
God for ever and ever.

## ALTERNATIVE OPENING PRAYER

### YEAR A

Heavenly Father,
in Christ Jesus
you challenge us to renounce violence
and to forsake revenge.

Teach us to recognize as your children
even our enemies and persecutors
and to love them without measure or discrimination.

We ask this through our Lord Jesus Christ, your Son,
who lives and reigns with you in the unity of the Holy Spirit,
God for ever and ever.

## YEAR B

God of pardon and deliverance,
your forgiving love, revealed in Christ,
has brought to birth a new creation.

Raise us up from our sins
to walk in your ways,
that we may witness to your power,
which makes all things new.

Grant this through our Lord Jesus Christ, your Son,
who lives and reigns with you in the unity of the Holy Spirit,
God for ever and ever.

## YEAR C

Compassionate God and Father,
you are kind to the ungrateful,
merciful even to the wicked.

Pour out your love upon us,
that with good and generous hearts
we may keep from judging others
and learn your way of compassion.

We make our prayer through our Lord Jesus Christ, your Son,
who lives and reigns with you in the unity of the Holy Spirit,
God for ever and ever.

# EIGHTH SUNDAY IN ORDINARY TIME

## OPENING PRAYER

Let us pray.

*A period of silent prayer follows.*

Direct the course of this world, Lord God,
and order it in your peace,
that your Church may serve you
in serenity and quiet joy.

We ask this through our Lord Jesus Christ, your Son,
who lives and reigns with you in the unity of the Holy Spirit,
God for ever and ever.

## ALTERNATIVE OPENING PRAYER

### YEAR A

Lord God,
your care for us surpasses
even a mother's tender love.

Through this word and sacrament
renew our trust in your provident care,
that we may abandon all anxiety
and seek first your kingdom.

We make our prayer through our Lord Jesus Christ, your Son,
who lives and reigns with you in the unity of the Holy Spirit,
God for ever and ever.

## YEAR B

God of tenderness,
desire of the human heart,
you led your people into the desert
and made them your own in love and fidelity.

By this word and sacrament
renew with us your covenant of love,
so that, forsaking the ways of the past,
we may embrace the new life of the kingdom.

We make our prayer through our Lord Jesus Christ, your Son,
who lives and reigns with you in the unity of the Holy Spirit,
God for ever and ever.

## YEAR C

O God, our teacher and judge,
hear our prayer
as we gather at the table of your word.

Enrich our hearts with the goodness of your wisdom
and renew us from within,
that all our actions, all our words,
may bear the fruit of your transforming grace.

We make our prayer through our Lord Jesus Christ, your Son,
who lives and reigns with you in the unity of the Holy Spirit,
God for ever and ever.

# NINTH SUNDAY IN ORDINARY TIME

## OPENING PRAYER

Let us pray.

A period of silent prayer follows.

O God,
you order the course of our lives
with unfailing providence.
Remove from our path whatever is harmful
and grant us those things that work to our good.

We ask this through our Lord Jesus Christ, your Son,
who lives and reigns with you in the unity of the Holy Spirit,
God for ever and ever.

## ALTERNATIVE OPENING PRAYER

### YEAR A

God of justice,
rock of our salvation,
open our minds and hearts to Jesus your Son.

Let us hold fast to his words
and express them in deeds,
that our faith may be built on a sure foundation
and our lives be judged worthy of you.

Grant this through our Lord Jesus Christ, your Son,
who lives and reigns with you in the unity of the Holy Spirit,
God for ever and ever.

## YEAR B

Holy God,
you sanctified this day
as a time for rest and worship.

As its blessed hours unfold,
place on our lips canticles of praise
and in our hearts the charity of Christ,
that this day may be a pledge and foretaste
of the eternal kingdom yet to come.

We ask this through our Lord Jesus Christ, your Son,
who lives and reigns with you in the unity of the Holy Spirit,
God for ever and ever.


## YEAR C

God of the nations,
whose will it is that all be saved
and come to knowledge of the truth,
grant that your gift of faith
may be alive in every heart,
so that, unworthy as we are,
we may welcome your Son
and find healing in his word.

We ask this through our Lord Jesus Christ, your Son,
who lives and reigns with you in the unity of the Holy Spirit,
God for ever and ever.

# TENTH SUNDAY IN ORDINARY TIME

## OPENING PRAYER

Let us pray.

A period of silent prayer follows.

Almighty God,
from whom every good gift proceeds,
grant that by your inspiration
we may discern those things that are right
and, by your merciful guidance, do them.

We ask this through our Lord Jesus Christ, your Son,
who lives and reigns with you in the unity of the Holy Spirit,
God for ever and ever.

## ALTERNATIVE OPENING PRAYER

### YEAR A

O God,
whose judgment shines like the light of day,
you invite sinners and outcasts
to the banquet of salvation.

Heal our pride and self-righteousness
as you send down upon us
the gentle rain of your mercy.

We make our prayer through our Lord Jesus Christ, your Son,
who lives and reigns with you in the unity of the Holy Spirit,
God for ever and ever.

## YEAR B

God our redeemer,
in Jesus, your promised Messiah,
you crushed the power of Satan.

Sustain your Church in the struggle against evil,
that, hearing your word and doing your will,
we may be fashioned into a household of true disciples
who share in the victory of the cross.

Grant this through our Lord Jesus Christ, your Son,
who lives and reigns with you in the unity of the Holy Spirit,
God for ever and ever.

## YEAR C

O God,
our very breath, our only hope,
in every age you take pity on us
and bring forth life from death.

Visit your people
and raise your Church to new life,
that we may join with all generations
in voicing our wonder and praise.

We make our prayer through our Lord Jesus Christ, your Son,
who lives and reigns with you in the unity of the Holy Spirit,
God for ever and ever.

# ELEVENTH SUNDAY IN ORDINARY TIME

## OPENING PRAYER

Let us pray.

A period of silent prayer follows.

O God,
the strength of all who hope in you,
accept our earnest prayer.
And since without you we are weak and certain to fall,
grant us always the help of your grace,
that in following your commands
we may please you in desire and in deed.

We ask this through our Lord Jesus Christ, your Son,
who lives and reigns with you in the unity of the Holy Spirit,
God for ever and ever.

## ALTERNATIVE OPENING PRAYER

### YEAR A

Compassionate God,
your word calls labourers to the harvest.
Send us who are blest with the gift of your kingdom
to announce its coming with gladness
and to manifest its healing power.

We make our prayer through our Lord Jesus Christ, your Son,
who lives and reigns with you in the unity of the Holy Spirit,
God for ever and ever.

## YEAR B

O God,
at whose bidding the seed will sprout
and the shoot grow toward full stature,
hear the prayer of your assembled people.

Make us trust in your hidden ways,
that we may pray with confidence
and wait upon your kingdom now growing in our midst.

We ask this through our Lord Jesus Christ, your Son,
who lives and reigns with you in the unity of the Holy Spirit,
God for ever and ever.

## YEAR C

Compassionate God,
you gather your people in prayer
and lavish your gifts upon us anew.

Sinners that we are,
you have forgiven us much.
Grant that our experience of your pardon
may increase our love
until it reflects your own immeasurable forgiveness.

We make our prayer through our Lord Jesus Christ, your Son,
who lives and reigns with you in the unity of the Holy Spirit,
God for ever and ever.

# TWELFTH SUNDAY IN ORDINARY TIME

## OPENING PRAYER

Let us pray.

A period of silent prayer follows.

Lord God,
teach us to hold your holy name
both in awe and in lasting affection,
for you never fail to help and govern
those whom you establish in your steadfast love.

We ask this through our Lord Jesus Christ, your Son,
who lives and reigns with you in the unity of the Holy Spirit,
God for ever and ever.

## ALTERNATIVE OPENING PRAYER

### YEAR A

True and faithful God,
you give courage to the fearful
and endurance to martyrs.

Sustain us as followers of your Son Jesus,
that with boldness and conviction
we may acknowledge him before the world.

We ask this through our Lord Jesus Christ, your Son,
who lives and reigns with you in the unity of the Holy Spirit,
God for ever and ever.

In the beginning, O God,
your word subdued the chaos;
in the fullness of time
you sent Jesus, your Son,
to rebuke the forces of evil
and bring forth a new creation.

By that same power,
transform all our fear
into faith and awe in your saving presence.

We ask this through our Lord Jesus Christ, your Son,
who lives and reigns with you in the unity of the Holy Spirit,
God for ever and ever.

## YEAR C

O God,
whose Son, our Messiah and Lord,
did not turn aside from the path of suffering
nor spare his disciples the prospect of rejection,
pour out your Spirit upon this assembly,
that we may abandon the security of the easy way
and follow in Christ's footsteps
toward the cross and true life.

Grant this through our Lord Jesus Christ, your Son,
who lives and reigns with you in the unity of the Holy Spirit,
God for ever and ever.

# THIRTEENTH SUNDAY
# IN ORDINARY TIME

## OPENING PRAYER

Let us pray.

A period of silent prayer follows.

Merciful God,
you willed that by the grace of adoption
we should become children of light;
grant that we not be cloaked in the darkness of error
but rather stand forth in the splendour of truth.

We ask this through our Lord Jesus Christ, your Son,
who lives and reigns with you in the unity of the Holy Spirit,
God for ever and ever.

## ALTERNATIVE OPENING PRAYER

### YEAR A

All-powerful God,
your incarnate Word commands our obedience
and offers us true life.

Make our ears attentive to the voice of your Son
and our hearts generous in answering his call,
that we may take up the cross with trust in his promises.

We ask this through our Lord Jesus Christ, your Son,
who lives and reigns with you in the unity of the Holy Spirit,
God for ever and ever.

## YEAR B

God of the living,
in whose image we have been formed
with imperishable life as our destiny,
dispel from your people the fear of death
and awaken within us the faith that saves.
Bid us rise from the death of sin
to take our place in the new creation.

We make our prayer through our Lord Jesus Christ, your Son,
who lives and reigns with you in the unity of the Holy Spirit,
God for ever and ever.

## YEAR C

Sovereign God, ruler of our hearts,
you call us to obedience
and sustain us in freedom.

Keep us true to the way of your Son,
that we may leave behind all that hinders us
and, with eyes fixed on him,
walk surely in the path of the kingdom.

Grant this through our Lord Jesus Christ, your Son,
who lives and reigns with you in the unity of the Holy Spirit,
God for ever and ever.

# FOURTEENTH SUNDAY IN ORDINARY TIME

## OPENING PRAYER

Let us pray.

A period of silent prayer follows.

God of power,
who raised up a fallen world
through the lowliness of your Son,
grant to your faithful people a holy joy,
so that those whom you have rescued from the slavery of sin
may delight in the happiness that never ends.

We ask this through our Lord Jesus Christ, your Son,
who lives and reigns with you in the unity of the Holy Spirit,
God for ever and ever.

## ALTERNATIVE OPENING PRAYER

### YEAR A

Father, Lord of heaven and earth,
by whose gracious will
the mysteries of the kingdom are revealed to the childlike,
make us learn from your Son humility of heart,
that in shouldering his yoke
we may find refreshment and rest.

We ask this through our Lord Jesus Christ, your Son,
who lives and reigns with you in the unity of the Holy Spirit,
God for ever and ever.

## YEAR B

God of the prophets,
in every age you send the word of truth,
familiar yet new,
a sign of contradiction.

Let us not be counted among those who lack faith,
but give us the vision
to see Christ in our midst
and to welcome your saving word.

Grant this through our Lord Jesus Christ, your Son,
who lives and reigns with you in the unity of the Holy Spirit,
God for ever and ever.


## YEAR C

Boundless, O God, is your saving power;
your harvest reaches to the ends of the earth.

Fill our hearts with zeal for your kingdom
and place on our lips the tidings of peace.
Grant us perseverance as heralds of the gospel
and joy as disciples of your Son, Jesus Christ our Lord,
who lives and reigns with you in the unity of the Holy Spirit,
God for ever and ever.

# FIFTEENTH SUNDAY IN ORDINARY TIME

## Opening Prayer

Let us pray.

A period of silent prayer follows.

O God,
you show the light of your truth to those who stray,
that they may return to the right path.
Grant that all who profess the Christian faith
may reject whatever is contrary to the gospel
and follow the way that leads to you.

We make our prayer through our Lord Jesus Christ, your Son,
who lives and reigns with you in the unity of the Holy Spirit,
God for ever and ever.

## Alternative Opening Prayer

### YEAR A

God of the heavens,
God of the earth,
all creation awaits your gift of new life.

Prepare our hearts
to receive the word of your Son,
that his gospel may grow within us
and yield a harvest that is a hundredfold.

We ask this through our Lord Jesus Christ, your Son,
who lives and reigns with you in the unity of the Holy Spirit,
God for ever and ever.

God of justice, God of salvation,
from every land you call a people to yourself.
Yours is the work we do,
yours the message we carry.

Keep your Church single-minded and faithful to you.
Let failure not discourage us
nor success beguile our hearts,
as you send us to proclaim the gospel.

We make our prayer through our Lord Jesus Christ, your Son,
who lives and reigns with you in the unity of the Holy Spirit,
God for ever and ever.

## YEAR C

In Christ you draw near to us,
God of mercy and compassion,
lifting us out of death,
binding up our wounds,
and nursing our spirits back to health.

Let such a tenderness as yours compel us
to go and do likewise.

Grant this through our Lord Jesus Christ, your Son,
who lives and reigns with you in the unity of the Holy Spirit,
God for ever and ever.

# SIXTEENTH SUNDAY IN ORDINARY TIME

## OPENING PRAYER

Let us pray.

A period of silent prayer follows.

Show favour to your servants, O Lord,
and shower upon us the gifts of your grace,
that, eager in faith, in hope, and in love,
we may always be watchful in keeping your commandments.

We ask this through our Lord Jesus Christ, your Son,
who lives and reigns with you in the unity of the Holy Spirit,
God for ever and ever.

## ALTERNATIVE OPENING PRAYER

### YEAR A

O God, patient and forbearing,
you alone know fully
the goodness of what you have made.

Strengthen our spirit when we are slow
and temper our zeal when we are rash,
that in your own good time
you may produce in us a rich harvest
from the seed you have sown and tended.

We make our prayer through our Lord Jesus Christ, your Son,
who lives and reigns with you in the unity of the Holy Spirit,
God for ever and ever.

## YEAR B

Compassionate God,
from far and near you gather your Church into one.

Safeguard the unity of your flock
through the teaching of Christ the Shepherd,
that all your scattered children may find in him
the guidance and nourishment they seek.

We ask this through our Lord Jesus Christ, your Son,
who lives and reigns with you in the unity of the Holy Spirit,
God for ever and ever.

## YEAR C

Eternal God,
you draw near to us in Christ
and make yourself our guest.

Amid the cares of our daily lives,
make us attentive to your voice
and alert to your presence,
that we may treasure your word above all else.

We ask this through our Lord Jesus Christ, your Son,
who lives and reigns with you in the unity of the Holy Spirit,
God for ever and ever.

# SEVENTEENTH SUNDAY
# IN ORDINARY TIME

## OPENING PRAYER

Let us pray.

A period of silent prayer follows.

O God, protector of those who hope in you,
without whom nothing is strong, nothing is holy,
enfold us in your gracious care and mercy,
that with you as our ruler and guide,
we may use wisely the gifts of this passing world
and fix our hearts even now on those which last for ever.

We ask this through our Lord Jesus Christ, your Son,
who lives and reigns with you in the unity of the Holy Spirit,
God for ever and ever.

## ALTERNATIVE OPENING PRAYER

### YEAR A

God of eternal wisdom,
you alone impart the gift of right judgment.

Grant us an understanding heart,
that we may value wisely
the treasure of your kingdom
and gladly forgo all lesser gifts
to possess that kingdom's incomparable joy.

We make our prayer through our Lord Jesus Christ, your Son,
who lives and reigns with you in the unity of the Holy Spirit,
God for ever and ever.

O God, you open wide your hand,
giving us food in due season.

Out of your never-failing abundance,
satisfy the hungers of body and soul
and lead all peoples of the earth
to the feast of the world to come.

We make our prayer through our Lord Jesus Christ, your Son,
who lives and reigns with you in the unity of the Holy Spirit,
God for ever and ever.

## YEAR C

Provident Father,
with the prayer your Son taught us always on our lips,
we ask, we seek, we knock at your door.

In our every need,
grant us the first and best of all your gifts,
the Spirit who makes us your children.

We ask this through our Lord Jesus Christ, your Son,
who lives and reigns with you in the unity of the Holy Spirit,
God for ever and ever.

# EIGHTEENTH SUNDAY
# IN ORDINARY TIME

## OPENING PRAYER

Let us pray.

*A period of silent prayer follows.*

Be present, Lord, to your grateful servants
and bless us with your unfailing kindness.
Since it is you who give us life and purpose,
restore in us the beauty of your creation
and keep intact the gifts you have restored.

We ask this through our Lord Jesus Christ, your Son,
who lives and reigns with you in the unity of the Holy Spirit,
God for ever and ever.

## ALTERNATIVE OPENING PRAYER

### YEAR A

Bountiful and compassionate God,
you place in the hands of your disciples
the food of life.

Nourish us at your holy table,
that we may bear Christ to others
and share with them
the gifts we have so richly received.

We make our prayer through our Lord Jesus Christ, your Son,
who lives and reigns with you in the unity of the Holy Spirit,
God for ever and ever.

## YEAR B

Lord, giver of lasting life,
satisfy our hunger through Christ, the Bread of Life,
and quench our thirst with your gift of belief,
that we may no longer work for food that perishes,
but believe in the One whom you have sent.

We ask this through our Lord Jesus Christ, your Son,
who lives and reigns with you in the unity of the Holy Spirit,
God for ever and ever.

## YEAR C

O God,
the giver of every gift that endures,
only by your grace can we rightly understand
the wonder of life
and why it is given.

By the word of your Son
challenge our foolishness,
confront our greed,
and shape our lives
to the wisdom of the gospel.

We ask this through our Lord Jesus Christ, your Son,
who lives and reigns with you in the unity of the Holy Spirit,
God for ever and ever.

# NINETEENTH SUNDAY IN ORDINARY TIME

## OPENING PRAYER

Let us pray.

A period of silent prayer follows.

Almighty and eternal God,
whom we dare to call Father,
impart to us more fully the spirit of adoption,
that we may one day gain the inheritance you have promised.

We ask this through our Lord Jesus Christ, your Son,
who lives and reigns with you in the unity of the Holy Spirit,
God for ever and ever.

## ALTERNATIVE OPENING PRAYER

### YEAR A

God of all power,
your sovereign word comes to us in Christ.

When your Church is in danger, make firm our trust;
when your people falter, steady our faith.
Show us in Jesus your power to save,
that we may always acclaim him as Lord,
who lives and reigns with you in the unity of the Holy Spirit,
God for ever and ever.

## YEAR B

God our Father and provider,
whose Son has given his flesh for the life of the world,
sustain your pilgrim Church on its journey
with the word of life and the bread of heaven.

Draw us nearer to him in whose name we gather,
that, following his way of sacrificial love,
we may come to the banquet of eternal life.

Grant this through our Lord Jesus Christ, your Son,
who lives and reigns with you in the unity of the Holy Spirit,
God for ever and ever.

## YEAR C

O God,
on whom our faith rests secure
and whose kingdom we await,
sustain us by word and sacrament
and keep us alert for the coming of the Son of Man,
that we may welcome him without delay.

We ask this through our Lord Jesus Christ, your Son,
who lives and reigns with you in the unity of the Holy Spirit,
God for ever and ever.

# TWENTIETH SUNDAY IN ORDINARY TIME

## OPENING PRAYER

Let us pray.

*A period of silent prayer follows.*

For those who love you, Lord,
you have prepared blessings which no eye has seen;
fill our hearts with longing for you,
that, loving you in all things and above all things,
we may obtain your promises,
which exceed every heart's desire.

We ask this through our Lord Jesus Christ, your Son,
who lives and reigns with you in the unity of the Holy Spirit,
God for ever and ever.

## ALTERNATIVE OPENING PRAYER

### YEAR A

God of the nations,
to your table all are invited
and in your family no one is a stranger.

Satisfy the hunger
of those gathered in this house of prayer,
and mercifully extend to all the peoples on earth
the joy of salvation and faith.

Grant this through our Lord Jesus Christ, your Son,
who lives and reigns with you in the unity of the Holy Spirit,
God for ever and ever.

## YEAR B

Wise and gracious God,
you spread a table before us
and nourish your people with the word of life
and the bread from heaven.

In our sharing of these holy gifts,
show us our unity in you
and give us a taste of the life to come.

We make our prayer through our Lord Jesus Christ, your Son,
who lives and reigns with you in the unity of the Holy Spirit,
God for ever and ever.


## YEAR C

To set the earth ablaze, O God,
your Son submitted to a baptism unto death,
and from his cup of suffering
you call the Church to drink.

Keep our eyes fixed on Jesus
and give us strength in time of trial
to run the race that lies before us.

We ask this through our Lord Jesus Christ, your Son,
who lives and reigns with you in the unity of the Holy Spirit,
God for ever and ever.

# TWENTY-FIRST SUNDAY IN ORDINARY TIME

## Opening Prayer

Let us pray.

A period of silent prayer follows.

O God,
you inspire the hearts of the faithful
with a single longing.

Grant that your people
may love what you command
and desire what you promise,
so that, amid the uncertain things of this world,
our hearts may be fixed where true joys are found.

We ask this through our Lord Jesus Christ, your Son,
who lives and reigns with you in the unity of the Holy Spirit,
God for ever and ever.

## Alternative Opening Prayer

### YEAR A

Living God,
you sent your Son among us
to reveal your wisdom
and make known your ways.

Increase our faith,
that we may confess Jesus as your Son,
take up his work on earth,
and trust his promise to sustain the Church.

We ask this through our Lord Jesus Christ, your Son,
who lives and reigns with you in the unity of the Holy Spirit,
God for ever and ever.

## YEAR B

In every age, O God,
you give your people freedom
to walk in faith
or to turn away.

Grant us grace
to remain faithful to your Holy One,
whose words are spirit and life,
Jesus Christ, our Lord,
who lives and reigns with you in the unity of the Holy Spirit,
God for ever and ever.


## YEAR C

To the banquet of your kingdom,
O God of the nations,
you have invited people of every race and tongue.

May all who are called to a place at your table
come, by the narrow way,
to the unending feast of life.

We make our prayer through our Lord Jesus Christ, your Son,
who lives and reigns with you in the unity of the Holy Spirit,
God for ever and ever.

# TWENTY-SECOND SUNDAY IN ORDINARY TIME

## OPENING PRAYER

Let us pray.

A period of silent prayer follows.

God of hosts,
from whom every good gift proceeds,
implant in our hearts the love of your name.
Nurture within us whatever is good
by binding us more closely to you,
and in your watchful care
tend the good fruit you have nurtured.

We ask this through our Lord Jesus Christ, your Son,
who lives and reigns with you in the unity of the Holy Spirit,
God for ever and ever.

## ALTERNATIVE OPENING PRAYER

### YEAR A

O God,
whose word burns like a fire within us,
grant us a bold and faithful spirit,
that in your strength we may be unafraid
to speak your word
and follow where you lead.

We make our prayer through our Lord Jesus Christ, your Son,
who lives and reigns with you in the unity of the Holy Spirit,
God for ever and ever.

## YEAR B

Father of light,
giver of every good and perfect gift,
bring to fruition the word of truth
sown in our hearts by your Son,
that we may rightly understand your commandments,
live your law of love,
and so offer you worship that is pure and undefiled.

Grant this through our Lord Jesus Christ, your Son,
who lives and reigns with you in the unity of the Holy Spirit,
God for ever and ever.

## YEAR C

God and judge of all,
you show us that the way to your kingdom
is through humility and service.

Keep us true to the path of justice
and give us the reward promised to those
who make a place for the rejected and the poor.

We ask this through our Lord Jesus Christ, your Son,
who lives and reigns with you in the unity of the Holy Spirit,
God for ever and ever.

# TWENTY-THIRD SUNDAY
# IN ORDINARY TIME

## OPENING PRAYER

Let us pray.

A period of silent prayer follows.

God of unfailing mercy,
who redeemed us and adopted us as your children,
look upon us with tender love,
that we who believe in Christ
may enjoy true freedom
and enter our promised inheritance.

We ask this through our Lord Jesus Christ, your Son,
who lives and reigns with you in the unity of the Holy Spirit,
God for ever and ever.

## ALTERNATIVE OPENING PRAYER

### YEAR A

Confirm, O God, in unity and truth
the Church you gather in Christ.

Encourage the fervent,
enlighten the doubtful,
and bring back the wayward.
Bind us together in mutual love,
that our prayer in Christ's name
may be pleasing to you.

Grant this through our Lord Jesus Christ, your Son,
who lives and reigns with you in the unity of the Holy Spirit,
God for ever and ever.

## YEAR B

God of power and compassion,
in Christ you reveal your will
to heal and to save.

Open our ears to your redeeming word
and move our hearts by the strength of your love,
so that our every word and work
may proclaim as Messiah
Jesus the Lord,
who lives and reigns with you in the unity of the Holy Spirit,
God for ever and ever.

## YEAR C

God of the ages,
you call the Church to keep watch in the world
and to discern the signs of the times.

Grant us the wisdom which your Spirit bestows,
that with courage we may proclaim your prophetic word
and complete the work that you have set before us.

We make our prayer through our Lord Jesus Christ, your Son,
who lives and reigns with you in the unity of the Holy Spirit,
God for ever and ever.

# TWENTY-FOURTH SUNDAY
# IN ORDINARY TIME

## OPENING PRAYER

Let us pray.

A period of silent prayer follows.

O God,
creator and ruler of all that is,
look kindly upon the prayers of your servants:
grant that we may serve you with undivided hearts
and so experience the power of your mercy.

We ask this through our Lord Jesus Christ, your Son,
who lives and reigns with you in the unity of the Holy Spirit,
God for ever and ever.

## ALTERNATIVE OPENING PRAYER

### YEAR A

O God, most high,
you are slow to anger and rich in compassion.

Keep alive in us the memory of your mercy,
that our angers may be calmed
and our resentments dispelled.
May we discover the forgiveness
promised to those who forgive
and become a people rich in mercy.

We ask this through our Lord Jesus Christ, your Son,
who lives and reigns with you in the unity of the Holy Spirit,
God for ever and ever.

Make us one, O God,
in acknowledging Jesus the Christ.
As we proclaim him by our words,
let us follow him in our works;
give us strength to take up the cross
and courage to lose our lives for his sake.

We ask this through our Lord Jesus Christ, your Son,
who lives and reigns with you in the unity of the Holy Spirit,
God for ever and ever.

## YEAR C

Undaunted you seek the lost, O God,
exultant you bring home the found.

Touch our hearts with grateful wonder
at the tenderness of your forbearing love.
Grant us delight in the mercy that has found us
and bring all to rejoice at the feast of forgiveness.

We ask this through our Lord Jesus Christ, your Son,
who lives and reigns with you in the unity of the Holy Spirit,
God for ever and ever.

# TWENTY-FIFTH SUNDAY IN ORDINARY TIME

## OPENING PRAYER

Let us pray.

A period of silent prayer follows.

Lord our God,
upon the two commandments
to love you and to love our neighbour
you have founded all your holy Law.
Give us the grace to keep these commandments
and so inherit eternal life.

We ask this through our Lord Jesus Christ, your Son,
who lives and reigns with you in the unity of the Holy Spirit,
God for ever and ever.

## ALTERNATIVE OPENING PRAYER

### YEAR A

God most high,
your ways are not our ways,
for your kindness is lavished equally upon all.

Teach us to welcome your mercy toward others,
even as we hope to receive mercy ourselves.

We ask this through our Lord Jesus Christ, your Son,
who lives and reigns with you in the unity of the Holy Spirit,
God for ever and ever.

## YEAR B

O God,
protector of the poor and defender of the just,
in your kingdom the last become first,
the gentle are strong,
and the lowly exalted.

Give us wisdom from above,
that we may find in your servant Jesus
the pattern of true discipleship
and the grace to persevere in following him,
who lives and reigns with you in the unity of the Holy Spirit,
God for ever and ever.

## YEAR C

God our Saviour,
you call us into your service.

Make us wise and resourceful:
children of the light who continue your work in this world
with untiring concern for integrity and justice.

We ask this through our Lord Jesus Christ, your Son,
who lives and reigns with you in the unity of the Holy Spirit,
God for ever and ever.

# TWENTY-SIXTH SUNDAY IN ORDINARY TIME

## OPENING PRAYER

Let us pray.

A period of silent prayer follows.

God of heaven and earth,
your incomparable power is shown above all
in your willingness to forgive and show mercy;
let your grace descend upon us without ceasing,
that we may strive for the things you have promised
and come to share the treasures of heaven.

We ask this through our Lord Jesus Christ, your Son,
who lives and reigns with you in the unity of the Holy Spirit,
God for ever and ever.

## ALTERNATIVE OPENING PRAYER

### YEAR A

O God,
you alone judge rightly
and search the depths of the heart.

Make us swift to do your will
and slow to judge our neighbour,
that we may walk with those
who follow the way of repentance and faith
and so enter your heavenly kingdom.

Grant this through our Lord Jesus Christ, your Son,
who lives and reigns with you in the unity of the Holy Spirit,
God for ever and ever.

## YEAR B

Pour out your Spirit, O God, over all the world
to inspire every heart
with knowledge and love of you.

Grant that we who confess Jesus as Lord
may shun whatever is contrary to this faith
and give witness to your love
that has saved us in Christ,
for he lives and reigns with you in the unity of the Holy Spirit,
God for ever and ever.

## YEAR C

O God of justice,
hear our cry and save us.

Make us heed your word to the prophets;
rouse us to the demand of the gospel
and impel us to carry it out.

We ask this through our Lord Jesus Christ, your Son,
who lives and reigns with you in the unity of the Holy Spirit,
God for ever and ever.

# TWENTY-SEVENTH SUNDAY
# IN ORDINARY TIME

## OPENING PRAYER

Let us pray.

A period of silent prayer follows.

Almighty and eternal God,
whose bounty is greater than we deserve or desire,
pour out upon us your abundant mercy;
forgive the things that weigh upon our consciences
and enrich us with blessings
for which our prayers dare not hope.

We ask this through our Lord Jesus Christ, your Son,
who lives and reigns with you in the unity of the Holy Spirit,
God for ever and ever.

## ALTERNATIVE OPENING PRAYER

### YEAR A

Yours, O God, is the vineyard and its harvest,
yours the kingdom of justice and peace.
You call your people to tend its growth.

Bless the work entrusted to our hands,
that we may offer you
an abundance of just works,
a rich harvest of peace.

We ask this through our Lord Jesus Christ, your Son,
who lives and reigns with you in the unity of the Holy Spirit,
God for ever and ever.

## YEAR B

Creator God,
in Christ you call man and woman
to the fullness of glory
for which you created them in your image.

Heal our hardened hearts,
renew our obedience to your spoken will,
and conform our lives to your gracious design.

Grant this through our Lord Jesus Christ, your Son,
who lives and reigns with you in the unity of the Holy Spirit,
God for ever and ever.

## YEAR C

God, the rock of our salvation,
whose gifts can never fail,
deepen the faith you have already bestowed
and let its power be seen in your servants.

We make our prayer through our Lord Jesus Christ, your Son,
who lives and reigns with you in the unity of the Holy Spirit,
God for ever and ever.

# TWENTY-EIGHTH SUNDAY IN ORDINARY TIME

## OPENING PRAYER

Let us pray.

A period of silent prayer follows.

Let your tireless grace accompany us, Lord God,
let it go before us and follow after,
that we may never slacken in our resolve
to pursue the practice of good works.

We ask this through our Lord Jesus Christ, your Son,
who lives and reigns with you in the unity of the Holy Spirit,
God for ever and ever.

## ALTERNATIVE OPENING PRAYER

### YEAR A

God of goodness and kindness,
you invite all peoples to the banquet
and offer them a feast beyond compare.

Give us your saving grace
to keep unstained the robe of our baptism
until that day when you welcome us
to heaven's joyful table.

We ask this through our Lord Jesus Christ, your Son,
who lives and reigns with you in the unity of the Holy Spirit,
God for ever and ever.

## YEAR B

God of wisdom,
whose word probes the motives of our hearts,
with you all things are possible.

Let worldly treasure not keep us from Jesus,
who looks on us with love.
Free us to leave all things and follow him,
who lives and reigns with you in the unity of the Holy Spirit,
God for ever and ever.

## YEAR C

O God,
our life, our health, our salvation,
look with mercy on your people.

Stir up in us a saving faith,
that believing, we may be healed,
and being healed, we may worthily give you thanks.

We ask this through our Lord Jesus Christ, your Son,
who lives and reigns with you in the unity of the Holy Spirit,
God for ever and ever.

# TWENTY-NINTH SUNDAY
# IN ORDINARY TIME

## OPENING PRAYER

Let us pray.

A period of silent prayer follows.

God ever faithful and true,
form our wills at all times to accord with your own,
and so direct our hearts
that we may render you undivided service.

We ask this through our Lord Jesus Christ, your Son,
who lives and reigns with you in the unity of the Holy Spirit,
God for ever and ever.

## ALTERNATIVE OPENING PRAYER

### YEAR A

O God, whose image we bear
and whose name we carry,
yours is the world and all it contains.

Recall us to our true allegiance,
so that above the powers and rulers of this world
you alone may claim our fullest loyalty and love.

We make our prayer through our Lord Jesus Christ, your Son,
who lives and reigns with you in the unity of the Holy Spirit,
God for ever and ever.

Most glorious God,
in Jesus you show us
that your will is to save.

Grant to us your people
the boldness to desire a place in your kingdom,
the courage to drink the cup of suffering,
and the grace to find in service
the glory you promise.

We ask this through our Lord Jesus Christ, your Son,
who lives and reigns with you in the unity of the Holy Spirit,
God for ever and ever.

## YEAR C

Lord, tireless guardian of your people,
always ready to hear the cries of your chosen ones,
teach us to rely, day and night, on your care.

Support our prayer lest we grow weary.
Impel us to seek your enduring justice
and your ever-present help.

Grant this through our Lord Jesus Christ, your Son,
who lives and reigns with you in the unity of the Holy Spirit,
God for ever and ever.

# THIRTIETH SUNDAY IN ORDINARY TIME

## OPENING PRAYER

Let us pray.

A period of silent prayer follows.

God of holiness,
enlarge within us your gifts of faith, hope, and love,
and enable us to cherish whatever you command,
that we may come to possess all that you promise.

We ask this through our Lord Jesus Christ, your Son,
who lives and reigns with you in the unity of the Holy Spirit,
God for ever and ever.

## ALTERNATIVE OPENING PRAYER

### YEAR A

Your love, O God, is boundless.
We who were strangers
have been made your children.
We who were defenceless
have been brought into your household.

Keep us mindful of your deeds of mercy,
that we may love you with our whole heart
and love our neighbour as ourselves.

We ask this through our Lord Jesus Christ, your Son,
who lives and reigns with you in the unity of the Holy Spirit,
God for ever and ever.

## YEAR B

Have pity on us, God our Saviour.
Grant us grace and courage to cast off our sins
and turn to you for healing.
Show us in Christ the sure path of salvation
and strengthen us to follow gladly
in the way of the gospel.

We ask this through our Lord Jesus Christ, your Son,
who lives and reigns with you in the unity of the Holy Spirit,
God for ever and ever.

## YEAR C

O God,
who alone can probe the depths of the heart,
you hear the prayer of the humble
and justify the repentant sinner.

As we stand before you,
grant us the gift of humility,
that we may see our own sins clearly
and refrain from judging our neighbour.

We make our prayer through our Lord Jesus Christ, your Son,
who lives and reigns with you in the unity of the Holy Spirit,
God for ever and ever.

# THIRTY-FIRST SUNDAY
# IN ORDINARY TIME

## OPENING PRAYER

Let us pray.

A period of silent prayer follows.

Almighty and merciful God,
from whom every blessing flows,
only by your gift
do your people offer you fitting service and praise;
grant, we beseech you,
that we may hasten without stumbling
toward the joys that you promise.

We ask this through our Lord Jesus Christ, your Son,
who lives and reigns with you in the unity of the Holy Spirit,
God for ever and ever.

## ALTERNATIVE OPENING PRAYER

### YEAR A

Sovereign God,
we have no father but you,
no teacher but Christ.

Conform our lives to the faith we profess,
preserve us from arrogance and pride,
and teach us in Christ the greatness of humility and service.

We make our prayer through our Lord Jesus Christ, your Son,
who lives and reigns with you in the unity of the Holy Spirit,
God for ever and ever.

## YEAR B

Lord our God,
you are the one God and there is no other.

Give us grace to hear and heed
the great commandment of your kingdom,
that we may love you with all our heart
and love our neighbour as ourselves.

We make our prayer through our Lord Jesus Christ, your Son,
who lives and reigns with you in the unity of the Holy Spirit,
God for ever and ever.

## YEAR C

Just and merciful God,
true Lord of every house,
sure delight of every heart,
come into our midst today
to speak your word and satisfy our hunger.
Enable us to see you clearly,
to welcome you with joy,
and to give justice and mercy
a place in our lives.

Grant this through our Lord Jesus Christ, your Son,
who lives and reigns with you in the unity of the Holy Spirit,
God for ever and ever.

# THIRTY-SECOND SUNDAY
# IN ORDINARY TIME

## OPENING PRAYER

Let us pray.

A period of silent prayer follows.

Almighty and merciful God,
drive from us whatever things are harmful
and make us ready in both body and mind
to accomplish your will in perfect freedom.

We ask this through our Lord Jesus Christ, your Son,
who lives and reigns with you in the unity of the Holy Spirit,
God for ever and ever.

## ALTERNATIVE OPENING PRAYER

### YEAR A

Brighten your Church, O God,
with the promise of your kingdom
and waken our hearts to its light.
Bid us hasten with faith undimmed
to greet the bridegroom's return
and to enter the wedding feast.

We ask this through our Lord Jesus Christ, your Son,
who lives and reigns with you in the unity of the Holy Spirit,
God for ever and ever.

God, our provider,
you are the orphan's hope
and the widow's bread.

Strengthen our faith,
that with simplicity of heart
we may come to trust in you alone
and hold back nothing in serving you.

Grant this through our Lord Jesus Christ, your Son,
who lives and reigns with you in the unity of the Holy Spirit,
God for ever and ever.

## YEAR C

God of all the living,
in the resurrection of Christ Jesus
you have given us the life
which even death cannot destroy.

Remember your unshakable promise
and strengthen us to live in this world
as your new creation.

We ask this through our Lord Jesus Christ, your Son,
who lives and reigns with you in the unity of the Holy Spirit,
God for ever and ever.

# THIRTY-THIRD SUNDAY
# IN ORDINARY TIME

## OPENING PRAYER

Let us pray.

A period of silent prayer follows.

Gracious Lord and God,
grant that we may always take delight in your service,
for only through our faithfulness to you,
the author of every good,
will full and lasting happiness be ours.

We ask this through our Lord Jesus Christ, your Son,
who lives and reigns with you in the unity of the Holy Spirit,
God for ever and ever.

## ALTERNATIVE OPENING PRAYER

### YEAR A

O God,
from whose own abundance
all gifts and skills are lavishly bestowed,
encourage us to use our talents
as generously as you have allotted them,
so that, being faithful to your purpose,
we may become sharers in your glory.

We make our prayer through our Lord Jesus Christ, your Son,
who lives and reigns with you in the unity of the Holy Spirit,
God for ever and ever.

Your creation, O God,
runs its appointed course,
as from the ends of the earth
you gather a people you call your own.

Confirm us in the strength of your abiding word.
Steady our hearts in the time of trial,
so that on the day of the Son of Man
we may without fear rejoice to behold his appearing.

We ask this through our Lord Jesus Christ, your Son,
who lives and reigns with you in the unity of the Holy Spirit,
God for ever and ever.

## YEAR C

Lord God of all the ages,
the One who is, who was, and who is to come,
stir up within us a longing for your kingdom,
steady our hearts in time of trial,
and grant us patient endurance
until the sun of justice dawns.

We make our prayer through our Lord Jesus Christ, your Son,
who lives and reigns with you in the unity of the Holy Spirit,
God for ever and ever.

# THIRTY-FOURTH WEEK
# IN ORDINARY TIME

## OPENING PRAYER

Let us pray.

A period of silent prayer follows.

Stir up the hearts of your faithful people, Lord God,
that they may cooperate more readily in the work of grace
and obtain in ever greater measure
the saving power of your goodness.

We ask this through our Lord Jesus Christ, your Son,
who lives and reigns with you in the unity of the Holy Spirit,
God for ever and ever.

Last Sunday in Ordinary Time

# CHRIST THE KING

## OPENING PRAYER

Let us pray.

A period of silent prayer follows.

Almighty and eternal God,
you chose to restore all things in Christ your Son,
who is king of heaven and earth.
Grant that all creation,
set free from the bondage of sin and death,
may offer homage to your majesty
and join in singing your eternal praise.

We ask this through our Lord Jesus Christ, your Son,
who lives and reigns with you in the unity of the Holy Spirit,
God for ever and ever.

## ALTERNATIVE OPENING PRAYER

### YEAR A

Almighty God,
you have conferred upon Christ Jesus
sovereignty over every age and nation.

Direct us, in the love of Christ,
to care for the least of his brothers and sisters,
that we may be subject to his dominion
and receive the inheritance of your kingdom.

Grant this through our Lord Jesus Christ, your Son,
who lives and reigns with you in the unity of the Holy Spirit,
God for ever and ever.

## YEAR B

Almighty and eternal God,
to Jesus Christ, the firstborn from the dead,
you have granted everlasting dominion
and a kingship that shall not pass away.

Remove from us every desire for privilege and power,
that we may imitate the sacrificial love of Christ our King
and, as a royal and priestly people,
serve you humbly in our brothers and sisters.

Grant this through our Lord Jesus Christ, your Son,
who lives and reigns with you in the unity of the Holy Spirit,
God for ever and ever.

## YEAR C

God and Father of our Lord Jesus Christ,
you gave us your Son,
the beloved one who was rejected,
the Saviour who appeared defeated.
Yet the mystery of his kingship illumines our lives.

Show us in his death
the victory that crowns the ages,
and in his broken body
the love that unites heaven and earth.

We ask this through our Lord Jesus Christ, your Son,
who lives and reigns with you in the unity of the Holy Spirit,
God for ever and ever.

# SOLEMNITIES OF THE LORD

## Introductory Rites

### SIGN OF THE CROSS

All make the sign of the cross, as the leader of prayer says:

In the name of the Father, and of the Son,
✠ and of the Holy Spirit.

All respond:  Amen.

### GREETING

The leader of prayer says:

Brothers and sisters,
let us praise and give thanks to the Lord,
the fountain of all goodness.
Bless the Father and the Son and the Holy Spirit.

or

Let us praise the Lord Jesus Christ,
who is present among us and in the Word,
and who keeps us united us in love.
Bless the Father and the Son and the Holy Spirit.

or

Blessed be God the Father,
who has sanctified and justified us,
in the name of the Lord Jesus Christ and in the Spirit of our God.
Bless the Father and the Son and the Holy Spirit.

or

Bless the Father and the Son and the Holy Spirit.

All respond:  Blessed be God for ever.

# OPENING RITE

Only one of the options for the opening rite is chosen on any Sunday. The following are suggested for Solemnities of the Lord.

## I. HYMN OF PRAISE (*GLORIA*)

INVITATION: After the greeting, the leader of prayer invites the people to praise God, using one of the following formularies or similar words.

With peoples everywhere,
let us glorify our God in joyful song:

or

With all the voices of heaven,
let us sing praise and honour and glory to God:

GLORIA: The hymn of praise is then sung.

or

## II. LITANY OF PRAISE

INVITATION: After the greeting, the leader of prayer invites the people to praise Christ, using the following formularies or similar words.

Rich in mercy is our Saviour
and great in kindness.
Praise the Lord Jesus Christ.

INVOCATIONS TO CHRIST: After a brief pause, the leader of prayer, or another minister or a cantor, sings or says one of the following forms of invocation or other similar invocations to Christ.

### A

The minister sings or says:

Lord Jesus, you are the way to the Father:
Lord, have mercy.

All respond: **Lord, have mercy.**

The minister sings or says:

Christ Jesus, you have the words of truth and consolation:
Christ, have mercy.

All respond: **Christ, have mercy.**

The minister sings or says:

Lord Jesus, you have given us the Spirit of life:
Lord, have mercy.

All respond: **Lord, have mercy.**

# B

The minister sings or says:

Lord Jesus, you are the High Priest of the eternal covenant:
Lord, have mercy.

All respond: **Lord, have mercy.**

The minister sings or says:

Christ Jesus, you are the cleansing Word of God's love:
Christ, have mercy.

All respond: **Christ, have mercy.**

The minister sings or says:

Lord Jesus, you are the Bread of life:
Lord, have mercy.

All respond: **Lord, have mercy.**

The opening prayer then follows (see pages 162-167).

# THE HOLY TRINITY
## Sunday after Pentecost

This feast, first celebrated in monastic communities in the 9th century as an expression of praise to the triune God, was extended to the entire Western Church in the 14th. It celebrates the mystery of God's self-revelation through the experiences of the people of Israel, the disciples of Jesus, and the Christian people since Pentecost.

## OPENING PRAYER

Let us pray.

A period of silent prayer follows.

God our Father,
you revealed the wonderful mystery of the Godhead
by sending into the world
the Word who speaks all truth
and the Spirit who makes us holy.

Grant that we may proclaim the fullness of faith
by acknowledging and worshipping
three Persons, eternal in glory,
one God of majesty and power.

We ask this through our Lord Jesus Christ, your Son,
who lives and reigns with you in the unity of the Holy Spirit,
God for ever and ever.

## ALTERNATIVE OPENING PRAYER

### YEAR A

Merciful and gracious Father,
you showed the fullness of your love
when you gave your only Son for our salvation
and sent down upon us the power of your Spirit.

Complete within us the work of your love,
that we who have communion in Christ
may come to share fully
the undying life he lives with you,
in the unity of the Holy Spirit,
God for ever and ever.

God our Father,
you have given us a share
in the life that is yours
with your Son and the Holy Spirit.

Strengthen that life within your Church,
that we may know your presence,
observe your commands,
and proclaim the gospel to every nation.

We ask this through our Lord Jesus Christ, your Son,
who lives and reigns with you in the unity of the Holy Spirit,
God for ever and ever.

## YEAR C

O God, your name is veiled in mystery,
yet we dare to call you Father;
your Son was begotten before all ages,
yet is born among us in time;
your holy Spirit fills the whole creation,
yet is poured forth now into our hearts.

Because you have made us and loved us
and called us by name,
draw us more deeply into your divine life,
that we may glorify you rightly, through your Son,
in the unity of the Holy Spirit,
God for ever and ever.

# THE BODY AND BLOOD OF CHRIST
## Sunday after The Holy Trinity

This feast, originally Corpus Christi, arose in 13th century Belgium in response to debates about the real presence and as a result of an upsurge in eucharistic piety. Its extension to the entire Western Church was first decreed by Urban IV in 1264. The feast celebrates the mystery of the nourishing and enduring presence of the Body and Blood of Christ in the eucharist.

## OPENING PRAYER

Let us pray.

A period of silent prayer follows.

Lord Jesus Christ,
in this most wonderful sacrament
you have left us the memorial of your passion;
deepen our reverence for the mystery of your body and blood,
that we may experience within us the fruit of your redemption.

You live and reign with the Father in the unity of the Holy Spirit,
God for ever and ever.Alternative Opening Prayer

### YEAR A

The bread you give, O God,
is Christ's flesh for the life of the world;
the cup of his blood
is your covenant for our salvation.

Grant that we who worship Christ in this holy mystery
may reverence him in the needy of this world
by lives poured out for the sake of that kingdom
where he lives and reigns with you in the unity of the Holy Spirit,
God for ever and ever.

## YEAR B

God ever faithful,
you have made a covenant with your people
in the gift of your Son,
who offered his body for us
and poured out his blood for the many.

As we celebrate this eucharistic sacrifice,
build up your Church
by deepening within us the life of your covenant
and by opening our hearts to those in need.

We ask this through our Lord Jesus Christ, your Son,
who lives and reigns with you in the unity of the Holy Spirit,
God for ever and ever.


## YEAR C

You have blessed all generations,
O God most high,
in Jesus, our compassionate Saviour,
for through him you invite us to your kingdom,
welcome us to your table,
and provide us with nourishment in abundance.

Teach us to imitate your unfailing kindness
and to build up Christ's body, the Church,
by generously handing on to others
the gifts we have received from your bounty.

We ask this through our Lord Jesus Christ, your Son,
who lives and reigns with you in the unity of the Holy Spirit,
God for ever and ever.

# THE SACRED HEART OF JESUS
## Friday following Second Sunday after Pentecost

This devotion, which dates back to the Middle Ages, flowered in France in the 17th century as a result of the visions of St Margaret Mary Alacoque (16 October). The feast was extended to the entire Western Church by Pius IX in 1856. It recalls the mystery of God, who is love, and honours the heart of Jesus as the source and centre of the incarnate love of God.

## OPENING PRAYER

Let us pray.

A period of silent prayer follows.

Almighty God,
as we honour the heart of Jesus, your beloved Son,
we recall the blessings which his love showers upon us;
fill us with the gifts of grace
that flow so richly from his Sacred Heart.

We ask this through our Lord Jesus Christ, your Son,
who lives and reigns with you in the unity of the Holy Spirit,
God for ever and ever.

or

God of mercy,
in the heart of your Son, wounded by our sins,
you lavish upon us the boundless treasures of your love;
grant that, in offering the homage of our faithful service,
we may also make fitting reparation for our sins.

We ask this through our Lord Jesus Christ, your Son,
who lives and reigns with you in the unity of the Holy Spirit,
God for ever and ever.

# ALTERNATIVE OPENING PRAYER

## YEAR A

God of love,
you set your heart upon the least of nations,
and in the heart of Jesus
you reveal your love to the merest of children.

Make us simple enough to receive your great love,
and strong enough to bear it to others.
Grant this through our Lord Jesus Christ, your Son,
who lives and reigns with you in the unity of the Holy Spirit,
God for ever and ever.

## YEAR B

God of life and love,
from the pierced heart of your Son
flowed water and blood,
cleansing the world
and giving birth to your Church.

Renew within your people
the love poured out on us in baptism,
and through the blessing-cup we share
keep us always faithful
to your life-giving covenant.

We make our prayer through our Lord Jesus Christ, your Son,
who lives and reigns with you in the unity of the Holy Spirit,
God for ever and ever.

## YEAR C

Eternal God,
in Christ you have sought us
with a shepherd's heart,
and we have rejoiced
to be found and restored.

Multiply in all the world
the wonders of your saving grace,
and gather your scattered people
until heaven resounds in jubilation
at humanity made whole
and creation restored

We ask this through our Lord Jesus Christ, your Son,
who lives and reigns with you in the unity of the Holy Spirit,
God for ever and ever.

# SOLEMNITIES AND FEASTS

## INTRODUCTORY RITES
### AND
### OPENING PRAYERS

# FEASTS OF THE LORD

## Introductory Rites

### SIGN OF THE CROSS

All make the sign of the cross, as the leader of prayer says:

**In the name of the Father, and of the Son,**
✠ **and of the Holy Spirit.**

All respond: **Amen.**

### GREETING

The leader of prayer says:

**Brothers and sisters,**
**let us praise and give thanks to the Lord,**
**the fountain of all goodness.**
**Bless the Father and the Son and the Holy Spirit.**

or

**Let us praise the Lord Jesus Christ,**
**who is present among us and in the Word,**
**and who keeps us united us in love.**
**Bless the Father and the Son and the Holy Spirit.**

or

**Bless the Father and the Son and the Holy Spirit.**

All respond: **Blessed be God for ever.**

### OPENING RITE

Only one of the options for the opening rite is chosen on any Sunday. The following are suggested for Feasts of the Lord.

#### I. HYMN OF PRAISE (*GLORIA*)

INVITATION: After the greeting, the leader of prayer invites the people to praise God, using one of the following formularies or similar words.

**With peoples everywhere,**
**let us glorify our God in joyful song:**

or

**With all the voices of heaven,**
**let us sing praise and honour and glory to God:**

GLORIA: The hymn of praise is then sung.
The opening prayer then follows (see pages 187-198).

or

## II. LITANY OF PRAISE

INVITATION: After the greeting, the leader of prayer invites the people to praise Christ, using the following formularies or similar words.

Rich in mercy is our Saviour
and great in kindness.
Praise the Lord Jesus Christ.

INVOCATIONS TO CHRIST: After a brief pause, the leader of prayer, or another minister or a cantor, sings or says one of the following forms of invocation or other similar invocations to Christ.

### A

The minister sings or says:

Lord Jesus, you are the way, the truth and the life:
Lord, have mercy.

All respond: **Lord, have mercy.**

The minister sings or says:

Christ Jesus, you are the source of our salvation:
Christ, have mercy.

All respond: **Christ, have mercy.**

The minister sings or says:

Lord Jesus, you are the light of the nations.
Lord, have mercy.

All respond: **Lord, have mercy.**

### B

The minister sings or says:

Lord Jesus, you are the incarnate Word of God's love:
Lord, have mercy.

All respond: **Lord, have mercy.**

The minister sings or says:

Christ Jesus, you are the high Priest of the eternal covenant:
Christ, have mercy.

All respond: **Christ, have mercy.**

The minister sings or says:

Lord Jesus, you are the Paschal Lamb of our salvation:
Lord, have mercy.

All respond: **Lord, have mercy.**

The opening prayer then follows (see pages 182-198).

# SOLEMNITIES OF MARY

## Introductory Rites

### SIGN OF THE CROSS

All make the sign of the cross, as the leader of prayer says:

In the name of the Father, and of the Son,
✠ and of the Holy Spirit.

All respond: **Amen.**

### GREETING

The leader of prayer says:

Blessed be God our Father,
who has made us heirs of the kingdom through Christ,
with all the saints in glory.
Bless the Father and the Son and the Holy Spirit.

or

Blessed be God the Father,
who has sanctified and justified us,
in the name of the Lord Jesus Christ
and in the Spirit of our God.
Bless the Father and the Son and the Holy Spirit.

or

Blessed be God our Father,
now manifested in Christ
who was born for our salvation.
Bless the Father and the Son and the Holy Spirit.

All respond: **Blessed be God for ever.**

# OPENING RITE

Only one of the options for the opening rite is chosen on any Sunday. The following are suggested for Solemnities of the Blessed Virgin Mary.

## I. HYMN OF PRAISE (*GLORIA*)

INVITATION: After the greeting, the leader of prayer invites the people to praise God, using one of the following formularies or similar words.

With peoples everywhere,
let us glorify our God in joyful song:

or

With all the voices of heaven,
let us sing praise and honour and glory to God:

GLORIA: The hymn of praise is then sung.

or.

## II. LITANY OF PRAISE

INVITATION: After the greeting, the leader of prayer invites the people to praise Christ, using one of the following formularies or similar words.

Let us rejoice in the mercy of Christ.
Praise the risen Saviour who was born of the Virgin Mary.

or

As we celebrate the mystery of God with us,
let us rejoice that our Saviour is rich in mercy
and great in kindness.
Praise the Lord Jesus Christ.

INVOCATIONS TO CHRIST: After a brief pause, the leader of prayer, or another minister or a cantor, sings or says the following forms of invocation or other similar invocations to Christ.

### A

The minister sings or says:

Son of God, you were born of the Virgin Mary for our salvation:
Lord, have mercy.

All respond: Lord, have mercy.

The minister sings or says:

Son of Mary, you raise us to new life in God's kingdom:
Christ, have mercy.

All respond: Christ, have mercy.

The minister sings or says:

Son of Man, you have given us Mary as our mother:
Lord, have mercy.

All respond: Lord, have mercy.

## B

The minister sings or says:

Lord Jesus, you have renewed us by the cleansing word of the Father:
Lord, have mercy.

All respond: Lord, have mercy.

The minister sings or says:

Christ Jesus, you have made us one by the Spirit of adoption:
Christ, have mercy.

All respond: Christ, have mercy.

The minister sings or says:

Lord Jesus, you have glorified us by your death and rising to new life:
Lord, have mercy.

All respond: Lord, have mercy.

The opening prayer then follows (see pages 189-190 and 199).

# SOLEMNITIES OF SAINTS

## Introductory Rites

### SIGN OF THE CROSS

All make the sign of the cross, as the leader of prayer says:

In the name of the Father, and of the Son,
✠ and of the Holy Spirit.

All respond: **Amen.**

### GREETING

The leader of prayer says:

Blessed be God our Father,
who has made us heirs of the kingdom through Christ,
with all the saints in glory.
Bless the Father and the Son and the Holy Spirit.

or

Blessed be God,
who has called us to share the lot of the saints in light.
Bless the Father and the Son and the Holy Spirit.

or

Blessed be God the Father, the Lord of heaven and earth,
who has revealed the mystery of his presence
to us his children.
Bless the Father and the Son and the Holy Spirit.

or

Bless the Father and the Son and the Holy Spirit.

All respond: **Blessed be God for ever.**

# OPENING RITE

Only one of the options for the opening rite is chosen on any Sunday. The following are suggested for the Solemnities of Saints.

## I. HYMN OF PRAISE (*GLORIA*)

INVITATION: After the greeting, the leader of prayer invites the people to praise God, using one of the following formularies or similar words.

With peoples everywhere,
let us glorify our God in joyful song:

or

With all the voices of heaven,
let us sing praise and honour and glory to God:

GLORIA: The hymn of praise is then sung.

or.

## II. LITANY OF PRAISE

INVITATION: After the greeting, the leader of prayer invites the people to praise Christ, using one of the following formularies or similar words.

With the communion of saints let us rejoice in the mercy of Christ.
Praise the risen Saviour.

or

As we celebrate the mystery of God's love for us,
let us rejoice that our Saviour is rich in mercy and great in kindness.
Praise the Lord Jesus Christ.

INVOCATIONS TO CHRIST: After a brief pause, the leader of prayer, or another minister or a cantor, sings or says one of the following forms of invocation or other similar invocations to Christ.

### A

The minister sings or says:

Lord Jesus, by your blood you have redeemed us from slavery to sin:
Lord, have mercy.

All respond: **Lord, have mercy.**

The minister sings or says:

Christ Jesus, by your rising you have claimed us as God's people:
Christ, have mercy.

All respond: **Christ, have mercy.**

The minister sings or says:

Paschal Lamb, by baptism you have raised us to new life in the Spirit:
Lord, have mercy.

All respond: Lord, have mercy.

## B

The minister sings or says:

Lord Jesus, you have called us out of darkness
into God's marvellous light:
Lord, have mercy.

All respond: Lord, have mercy.

The minister sings or says:

Christ Jesus, you have clothed us with holiness and love:
Christ, have mercy.

All respond: Christ, have mercy.

The minister sings or says:

Lord Jesus, you have made us a new creation in the Spirit:
Lord, have mercy.

All respond: Lord, have mercy.

The opening prayer then follows (see pages 181, 183-186, 192).

## 2 FEBRUARY
# THE PRESENTATION OF THE LORD

This feast originated in Jerusalem before the 5th century and was adopted at Rome during the 7th. It is celebrated forty days after Christmas to commemorate the prescribed Mosaic ritual following the birth of a child. The feast recalls the encounter of Jesus with Simeon and Anna in the temple – the Lord meets his people. It celebrates Christ as "the light to enlighten all nations," and so candles are traditionally blessed during the introductory rites of the Eucharist

## THANKSGIVING FOR THE LIGHT

The community assembles in some other place distinct from the church to which the procession will move. All carry unlighted candles. A suitable song or acclamation may be sung as the assembly and ministers gather and the candles of the people are lighted. Then the leader of prayer greets the assembly with the sign of the cross and the liturgical greeting, as usual.

### SIGN OF THE CROSS

All make the sign of the cross, as the leader of prayer says:

In the name of the Father, and of the Son,
✠ and of the Holy Spirit.

All respond: **Amen.**

### GREETING

The leader of prayer says:

Blessed be Jesus Christ, the life-giving Word,
who is the true light of the world,
and the revelation of the Father's glory.
Bless the Father and the Son and the Holy Spirit.

All respond: **Blessed be God for ever.**

INTRODUCTORY REMARKS: Then the leader gives a brief introduction, using these or similar words:

Forty days ago we celebrated the joyful feast
of the birth of our Lord Jesus Christ.
Today we recall the holy day
on which he was presented in the temple,
fulfilling the law of Moses
and at the same time, going to meet his faithful people.

Led by the Spirit, Simeon and Anna came to the temple,
recognized Christ as their Lord,
and proclaimed him with joy.

United by the Spirit,
may we go now to the house of the God
to welcome Christ the Lord.
There we shall recognize him in the word that is proclaimed
until he comes again in glory.

INVITATION TO PRAYER: The leader of prayer says:

Let us pray.

PRAYER: After a brief pause, with hands extended, the leader says the collect prayer.

Almighty God,
true light of the world
and source of light eternal,
shine upon the hearts of the faithful,
that all in this holy temple
who are brightened by the glow of these candles
may advance with joy toward the light of your glory.
We ask this through Christ our Lord.

---

If the leader of prayer is a deacon, one of the following is used:

Lord God, unquenchable source of light,
on this day you revealed to the just man Simeon
the light to enlighten all nations.
Bless ✠ these candles and make them holy.
Accept the prayers of your people
who will carry them in praise of your name,
that they may walk in the path of goodness
until they reach that light which never fails.
We ask this through Jesus Christ our Lord.

or

Almighty God,
true light of the world
and source of light eternal,
shine upon the hearts of the faithful,
that all in this holy temple
who are brightened by the glow of these candles
may advance with joy toward the light of your glory.
We ask this through Christ our Lord.

---

INVITATION TO THE PROCESSION: If incense is used, grains of incense are placed in the thurible. The leader takes a candle and then says:

## Let us go in peace to meet the Lord.

PROCESSION: A processional song is sung as the procession moves to the church. If incense is used, a minister carrying the censer goes first, followed by those carrying the cross and candles, the leader of prayer and the assembly, carrying candles. A reader carries the Lectionary in the procession and waits at the ambo with the Lectionary for the Enthronement of the Word after the opening prayer. The opening rite is omitted.

When the procession reaches the altar, the ministers venerate it and take their places. At this time the Lectionary may be enthroned and incensed. Since the Lectionary was carried into the assembly as part of the procession, the Procession of the Word of God does not take place after the opening prayer. When the assembly has taken its place, the celebration continues with the opening prayer.

## OPENING PRAYER

### Let us pray.

A period of silent prayer follows.

God of power and majesty,
your only-begotten Son,
having taken upon himself our flesh and blood,
was presented this day in the temple;
bring us also into your presence
with hearts that are cleansed and purified.

We ask this through our Lord Jesus Christ, your Son,
who lives and reigns with you in the unity of the Holy Spirit,
God for ever and ever.

## ALTERNATIVE OPENING PRAYER

Inspired by your Spirit, Lord,
we gather in your temple to welcome your Son.

Enlighten our minds
and lay bare our inmost thoughts.
Purify your people, and make us obedient to the demands of your law,
so that we may mature in wisdom
and grow to full stature in your grace.

We ask this through our Lord Jesus Christ, your Son,
who lives and reigns with you in the unity of the Holy Spirit,
God for ever and ever.

LITURGY OF THE WORD: The readings begin as usual, however the procession of the Word is omitted.

# 19 MARCH
# JOSEPH,
# HUSBAND OF THE VIRGIN MARY

A carpenter, though born of the royal house of David, Joseph was an upright man who, as husband of the Virgin Mary, cared for Mary and the child Jesus. Venerated in the East after the 4th century, his cult flowered in the West during the 15th, following the development of medieval nativity plays, the Christmas crib, and increasing devotion to Mary.

## OPENING PRAYER

Let us pray.

A period of silent prayer follows.

Grant, almighty God,
that through the prayers of blessed Joseph
your Church may help bring to fulfillment
the mysteries of salvation,
whose beginnings you entrusted to his faithful care.

We ask this through our Lord Jesus Christ, your Son,
who lives and reigns with you in the unity of the Holy Spirit,
God for ever and ever.

## ALTERNATIVE OPENING PRAYER

O God,
ever faithful to your covenant,
you strengthened Saint Joseph
to embrace the mystery of your will
and to welcome your Word, made flesh of the Virgin Mary.

Keep your Church also steadfast in faith,
ready to trust in your promises
and eager to fulfill your saving purpose.

We ask this through our Lord Jesus Christ, your Son,
who lives and reigns with you in the unity of the Holy Spirit,
God for ever and ever.

# 25 MARCH
# THE ANNUNCIATION OF THE LORD

This feast originated in the East during the 6th century and gained universal observance in the West during the 8th. It is a feast of the Lord, commemorating the announcement to the Virgin Mary of the Word made flesh, Mary's acceptance of God's will, and the conception of Christ nine months before Christmas. Its occurrence close to Easter links the incarnation with the whole mystery of human redemption in Christ.

## OPENING PRAYER

Let us pray.

A period of silent prayer follows.

Eternal God,
you chose that your Word
should take flesh in the womb of the Virgin Mary.

Grant that we who confess him to be our Redeemer,
truly God and truly human,
may also share in his divine nature.

We ask this through our Lord Jesus Christ, your Son,
who lives and reigns with you in the unity of the Holy Spirit,
God for ever and ever.

## ALTERNATIVE OPENING PRAYER

God most high,
you extended your gracious mercy
to the whole human race
through your Son, Jesus Christ,
who took flesh of the Virgin Mary.
You gave him to the world as your servant,
whose delight was to do your will.

Keep the Church, which is his body,
faithful to your purpose,
that all the ends of the earth
may know your saving power.

Grant this through our Lord Jesus Christ, your Son,
who lives and reigns with you in the unity of the Holy Spirit,
God for ever and ever.

# 24 JUNE
# THE BIRTH OF JOHN THE BAPTIST
## Vigil

This feast was observed on this date by the 4th century. It celebrates the holy birth of "the greatest of all the prophets," the one who leaped for joy in his mother's womb, who prepared the way for Christ, announced his presence, and baptized him in the Jordan.

## OPENING PRAYER

Let us pray.

*A period of silent prayer follows.*

Grant, almighty God,
that your people may walk in the way of salvation
and, by heeding the summons of John the Baptist,
may follow faithfully Christ our Lord,
whose coming John foretold.

We make our prayer through our Lord Jesus Christ, your Son,
who lives and reigns with you in the unity of the Holy Spirit,
God for ever and ever.

## ALTERNATIVE OPENING PRAYER

O God, you raise up prophets in every age.
Let your Spirit, who filled John the Baptist from his mother's womb,
fill us with joy as we celebrate his birth.

May the example of his life,
the urgency of his preaching,
and the power of his prayers
make us ready to receive the one he announced,
Jesus Christ, your Son,
who lives and reigns with you in the unity of the Holy Spirit,
God for ever and ever.

# THE BIRTH OF JOHN THE BAPTIST
## during the Day

### OPENING PRAYER

Let us pray.

A period of silent prayer follows.

Just and gracious God,
who raised up blessed John the Baptist
to prepare a holy people for Christ the Lord,
give to your Church gladness of spirit
and guide the hearts of all the faithful
along the path of salvation and peace.

We ask this through our Lord Jesus Christ, your Son,
who lives and reigns with you in the unity of the Holy Spirit,
God for ever and ever.

### ALTERNATIVE OPENING PRAYER

God most high,
from his mother's womb you destined John the Baptist
to preach repentance,
to challenge hardened hearts,
and so to herald salvation.

Grant us to embrace the conversion he proclaimed
and to follow the one whose coming he announced,
our Lord Jesus Christ, your Son,
who lives and reigns with you in the unity of the Holy Spirit,
God for ever and ever.

# 29 JUNE
# PETER AND PAUL, APOSTLES
## Vigil

This preeminent feast day of the city of Rome has been observed on this date since the mid-3rd century. It commemorates the martyrdoms at Rome under Nero, between 64-67, of Peter the "chief of the apostles" and Paul the "apostle to the Gentiles." It recalls their faith, their courage, and their leadership during the difficult days of the birth of the Church.

## OPENING PRAYER

Let us pray.

A period of silent prayer follows.

Sustain us, Lord our God,
through the prayers of the apostles Peter and Paul.
By their preaching you first gave your Church
the message of eternal life;
through their intercession
grant us now the means of salvation.

We ask this through our Lord Jesus Christ, your Son,
who lives and reigns with you in the unity of the Holy Spirit,
God for ever and ever.

## ALTERNATIVE OPENING PRAYER

O God,
source of every good gift
and sure foundation of our unity,
as we honour and revere Saints Peter and Paul,
grant your Church a share
in their zeal for preaching the gospel.
Strengthen our faith to be witnesses,
even unto death,
of the one Lord, Jesus Christ,
who lives and reigns with you in the unity of the Holy Spirit,
God for ever and ever.

# PETER AND PAUL, APOSTLES

## during the Day

### OPENING PRAYER

Let us pray.

A period of silent prayer follows.

Lord our God,
you give us this joyful day of celebration
to honour the apostles Peter and Paul.

Keep your Church in all things true to their teaching,
because in them our faith had its beginning.
We ask this through our Lord Jesus Christ, your Son,

who lives and reigns with you in the unity of the Holy Spirit,
God for ever and ever.

### ALTERNATIVE OPENING PRAYER

Lord, living God,
you crowned the faith of Peter
and the tireless preaching of Paul
with a share in Christ's triumphant death.

Renew our faith through their intercession
and, by the example of their lives,
rekindle our zeal for proclaiming the gospel.

Grant this through our Lord Jesus Christ, your Son,
who lives and reigns with you in the unity of the Holy Spirit,
God for ever and ever.

# 6 AUGUST
# THE TRANSFIGURATION OF THE LORD

This feast had its origin in the East in the 4th century as the commemoration of the dedication of the church of the Transfiguration on Mount Tabor. It was observed in the West from the 8th century and extended to the entire Western Church in the 15th. The feast celebrates the divine radiance shining in Christ's human flesh and God's glory shining forth in the lives of Christians.

## OPENING PRAYER

Let us pray.

A period of silent prayer follows.

Lord God,
in the transfiguration of your only-begotten Son
you confirmed the mysteries of faith
by the witness of your prophets,
and wonderfully foreshadowed
our full adoption as your children.

Grant that we, your people,
heeding the voice of your beloved Son,
may become heirs with him to eternal glory.

We ask this through our Lord Jesus Christ, your Son,
who lives and reigns with you in the unity of the Holy Spirit,
God for ever and ever.

## ALTERNATIVE OPENING PRAYER

### YEAR A

God of glory,
it is good for us to be here.

Reveal your Son to us now
in the message of the prophets
and the witness of the apostles,
that we may heed his voice
and receive him in faith.

We ask this through our Lord Jesus Christ, your Son,
who lives and reigns with you in the unity of the Holy Spirit,
God for ever and ever.

## YEAR B

Upon a high mountain,
O God of majestic glory,
you revealed Jesus
in the mystery of his transfiguration
as your Son, the Beloved,
to whom we must listen.

By the word of his gospel,
shining for ever as a light in the darkness,
give us hope in the midst of suffering
and faith to perceive, even in the passion and cross,
the glory of the risen Christ,
who lives and reigns with you in the unity of the Holy Spirit,
God for ever and ever.


## YEAR C

God and Father of Jesus,
you transfigured your Chosen One
and in heavenly light
revealed him as your Son.

Open our ears to the living Word
and our eyes to his glorious presence,
that we may be strengthened
in time of fear and uncertainty,
and one day pass over to share your glory.

Grant this through our Lord Jesus Christ, your Son,
who lives and reigns with you in the unity of the Holy Spirit,
God for ever and ever.

## 15 AUGUST
# THE ASSUMPTION OF THE VIRGIN MARY INTO HEAVEN
## Vigil

This feast originated in Jerusalem before the 5th century as the "Falling-Asleep of the Mother of God." It was adopted in Rome in the mid-7th century and was renamed the "Assumption" in the 8th. It celebrates Mary's passing over, body and soul, from this world into the glory of her risen Son.

### OPENING PRAYER

Let us pray.

A period of silent prayer follows.

Almighty God,
you looked with favour upon a humble virgin and raised her up,
so that she became the mother of your only Son
and was crowned this day in heaven with incomparable glory.

Through the prayers of blessed Mary
may we who are saved by the mystery of your redemption
be raised by you to everlasting life.

Grant this through our Lord Jesus Christ, your Son,
who lives and reigns with you in the unity of the Holy Spirit,
God for ever and ever.

### ALTERNATIVE OPENING PRAYER

Gracious God,
you chose the Virgin Mary
to bear your incarnate Word,
and at her life's end
you brought her in body and spirit to heavenly glory.

Grant that, like Mary,
we may hear your word and keep it
and one day share with her
the risen life of Christ your Son,
who lives and reigns with you in the unity of the Holy Spirit,
God for ever and ever.

# THE ASSUMPTION OF THE VIRGIN MARY INTO HEAVEN

## during the Day

### OPENING PRAYER

Let us pray.

A period of silent prayer follows.

God of power and life,
who chose the sinless Virgin Mary to be mother of your Son
and raised her, body and soul, to the glory of heaven,
set our hearts upon the things that are above
and lift us up to share in her glory.

We ask this through our Lord Jesus Christ, your Son,
who lives and reigns with you in the unity of the Holy Spirit,
God for ever and ever.

### ALTERNATIVE OPENING PRAYER

Faithful to your promise, O God,
you have lifted up the lowly,
clothing with heavenly splendour
the woman who bore Christ, our life and resurrection.

Grant that the Church, prefigured in Mary,
may bear Christ to the world
and come to share his triumph.

We ask this through our Lord Jesus Christ, your Son,
who lives and reigns with you in the unity of the Holy Spirit,
God for ever and ever.

# 14 SEPTEMBER
# THE HOLY CROSS

Originally this day commemorated the dedication of Constantine's Basilica of the Holy Sepulcher in the 4th century; after the celebration, the wood of the cross was venerated. The feast spread in the West after the recovery of the relics of the cross from Persia in the 7th century. A feast of the Lord, it celebrates the "lifting up" of the Son of Man on the cross, into glory, and the paradox of the cross as a symbol of humiliation and death, yet the source of victory and life.

## OPENING PRAYER

Let us pray.

A period of silent prayer follows.

All-powerful God,
in obedience to your will,
your only Son suffered death on the cross
to save the human race.

Grant that we who embrace this mystery on earth
may share the triumph of his redemption in heaven.

We ask this through our Lord Jesus Christ, your Son,
who lives and reigns with you in the unity of the Holy Spirit,
God for ever and ever.

## ALTERNATIVE OPENING PRAYER

Lifted up among us, O God,
is Jesus the crucified:
sign of your steadfast love
and pledge of your will to save.

To those who look upon the cross with faith
grant healing of soul
and life eternal.

We ask this through our Lord Jesus Christ, your Son,
who lives and reigns with you in the unity of the Holy Spirit,
God for ever and ever.

# 1 NOVEMBER
# ALL SAINTS

This feast began in the East to commemorate all martyrs and was progressively adopted in the West. It was celebrated on this day in the 8th century and was soon widely observed. Honoured today are all holy men and women in glory with Christ: known or unknown, mighty or lowly, all whose lives were modeled on the Beatitudes and on the great commandment of love.

## OPENING PRAYER

Let us pray.

A period of silent prayer follows.

All-holy and eternal God,
you have given us this feast
to celebrate on one day
the holy men and women of every time and place.

Through their manifold intercession
grant us the full measure of your mercy,
for which we so deeply long.

We ask this through our Lord Jesus Christ, your Son,
who lives and reigns with you in the unity of the Holy Spirit,
God for ever and ever.

## ALTERNATIVE OPENING PRAYER

All-holy God,
you call your people to holiness.

As we keep the festival of your saints,
give us their meekness and poverty of spirit,
a thirst for righteousness,
and purity of heart.
May we share with them the richness of your kingdom
and be clothed in the glory you bestow.

Grant this through our Lord Jesus Christ, your Son,
who lives and reigns with you in the unity of the Holy Spirit,
God for ever and ever.

# 2 NOVEMBER
# THE COMMEMORATION
# OF ALL THE FAITHFUL DEPARTED

This day of commemoration began early in the Middle Ages with annual prayers for the dead in monastic communities. Fixed on this day, it spread more widely after the 10th century and now ranks with the principal feast days in the liturgical calendar. Commonly know as All Souls, it expresses Christian faith in the communion of saints and our need to pray for one another in the Church, especially those souls in purgatory, "who have been buried in their human imperfection."

## Introductory Rites

### SIGN OF THE CROSS

All make the sign of the cross, as the leader of prayer says:

In the name of the Father, and of the Son,
✠ and of the Holy Spirit.

All respond: Amen.

### GREETING

The leader of prayer says:

Blessed be the God of life,
who broke the bonds of death
by raising Jesus from the dead
through the power of the Holy Spirit.
Bless the Father and the Son and the Holy Spirit.

or

Blessed be God who has given us the victory
through our Lord Jesus Christ.
Bless the Father and the Son and the Holy Spirit.

or

Blessed be the God and Father of our Lord Jesus Christ,
who in his great mercy has given us a new birth
by raising Jesus Christ from he dead.
Bless the Father and the Son and the Holy Spirit.

All respond: Blessed be God for ever.

# OPENING RITE

Only one of the options for the opening rite is chosen. The following is suggested for All Souls.

## I. LITANY OF PRAISE

INVITATION: After the greeting, the leader of prayer invites the people to praise Christ, using one of the following formularies or similar words.

Let us praise the Lord Jesus Christ
who has raised us to new life.

or

Let us rejoice in the mercy of Christ.
Praise the risen Saviour who is exalted at the right hand of God.

or

As we celebrate the mystery of our new life with Christ,
let us acknowledge that our Saviour is rich in mercy and great in kindness.
Praise the Lord Jesus Christ.

INVOCATIONS TO CHRIST: After a brief pause, the leader of prayer, or another minister or a cantor, sings or says one of the following forms of invocation or other similar invocations to Christ.

### A

The minister sings or says:

Lord Jesus, by your blood you have redeemed us from slavery to sin:
Lord, have mercy.

All respond: Lord, have mercy.

The minister sings or says:

Christ Jesus, by your rising you have claimed us as God's people:
Christ, have mercy.

All respond: Christ, have mercy.

The minister sings or says:

Paschal Lamb, by baptism you have raised us to new life in the Spirit:
Lord, have mercy.

All respond: Lord, have mercy.

### B

The minister sings or says:

Lord Jesus, you have called us out of darkness into your own marvellous light:
Lord, have mercy.

All respond: Lord, have mercy.

Christ Jesus, you have clothed us with holiness and love:
Christ, have mercy.

**Christ, have mercy.**

Lord Jesus, you have made us a new creation in the Spirit:
Lord, have mercy.

**Lord, have mercy.**

## OPENING PRAYER

Let us pray.

A period of silent prayer follows.

God, our Creator and Redeemer,
by your power your only Son has conquered death
and has passed from this world into your kingdom.

Grant that all the faithful departed
may share his triumph over death
and enjoy for ever the vision of your glory.

We ask this through our Lord Jesus Christ, your Son,
who lives and reigns with you in the unity of the Holy Spirit,
God for ever and ever.

## ALTERNATE OPENING PRAYER

### YEAR A

Father, Lord of heaven and earth,
through your Son
you have revealed the mystery of our salvation,
hidden from the beginning of the ages.

Welcome all our departed brothers and sisters
to the victory feast of your kingdom
where they shall reign with you in glory.
Deepen within us the mystery of Christ's death and resurrection
that all who have died in the waters of baptism
may be changed into his image
and yield a harvest of everlasting life.

We ask this through our Lord Jesus Christ, your Son,
who lives and reigns with you in the unity of the Holy Spirit,
God for ever and ever.

## YEAR B

Lord of hosts,
how great is the mystery of our salvation:
when death came through human sin
you sent your Son as the Word made flesh
to bring us new life.

Grant that all the faithful departed
may share in the banquet of your glory.
Teach us the way of your Son,
that those who accept him and believe in his name
may willingly give their lives for the sake of the gospel.

We ask this through our Lord Jesus Christ, your Son,
who lives and reigns with you in the unity of the Holy Spirit,
God for ever and ever.


## YEAR C

To bring forth life from death, O God,
you raised up your Son from the depths of the grave
and revealed him as the source of life.

Raise up all the faithful departed
to share the life of your risen Son.
Touch our lives,
that we who have not seen him
may believe the message announced to us
and live in the hope of lasting glory.

We ask this through our Lord Jesus Christ, your Son,
who lives and reigns with you in the unity of the Holy Spirit,
God for ever and ever.

# 9 NOVEMBER
# THE DEDICATION OF
# THE LATERAN BASILICA IN ROME

The Lateran Basilica, the cathedral of the diocese of Rome, was dedicated to Christ the Saviour in the 4th century. The anniversary has been celebrated as a feast of the Latin Church on this date since the 12th century. It honours the local Church of Rome as a link with earliest Christian tradition and as a sign of our communion in Christ.

## OPENING PRAYER

Let us pray.

*A period of silent prayer follows.*

God of majesty,
you choose living stones
to fashion for yourself an eternal dwelling place.
Increase the spiritual gifts you have given to your Church,
that your faithful people may continue to grow
and so build up the new and heavenly Jerusalem.

We ask this through our Lord Jesus Christ, your Son,
who lives and reigns with you in the unity of the Holy Spirit,
God for ever and ever.

or

God of blessings,
you gave to your assembled people the name of Church:
grant that all who gather in your name
may love, reverence, and follow you,
and under your governance
be brought to the life of glory that you promise.

We ask this through our Lord Jesus Christ, your Son,
who lives and reigns with you in the unity of the Holy Spirit,
God for ever and ever.

## ALTERNATIVE OPENING PRAYER

God all-holy,
in every place on earth
you gather your people into your presence
to proclaim the wonders of your love.

As we celebrate the dedication
of the cathedral church of Rome,
deepen our unity with your faithful throughout the world,
and build us up into a house of prayer for all nations.

We ask this through our Lord Jesus Christ, your Son,
who lives and reigns with you in the unity of the Holy Spirit,
God for ever and ever.

# THE IMMACULATE CONCEPTION OF THE VIRGIN MARY

This feast had its origin in the East as the "Conception of Mary by St Anne." It spread through the West during the Middle Ages as the "Immaculate Conception" and was extended to the entire Western Church in the 18th century. The feast celebrates Mary, preserved from sin from the moment of conception; she is the firstfruits of her Son's redemption and a prophetic model of what the Church is called to be.

## OPENING PRAYER

Let us pray.

A period of silent prayer follows.

Lord our God,
through the immaculate conception of the Virgin Mary
you prepared a worthy dwelling for your Son.

As you preserved her from all taint of sin
by the salvation his death would bring,
so, through her intercession, cleanse us from our faults
and lead us safely into your presence.

We ask this through our Lord Jesus Christ, your Son,
who lives and reigns with you in the unity of the Holy Spirit,
God for ever and ever.

## ALTERNATIVE OPENING PRAYER

God most high,
from the first moment of her conception
you favoured the Virgin Mary with your grace,
that she might become the mother of the world's Redeemer.

As you blessed the daughter of Israel,
so grant us the grace
to be fully engaged in your service,
eager to do your will.
Hasten that day of gladness
when you will bring to completion your saving work,
through Jesus Christ our Lord,
who lives and reigns with you in the unity of the Holy Spirit,
God for ever and ever.

# ORDINARY PARTS

### SUNDAY CELEBRATION
### OF THE
### LITURGY OF THE WORD

# SUNDAY CELEBRATION OF THE WORD

# OUTLINE

**INTRODUCTORY RITE**

> Gathering of the Community
> Gathering Song
> Liturgical Greeting
> Introductory Remarks
> Opening Rite
> Opening Prayer

**LITURGY OF THE WORD**

> Procession and Enthronement of the Word of God
> First Reading
> Responsorial Psalm
> Second Reading
> Gospel Acclamation
> Gospel
> Homily [Reflection]
> Profession of Faith
> General Intercessions
> Proclamation of Praise
>
> Lord's Prayer
> Sign of Peace

**CONCLUDING RITE**

> Announcements
> Collection
> Blessing
> Dismissal

# INTRODUCTORY RITES

## GATHERING OF THE COMMUNITY

As the community gathers the members welcome one another. Some members may be chosen to greet and welcome others as they enter the church.

The usual presidential chair, a sign of the office of the bishop or presbyter (*A Book of Blessings*, no. 881), remains empty. If a deacon presides, a special chair is placed to the right of the presidential chair. If a lay person leads the prayer of the community, a chair is placed in another suitable place, preferably in the sanctuary.

The ministers gather in a suitable place to make the necessary preparations for the celebration. In advance of the celebration, the Lectionary is placed on a suitably covered table or stand near the entrance of the church. When all is ready the ministers may take their places with or without a procession or other liturgical form of entrance. The lector who will carry the Lectionary at the beginning of the liturgy of the word, and the ministers who will carry the candles and incense, if it is used, remain near the entrance, but where they can participate in the introductory rites.

When all is ready, the leader of prayer goes to the place from which he or she will preside. The altar or ambo (lectern) is never used for this purpose.

## GATHERING SONG

A psalm, acclamation or hymn is sung as the first act of worship of the assembly. The song expresses the unity of the community and is most appropriately a song of praise. A song that is seasonal in character may also be used.

## SIGN OF THE CROSS

Immediately after the song, all make the sign of the cross, as the leader of prayer says:

In the name of the Father, and of the Son,
✠ and of the Holy Spirit.

All respond: **Amen.**

## GREETING

The leader of prayer then greets the assembly, using one of the following forms. Seasonal greetings are found in the Proper of Seasons.

1. Blessed be God,
   whom we glorify with one heart and voice,
   who enables us, through the Spirit,
   to live in harmony as followers of Christ Jesus.
   Bless the Father and the Son and the Holy Spirit.

   or

2. Brothers and sisters, let us praise our Lord Jesus Christ,
   who loved us and gave himself for us.
   Bless the Father and the Son and the Holy Spirit.

   or

3. Blessed be the God of all consolation,
   who has shown us his great mercy.
   Bless the Father and the Son and the Holy Spirit.

   or

4. With one heart and one mind
   let us bless the Lord Jesus Christ,
   who is the way, the truth and the life.
   Bless the Father and the Son and the Holy Spirit.

   or

5. Brothers and sisters,
   let us praise and give thanks to the Lord,
   the fountain of all goodness.
   Bless the Father and the Son and the Holy Spirit.

   or

6. Let us praise the Lord Jesus Christ,
   who is present among us and in the Word,
   and who keeps us united in love.
   Bless the Father and the Son and the Holy Spirit.

   or

7. Blessed be God our Father,
   who has made us heirs of the kingdom with Christ,
   so that we may be glorified with him.
   Bless the Father and the Son and the Holy Spirit.

   or

8. Blessed be God the Father
who has sanctified and justified us
in the name of the Lord Jesus Christ
and in the Spirit of our God.
Bless the Father and the Son and the Holy Spirit.
or

9. Blessed be the Lord Jesus Christ,
who loves us and gave himself for us.
Now he lives in us
and we live in him by faith.
Bless the Father and the Son and the Holy Spirit.
or

10. Blessed be God,
who gives us righteousness and peace and joy
in the Holy Spirit.
Bless the Father and the Son and the Holy Spirit.
or

11. Blessed be the Holy Spirit,
who dwells in the Church
and is the source of all gifts and service,
Bless the Father and the Son and the Holy Spirit.
or

12. Bless the Father and the Son and the Holy Spirit.

All respond: Blessed be God for ever.

---

A deacon greets those present using one of the following greetings, or similar words.

1. The grace of our Lord Jesus Christ, the love of God,
and the fellowship of the Holy Spirit be with you all.
or

2. The grace and peace of God the Father
and the Lord Jesus Christ be with you.
or

3. The Lord be with you.
All respond: And also with you.

## INTRODUCTORY REMARKS

The leader of prayer may introduce the celebration in these or similar words, especially if the Sunday celebration of the word is not held regularly. The words should be suited to the particular occasion, and should call to mind the unity of this assembly with Sunday celebrations of the eucharist taking place elsewhere. These remarks may also be made before the gathering song.

Today, we, the people of God,
gather to hear and respond to God's word,
to return praise and thanks,
[and to share Christ's sacrament.]
We look forward to that day
when we will once more celebrate the Eucharist,
as Christ commanded us to do in his memory.
Our community makes its worship
in union with the Church throughout the world,
with *N.* our Pope, *N.* our bishop,
our pastor, Father *N.*, who is unable to be with us,
and with our brothers and sisters in neighbouring parishes
who keep holy this day
in the celebration of the Lord's sacrifice and supper.

or

Where there is no resident pastor, the minister might say:

Today, we the people of God
gather to hear and respond to God's word,
to give God praise and thanks,
[and to share Christ's sacrament.]
We look forward to that day
when we will again celebrate the Eucharist,
as Christ commanded us to do in his memory.
Our community worships in union with the whole Church,
with *N.* our Pope, *N.* our bishop,

and with our brothers and sisters in neighbouring parishes
who keep holy this day
in the celebration of the Lord's sacrifice and supper.

# Opening Rites

The opening rite assists the assembly to listen to the word of God by calling to mind the love of God revealed in Christ. Only one of the following rites are chosen. Although these may be varied from Sunday to Sunday, it is recommended that one form be used throughout a liturgical season or for a period of time in order that the character and unity of the season may be fostered. The *Gloria* is not used during Advent or Lent.

I.   Rite of Thanksgiving and Sprinkling of Water (page 208)

II.  Penitential Rite (page 210)

III. Litany of Praise (page 212)

IV.  Sung *Lord, have mercy or Kyrie*, eleison (page 214)

V.   Sung *Gloria* (page 215)

VI.  Other Opening Rites (page 215)


RECOMMENDED USE: During the liturgical year the following forms of the opening rite are recommended.

Advent: The litany of praise

Christmas: The sung *Gloria*

Lent: The penitential rite or sung *Kyrie*

Easter: The rite of sprinkling of water

Ordinary Time: A variety of rites

The forms of the opening rite recommended for each season are found before the opening prayers of each season.

## I. SPRINKLING OF HOLY WATER

INVITATION TO PRAYER: After the greeting, a server brings a vessel of water, which was previously blessed. If this is not possible, unblessed water may be used. Then the leader of prayer invites the people to pray, using one of the following formularies or similar words.

My brothers and sisters in Jesus Christ,
let us praise God our Father,
who called us in baptism to be his people.

or

Brothers and sisters,
let us invoke and bless the name of God the all-holy,
that this water may be for us a sign of the new life in Christ
which in baptism we have all received.

SILENT PRAYER: All pause in silence for a moment of personal prayer.

ACCLAMATIONS OR PRAYER OF THANKSGIVING OVER THE WATER: After a brief period of silence the leader of prayer sings or says one of the following forms.

### A – Outside the Easter Season

The leader of prayer says:

Praised be the Lord, the Creator.

All respond: Praised be the name of the Lord.

The leader of prayer says:

Praised be the Lord, the Resurrection and the Life.

All respond: Praised be the name of the Lord.

The leader of prayer says:

Praised be the Lord, the Spirit of holiness.

All respond: Praised be the name of the Lord.

With hands extended, the leader of prayer concludes:

Lord God,
Creator and giver of life,
we thank you for this water which we use in faith.
Wash away the sin that divides us,
make new life spring up within us,
and lead us, whole and complete, into your presence
to bless your glorious name.

We ask this through Christ our Lord.

All respond: Amen.

## B – In the Easter Season

Another form for the Easter Season is found in the Proper of Seasons for Easter, page 68. With hands extended, the leader of prayer sings or says:

Lord God almighty,
hear the prayers of your people.
We thank you for this gift of water
which recalls the wonder of our creation
and the still greater work of our redemption.

You created water to make the fields fruitful
and to refresh and cleanse our bodies.

You made water the channel of your loving kindness:
through water you delivered your people from bondage
and quenched their thirst in the desert.
The prophets used water to symbolize
the new covenant you would make with the human race.
Through water, which Christ made holy in the Jordan,
you have restored our sinful nature in the sacrament of rebirth.

May this water remind us of our own baptism,
and may we rejoice with our brothers and sisters
who have been baptized in this Easter season.

We ask this through Christ our Lord.

All respond: **Amen.**

SPRINKLING: Taking the sprinkler the leader of prayer moves through the church to sprinkle the assembly with water. If the church is large, other ministers may assist the leader in the sprinkling the assembly by moving through the church.

SONG: Meanwhile an appropriate psalm, acclamation or song is sung.

The opening prayer then follows.

## II. PENITENTIAL RITE

INVITATION TO REPENTANCE: After the greeting, the leader of prayer invites the people to acknowledge their sins in silence and to repent of them, using one of the following formularies or similar words.

As we prepare to listen to the Word of God,
we confess that we are sinners
and ask the Lord for pardon and strength.

or

Gathered together in Christ,
let us ask forgiveness with confidence,
for God is full of gentleness and compassion.

or

My brothers and sisters,
let us acknowledge our sins,
that we may receive God's word with faith.

SILENT PRAYER: All pause in silence for a moment of personal prayer.

CONFESSION OF SIN: Then one of the following forms is used.

### A

All say:

I confess to almighty God
and to you, my brothers and sisters,
that I have sinned through my own fault.

All strike their breast as a sign of sorrow.

in my thoughts and in my words,
in what I have done,
and in what I have failed to do;
and I ask blessed Mary, ever virgin,
all the angels and saints,
and you, my brothers and sisters,
to pray for me to the Lord our God.

CONCLUSION: With hands joins the leader of prayer concludes:

May almighty God have mercy on us,
forgive us our sins,
and bring us to everlasting life.

All respond: Amen.

or

## B

The leader of prayer says:

**Have mercy on us, Lord.**

All respond: **For we have sinned against you.**

The leader of prayer says:

**Show us your steadfast love, O God.**

All respond: **And grant us your salvation.**

CONCLUSION: With hands joined, the leader of prayer concludes:

**May almighty God have mercy on us,
forgive us our sins,
and bring us to everlasting life.**

All respond: **Amen.**

The opening prayer then follows.

## III. LITANY OF PRAISE

INVITATION: After the greeting, the leader of prayer invites the people to praise Christ, using one of the following formularies or similar words.

Before listening to the word,
let us praise the Lord Jesus Christ.

or

Rejoice in the mercy of Christ.
Praise the risen Saviour.

or

Rich in mercy is our Saviour
and great in kindness.
Praise the Lord Jesus Christ.

INVOCATIONS TO CHRIST: After a brief pause, the leader of prayer, or another minister or a cantor, sings or says one of the following forms of invocation or other similar invocations to Christ. Other forms are found in the Proper of Seasons.

### A

The minister sings or says:

Lord Jesus, you were sent to heal the contrite:
Lord, have mercy.

All respond: Lord, have mercy.

The minister sings or says:

You came to call sinners:
Christ, have mercy.

All respond: Christ, have mercy.

The minister sings or says:

You plead for us at the right hand of the Father:
Lord, have mercy.

All respond: Lord, have mercy.

### B

The minister sings or says:

Lord Jesus, you came to gather the nations
into the peace of God's kingdom:
Lord, have mercy.

All respond: Lord, have mercy.

*The minister sings or says:*

You come in Word and Spirit to strengthen us in holiness:
Christ, have mercy.

*All respond:* Christ, have mercy.

*The minister sings or says:*

You will come in glory with salvation for your people:
Lord, have mercy.

*All respond:* Lord, have mercy.

### C

*The minister sings or says:*

Lord Jesus, you are the mighty God and Prince of Peace:
Lord, have mercy.

*All respond:* Lord, have mercy.

*The minister sings or says:*

Lord Jesus, you are Son of God and Son of Mary:
Christ, have mercy.

*All respond:* Christ, have mercy.

*The minister sings or says:*

Lord Jesus, you are Word made flesh and radiance of God's glory:
Lord, have mercy.

*All respond:* Lord, have mercy.

### D

*The minister sings or says:*

Lord Jesus, you came to reconcile us to one another and to God:
Lord, have mercy.

*All respond:* Lord, have mercy.

*The minister sings or says:*

Lord Jesus, you heal the wounds of sin and division:
Christ, have mercy.

*All respond:* Christ, have mercy.

*The minister sings or says:*

Lord Jesus, you intercede for us at the throne of grace:
Lord, have mercy.

*All respond:* Lord, have mercy.

*The opening prayer then follows.*

## IV. LORD, HAVE MERCY (*KYRIE*)

INVITATION: After the greeting, the leader of prayer invites the people to acclaim Christ, using one of the following formularies or similar words.

You are called by God to rejoice in the embrace of mercy.
Acclaim Christ our Saviour.

or

God is making all things new.
Acclaim Christ, the first fruits of the new creation.

or

You are called by God out of darkness
into the dawn of radiant light.
Acclaim Christ, the sun of justice.

INVOCATIONS TO CHRIST: One of the following forms of invocation of praise and petition to Christ the Lord is sung.

| A | B |
|---|---|
| Lord, have mercy. | Kyrie, eleison. |
| Christ, have mercy. | Christe, eleison. |
| Lord, have mercy. | Kyrie, eleison. |

The opening prayer then follows.

## V. HYMN OF PRAISE (GLORIA)

This option is not used during Advent or Lent.

INVITATION: After the greeting, the leader of prayer invites the people to praise God, using one of the following formularies or similar words.

Let us sing the praises of the Lord,
the God who made us,
whose glory is from age to age.

or

With people everywhere,
let us glorify our God in joyful song:

or

With all the voices of heaven,
let us sing praise and honour and glory to God:

GLORIA: The hymn of praise is then sung.

The opening prayer then follows.

## VI. OTHER OPENING RITES

Other opening rites are used on particular occasions and follow the prescriptions of the respective liturgical books. These occur on certain special feasts (for example, Presentation of the Lord or Passion Sunday), or when special rites are celebrated (for example, a baptism or funeral). When such rites are celebrated, the general structure of the Introductory Rites are modified.

The opening prayer immediately follows any other opening rites.

## OPENING PRAYER

INVITATION TO PRAYER: The leader of prayer says:

## Let us pray.

SILENT PRAYER: The leader of prayer pauses in silence to give the community time to pray.

COLLECT PRAYER: With hands extended, the leader of prayer sings or says the prayer proper to the Sunday or Solemnities. This prayer is found in the Proper of the Season.

ASSENT: At the end the people give their assent to the prayer.

All respond: **Amen.**

# LITURGY OF THE WORD

## PROCESSION AND ENTHRONEMENT OF THE WORD

PROCESSION: After the Opening Prayer, the community remains standing. The Lectionary is carried in procession through the church by a reader, accompanied by ministers carrying candles and, if used, incense. Without reverencing the altar, the ministers proceed to the ambo (lectern). These stand at the lectern (ambo), facing the assembly.

ACCLAMATION: During the procession an appropriate acclamation or song is sung by the community. If the acclamation is short, organ or instrumental music may be played until the reader reaches the ambo and elevates the Lectionary. The acclamation may then be sung. If it is not possible to sing an acclamation or hymn, organ or instrumental music may be played. Suggestions for acclamations are the *Trisagion*, CBW II 632-633, CBW III 558 ; *Alleluia* or the Lenten version *Praise to you Lord, King of eternal glory!* or another appropriate acclamation such as *Speak Lord* or *Open my Heart,* or *Your Words, O Lord.*

ENTHRONEMENT: The reader holds up the Lectionary for all to see, and the candle bearers stand on either side of the minister holding the Lectionary while the acclamation is begun or continues.

As the acclamation begins, or after holding the Lectionary for a brief period of time, the lector places the Lectionary on the ambo and may place some incense in the thurible and incense the Lectionary. The hymn or acclamation continues, otherwise the organ or instrumental music continues during the incensing of the Lectionary.

INVITATION: Following the incensing of the Lectionary and after the hymn or acclamation is completed, the leader of prayer says:

May the Word of God always be heard in this place,
as it unfolds the mystery of Christ before us
and achieves our salvation within the Church.

READINGS: All are seated. The leader of prayer may give a brief, well-prepared, introduction to the readings, but this is not required or recommended. The leader of prayer and the community are seated and a reader proclaims the first reading.

During the liturgy of the word there are proper times for silence, for example, before the first reading, after the first and second readings, after the homily.

## FIRST READING

When the community is seated, the first reader proclaims the Word of God from the Lectionary in the usual way.

SILENT REFLECTION: The reading is always followed by a period of silence. At the end of the period of silence, the reader returns to his or her seat.

## Responsorial Psalm

The community then prays the Psalm. It may be led by a cantor (psalmist), who sings or recites the psalm verses, but the refrain is always selected so that it can be sung easily by the entire community. The cantor leads the Psalm from the lectern.

If it is difficult for the community to use a new refrain each Sunday, one of the seasonal psalms may be used, and repeated during all the Sundays of that season. A variety of seasonal psalms is provided in the *Catholic Book of Worship* at the beginning of each liturgical season.

# SECOND READING

After the psalm, a second reader goes to the lectern. The second reading is proclaimed as usual. A different reader should proclaim the second reading.

SILENT REFLECTION: The reading is followed by a period of silence.

## Gospel Acclamation

Following the period of silence the community stands for the Gospel Acclamation. The reader for the Gospel, a third reader, and not the leader of prayer or preacher (homily reader), proceeds to the lectern. If candles have not been placed by the lectern, candle bearers may stand at either side of it.

The Gospel Acclamation is sung in the usual manner by the congregation, led by a cantor who intones it. If it is not sung it is omitted. The appropriate Gospel verse, however, may be recited with a sung "Alleluia!", or the "Alleluia!" may be sung alone without the Gospel verse. During Lent the "Alleluia!" is replaced by "Praise to you, Lord, king of eternal glory!" or a similar acclamation.

## Gospel

The Gospel is proclaimed by the Gospel reader. A lay reader does not say "The Lord be with you." but says immediately:

### A reading from the holy gospel according to . . . .

All answer: **Glory to you, Lord.**

The reader traces a small cross on the Lectionary, and then on the forehead, the lips and the heart, asking that the Good News of Christ will remain always in our minds, on our lips, and in our hearts.

If incense is used, the Lectionary is incensed.

At the end of the Gospel, the reader says:

### The gospel of the Lord.

All answer: **Praise to you Lord Jesus Christ.**

The *Alleluia*, or another acclamation, may be sung instead or afterward. After the response of the community the reader kisses the Lectionary. The community sits and the ministers return to their own seats.

A deacon greets the assembly before announcing the gospel. The deacon says:

The Lord be with you.

All respond: And also with you.

A reading from the holy gospel according to . . . .

All respond: Glory to you, Lord.


At the end of the Gospel, the deacon says:

The gospel of the Lord.

All respond: Praise to you Lord Jesus Christ.


## HOMILY (REFLECTION)

A person authorized to preach by the bishop may then give a reflection on the readings. If no one is so authorized, another person, not a reader who has read the first or second readings or the Gospel, reads the homily for the day provided by the diocese or by the pastor. This may be done by the leader of prayer. The reflection or homily is given from the ambo (lectern). Following it, the person who gives it returns to his or her seat.

SILENT REFLECTION: After the homily, there follows a period of silence so that the community may further reflect on God's Word.

If there is no homily, there is a longer period of silent reflection.


## PROFESSION OF FAITH

After a period of silence following the Homily, the assembly stands and the leader of prayer leads the community in the Profession of Faith, using one of the following forms. This may vary from Sunday to Sunday, according to the spirit of the season and the solemnity of the day. On Easter Sunday the Renewal of Baptismal Promises is used (see pages 336-337).

The leader of prayer may begin the profession of faith or introduce it in these or similar words:

Brothers and sisters,
let us reaffirm our faith, the faith of the Church.

or

In union with the whole Church, let us profess our faith.

or

Let us profess the faith of the Church we received on the day of our baptism.

## I. NICENE CREED

All say:

We believe in one God,
the Father, the Almighty,
maker of heaven and earth,
of all that is seen and unseen.

We believe in one Lord, Jesus Christ,
the only Son of God,
eternally begotten of the Father,
God from God, Light from Light,
true God from true God,
begotten not made,
one in Being with the Father:
through him all things were made.
For us men and for our salvation
he came down from heaven:

All make a profound bow during the next two lines.

by the power of the Holy Spirit,
he was born of the Virgin Mary and became man.
For our sake he was crucified under Pontius Pilate;
he suffered, died, and was buried.
On the third day he rose again in fulfilment of the Scriptures;
he ascended into heaven,
and is seated at the right hand of the Father.
He will come again in glory to judge the living and the dead,
and his kingdom will have no end.

We believe in the Holy Spirit, the Lord, the giver of life,
who proceeds from the Father and the Son.
With the Father and the Son he is worshipped and glorified.
He has spoken through the prophets.
We believe in one holy catholic and apostolic Church.
We acknowledge one baptism for the forgiveness of sins.
We look for the resurrection of the dead,
and the life of the world to come. Amen.

## II. APOSTLES' CREED

I believe in God,
the Father Almighty,
Creator of heaven and earth.

I believe in Jesus Christ, his only Son, our Lord.
He was conceived by the power of the Holy Spirit,
and born of the Virgin Mary.
He suffered under Pontius Pilate,
was crucified, died, and was buried.
He descended to the dead.
On the third day he rose again;
he ascended into heaven,
and is seated at the right hand of the Father.
He will come again to judge the living and the dead.

I believe in the Holy Spirit,
the holy catholic Church,
the communion of saints,
the forgiveness of sins,
the resurrection of the body,
and the life everlasting. Amen.

On Easter Sunday the baptismal renewal of faith is used (see page 336).

# General Intercessions

INVITATION TO PRAYER: After the Profession of Faith the leader of prayer introduces the intercessions in these or similar words:

Gathered together in Christ as sisters and brothers
let us pray to God
for the needs of the Church and the world:

or

In response to God's Word proclaimed in our midst,
we pray to God
for the needs of the Church and the world:

or

Gathered together in Christ as brothers and sisters
let us call to mind God's many blessings
as we make our prayers
for the Church and the world:

INTERCESSIONS: The various intentions are then presented by a reader or another minister from the lectern. The intentions should be prepared to reflect the needs of the particular community as well as the concerns of the universal Church. During the Sunday Celebration of the Word there should always be a petition for vocations to the priesthood. The sick and the dead can appropriately be prayed for. The last petition may invite the assembly to pray in silence for the other intentions it may have. Normally the order of prayers would be:

a)   for the Church community and its ministers;

b)   for civil authorities and the pressing needs of the world;

c)   for the suffering and the oppressed;

d)   for the local community.

Sample intercessions are found on pages 307-313, in the Appendix.

PRAYER OF THE ASSEMBLY: The person reading the intercessions concludes each one by saying: "We pray:" or "We pray to the Lord:" and the community answers, "Lord, hear our prayer" or another familiar response. The response should not be varied too often.

Provided that the community can sing the responses, and that the petitions are adapted to the particular circumstances, adapted forms of the sung petitions in CBW II 78 (morning) or 69 (evening), CBW III 14J or 14K may be used instead.

When the petitions are completed, the minister who announces them returns to his or her place. The leader of prayer concludes the intercessions with the Proclamation of Praise.

# PROCLAMATION OF PRAISE

The leader of prayer then leads the community in the Prayer of Praise. The community joins together in giving praise and thanks for all that God has done, especially for the word that they have received, and that greatest of all God's gifts, the eternal and saving Word, Jesus Christ. All remain standing.

PRAYER OR HYMN OF PRAISE: Twelve options are provided. Although these may be varied from Sunday to Sunday according to the spirit of the liturgy of that day, when first used a prayer should be prayed a number of times in order that the community may become familiar with it. The prayers, litanies and psalms of praise use acclamations sung by the assembly. The sung canticles or songs of praise are sung by the whole assembly. Only one of the following forms is used each Sunday.

I.     Prayer of Praise *(Te Deum)* (p. 224)

II.    Prayer of Praise (Ephesians 1, adapted) (p. 226)

III.   Prayer of Praise (p. 228)

IV.    Prayer of Praise (Daniel 3, adapted) (p. 230)

V.     Prayer of Praise (Colossians 1, adapted) (p. 232)

VI.    Prayer of Praise for Easter (p. 234)

VII.   Prayer of Praise (Romans 8, adapted) (p. 236)

VIII.  Prayer of Praise *(Clement of Rome)* (p. 238)

IX.    Prayer of Praise (Based on Psalms 135-136) (p. 240)

X.     Prayer of Praise (p. 242)

XI.    Litany of Praise (p. 244)

XII.   Song of Praise (p. 246)

ACCLAMATIONS: The Prayers, Psalms and Litanies of Praise have sung acclamations addressed to God. These acclamations are sung by all. Some suitable acclamations are given below. Other similar acclamations addressed to God can be selected by those planning the liturgy, keeping in mind the context of the particular prayer used and suitability for singing by the whole community. The acclamations from the Eucharistic Prayers should not be used. Only one acclamation should be used throughout the prayer. One acclamation should be used for a period of time in order that the assembly may have time to learn it. Each of the following acclamations can be used for any of the prayers:

"Alleluia!" (or triple Alleluia!) (Outside Lent)

"All the ends of the earth have seen the power of God." (David Haas & Marty Haugen, refrain) (CBW III, 29B, 548)

"It is good to give you thanks, O Lord." (CBW II, 252; CBW III, 143)

"Give thanks to the Lord, his love is everlasting." (CBW II, 263; CBW III, 91, 92, 146)

"Forever I will sing the goodness of the Lord." (CBW II, 265; CBW III, 27, 64,148, 448)

"Give the Lord glory and honour." (CBW II, 313; CBW III, 196)

"Strong is God's love for us. Alleluia!" (CBW II, 428; CBW III, 546) (Outside Lent)

"How great is your name, O Lord our God, through all the earth." (CBW II, 409; CBW III, 553)

"Glory to God in the highest." (Various settings) (Outside Lent)

"Glory and praise for evermore." (CBW III, 684)

"Glory to you, O God." (CBW III, 584, antiphon 2)

## I. PRAYER OF PRAISE (Te Deum)

The leader of prayer says:

Let us praise the Lord.

After a brief pause, he or she continues:

We praise you, O God,
we acclaim you as Lord;
all creation worships you,
the Father everlasting.

To you, most holy and glorious God,
we voice our praise and sing:

The community sings the acclamation.

The leader of prayer continues:

To you all angels, all the powers of heaven,
the cherubim and seraphim, sing in endless praise:
Holy, holy, holy Lord, God of power and might,
heaven and earth are full of your glory.

We join in their hymn
as we voice our praise and sing:

The community sings the acclamation.

The leader of prayer continues:

The glorious company of apostles praise you.
The noble fellowship of prophets praise you.
The white-robed army of martyrs praise you.
Throughout the world the holy Church acclaims you:
Father, of majesty unbounded,
your true and only Son, worthy of all praise,
the Holy Spirit, advocate and guide.

Our own voices praise you as we sing:

The community sings the acclamation.

The leader of prayer continues:

You, Christ, are the king of glory,
the eternal Son of the Father.
When you took our flesh to set us free
you humbly chose the Virgin's womb.

You overcame the sting of death
and opened the kingdom of heaven to all believers.
You are seated at God's right hand in glory.
We believe that you will come to be our judge.

Come then, Lord, and help your people,
bought with the price of your own blood,
and bring us with your saints
to glory everlasting.

Through you, our Lord and Saviour,
to the God of all glory,
we voice our praise and sing:

The community sings the acclamation.

WITHOUT COMMUNION: If Communion will not be distributed, the Lord's Prayer and the Sign of Peace follow the Prayer of Praise (see pages 246-247).

A   Taught by our Saviour's command,
and formed by the Word of God, we dare to say (sing):

B   With trust in our Father in heaven,
we pray as Jesus taught us, saying (singing):

WITH COMMUNION: If Communion will be distributed, the Sign of Peace follows the Prayer of Praise (see page 255).

Let us seal our prayer with a sign of unity and reconciliation
as we offer one another a sign of peace.

## II. PRAYER OF PRAISE (Ephesians, 1.3-14, adapted)

*The leader of prayer says:*

Let us praise the Lord.

*After a brief pause, he or she continues:*

Blessed are you,
God and Father of our Lord Jesus Christ,
for you have blessed us in him
with every spiritual blessing of heaven.
Before the foundation of the world,
you chose us in him,
to be holy and blameless before you.

For such marvellous deeds, O God,
we voice our praise and sing:

*The community sings the acclamation.*

*The leader of prayer continues:*

In love you destined us
for adoption as your children
through Jesus Christ,
according to the good pleasure of your will:
how worthy of praise is your glorious grace,
that you freely bestowed on us in your Beloved.
In him we have redemption through his blood,
and the forgiveness of our trespasses:
such are the riches of your grace
that you lavished on us.

For such marvellous deeds, O God,
we voice our praise and sing:

*The community sings the acclamation.*

*The leader of prayer continues:*

With all wisdom and insight, gracious God,
you have made known to us the mystery of your will,
according to your good pleasure
that you set forth in Christ
as a plan for the fullness of time:
to gather up all things in him,
things in heaven and things on earth.
In Christ, we obtained an inheritance,
having been destined according to your purpose,
so that we, who were the first to set our hope on Christ,
might live for the praise of your glory.

We acclaim you, glorious God,
as we voice our praise and sing:

*The community sings the acclamation.*

*The leader of prayer continues:*

In Christ we heard the word of truth,
the gospel of our salvation,
and believed in him.
Through Christ we were marked with the seal of the promised Spirit,
who is the pledge of our inheritance
until we come into its possession,
to the praise of your glory.

And so, O God, our strength,
we voice our praise and sing:

*The community sings the acclamation.*

WITHOUT COMMUNION: If Communion will not be distributed, the Lord's Prayer and the Sign of Peace follow the Prayer of Praise (see pages 246-247).

A   Taught by our Saviour's command,
and formed by the Word of God, we dare to say (sing):

B   With trust in our Father in heaven,
we pray as Jesus taught us, saying (singing):

WITH COMMUNION: If Communion will be distributed, the Sign of Peace follows the Prayer of Praise (see page 255).

Let us seal our prayer with a sign of unity and reconciliation
as we offer one another a sign of peace.

### III. PRAYER OF PRAISE*

The leader of prayer says:

**Let us praise the Lord.**

After a brief pause, he or she continues:

Blessed are you, Lord our God,
king of all ages:
from eternity you have called us to be your people,
to sing your praise at all times.
Bless us in our work and prayer,
and grant that our lives may give you glory
through our words, our witness, and our worship.

We give you praise, Father,
through Jesus Christ our brother and our Lord,
in the communion of the Holy Spirit,
God for endless ages,
as we voice our praise and sing:

The community sings the acclamation.

The leader of prayer continues:

All praise leads to you, Father in heaven,
for leading us from the darkness of sin
into the light of your kingdom.

We bless you for sending your Son to save us,
to die for us that we might die to sin,
to be raised that we may share your life.
We thank you for giving us your spirit of love
to live in our hearts and lead us to you.

All glory, praise and honour be yours,
Father, Son, and Holy Spirit,
now and for endless ages.
To you, we voice our praise and sing:

The community sings the acclamation.

---

* **Liturgies with Lay Presiders,** copyright © Liturgy Commission, Archdiocese of Edmonton, 1988. All rights reserved. Used with permission.

The leader of prayer continues:

Blessed are you, Lord God,
Creator of all that is,
and Father of your chosen people:
we praise and thank you for your love.
Bring us to continue to praise you
by our lives and by our worship.
Send the Spirit of your Son into the hearts of all people,
and lead them to eternal joy with you.

Gracious God, we ask this grace
through Jesus Christ, our Lord and our brother,
in the love of the Holy Spirit,
as we voice our praise and sing:

The community sings the acclamation.

WITHOUT COMMUNION: If Communion will not be distributed, the Lord's Prayer and the Sign of Peace follow the Prayer of Praise (see pages 246-247).

**A**   Taught by our Saviour's command,
and formed by the Word of God, we dare to say (sing):

**B**   With trust in our Father in heaven,
we pray as Jesus taught us, saying (singing):

WITH COMMUNION: If Communion will be distributed, the Sign of Peace follows the Prayer of Praise (see page 255).

Let us seal our prayer with a sign of unity and reconciliation
as we offer one another a sign of peace.

### IV. PRAYER OF PRAISE (Daniel 3, adapted)

The leader of prayer says:

Let us praise the Lord.

After a brief pause, he or she continues:

Blessed are you, Lord, God of our ancestors,
to you be praise for ever.
Blessed is your glorious holy name,
praised and highly exalted for ever.
Blessed are you in the temple of your glory,
to you be praise for ever.

We, your people, the work of your hands,
glorify and exalt your holy name
as we voice our praise and sing:

The community sings the acclamation.

The leader of prayer continues:

All you works of the Lord, bless the Lord,
who is praised and exalted for ever.
Angels of the Lord, bless the Lord,
praised and exalted for ever.
You heavens above, bless the Lord.
Sun and moon, bless the Lord.
Stars of the heavens, bless the Lord,
praised and exalted for ever.

With all the wonders of the heavens,
we voice our praise and sing:

The community sings the acclamation.

The leader of prayer continues:

Let the earth bless the Lord,
who is praised and exalted for ever.
Mountains and hills, bless the Lord,
praised and exalted for ever.
All that grows in the ground, bless the Lord.
Seas and rivers, bless the Lord.
Fish and whales
and all that live in the waters, bless the Lord.
Birds of the air, bless the Lord.
Wild animals and cattle, bless the Lord,
praised and exalted for ever.

With earth and seas,
and with all you creatures of our God,
we voice our praise and sing:

The community sings the acclamation.

The leader of prayer continues:

All people on earth, bless the Lord,
who is praised and exalted for ever.
Those who serve the Lord, bless the Lord.
All who are holy and humble in heart, bless the Lord,
praised and exalted for ever.

With all the peoples of the earth,
whose life and service is your glory,
we voice our praise and sing:

The community sings the acclamation.

The leader of prayer continues:

All who worship the Lord,
sing praise and give thanks,
and bless the God of gods,
whose love is everlasting:
Glory and honour be yours,
Father, Son, and Holy Spirit,
now and for endless ages,
as we voice our praise and sing:

The community sings the acclamation.

WITHOUT COMMUNION: If Communion will not be distributed, the Lord's Prayer and the Sign of Peace follow the Prayer of Praise (see pages 246-247).

**A**  Taught by our Saviour's command,
and formed by the Word of God, we dare to say (sing):

**B**  With trust in our Father in heaven,
we pray as Jesus taught us, saying (singing):

WITH COMMUNION: If Communion will be distributed, the Sign of Peace follows the Prayer of Praise (see page 255).

Let us seal our prayer with a sign of unity and reconciliation
as we offer one another a sign of peace.

## V. PRAYER OF PRAISE (Colossians 1. 12-20, 22-23, 26-27)

The leader of prayer says:
Let us praise God, the Father of our Lord Jesus Christ.

After a brief pause, he or she continues.
With great joy we give you thanks, O God,
for you have enabled us
to share in the inheritance of the saints in the light.
You have rescued us from the power of darkness
and transferred us into the kingdom of your beloved Son,
in whom we have redemption, the forgiveness of sins.
Through Jesus Christ we voice our praise and sing.

The community sings the acclamation.

The leader of prayer continues:
We praise you, the invisible God,
for revealing your glory in Jesus Christ,
the firstborn of all creation.
In Christ all things in heaven and on earth were created,
things visible and invisible,
– whether thrones or dominions or rulers or powers –
all things have been created through him and for him.
Christ is before all things,
and in him all things hold together.
Through Jesus Christ we voice our praise and sing.

The community sings the acclamation.

The leader of prayer continues:
We bless you, Father of our Lord Jesus Christ,
for you have made Christ the head of the body, the church;
he is the beginning, the firstborn from the dead,
so that he might have first place in everything.

For in him all the fullness of your Godhead was pleased to dwell,
and through him you were pleased to reconcile all things to yourself,
making peace through the blood of his cross.
Through Jesus Christ we voice our praise and sing.

The community sings the acclamation.

*The leader of prayer continues:*

We give you glory and honour, O God of our salvation,
for in his human body
Christ has now reconciled us to you through death,
in order to present us before you,
holy and blameless and irreproachable,
provided we stand secure and steadfast in the faith,
without shifting from the hope promised by the gospel
that we have heard.

Through Jesus Christ we voice our praise and sing.

*The community sings the acclamation.*

*The leader of prayer continues:*

We rejoice, O God,
for Christ is the Good News
proclaimed to every creature under heaven.
He is the mystery
hidden throughout the ages and generations
but now revealed to us, his saints.
He is the hope of glory,
living among us and announced to every people.

Through Jesus Christ we voice our praise and sing.

*The community sings the acclamation.*

WITHOUT COMMUNION: If Communion will not be distributed, the Lord's Prayer and the Sign of Peace follow the Prayer of Praise (see pages 246-247).

**A**   Taught by our Saviour's command,
and formed by the Word of God, we dare to say (sing):

**B**   With trust in our Father in heaven,
we pray as Jesus taught us, saying (singing):

WITH COMMUNION: If Communion will be distributed, the Sign of Peace follows the Prayer of Praise (see page 255).

Let us seal our prayer with a sign of unity and reconciliation
as we offer one another a sign of peace.

## VI. PRAYER OF PRAISE FOR THE EASTER SEASON

Adapted from: 1 Cor 5.7; Rom 6.9-11; 1 Cor 15.20-22; Phil 2.9-11; Rev 5.9,10,13.

The leader of prayer says:

Let us praise the Lord.

After a brief pause, the leader of prayer continues:

God of our salvation, we give you thanks
for Christ our Passover has been sacrificed.
Therefore, we celebrate the festival,
as we voice our praise and sing.

The community sings the acclamation.

The leader of prayer continues:

God of life, we praise you
for Christ, being raised from the dead, will never die again;
death no longer has dominion over him.
The death that he died, he died to sin, once and for all;
but the life that he lives, he lives to you, O God.
So we also should consider ourselves dead to sin,
and alive to you in Christ Jesus.
Therefore, we celebrate the festival,
as we voice our praise and sing.

The community sings the acclamation.

The leader of prayer continues:

God of mercy and love, we bless you
for Christ has been raised from the dead,
the first fruits of those who have died.
For since death came through human means,
the resurrection of the dead has also come through human means.
For as in Adam all have died,
so also in Christ all shall be made alive.
Therefore, we celebrate the festival,
as we voice our praise and sing.

The community sings the acclamation.

*The leader of prayer continues:*

God of majesty, we glorify you
for now Christ reigns on high,
having been exalted by you and given the name above all names.
So that at the name of Jesus every knee should bend,
in the heavens, on the earth, and in the depths.
And every tongue proclaim:
Jesus Christ is Lord,
to your glory, our God and Father.
Therefore, we celebrate the festival,
as we voice our praise and sing.

*The community sings the acclamation.*

*The leader of prayer continues:*

God of power and might, we rejoice
in Christ, the Lamb that was slain,
for with his blood he has redeemed for you,
saints from every family, language, people and nation,
and made us a kingdom of priests to serve you on earth.
To you, O God, who sits upon the throne of glory,
and to Christ the Lamb,
be worship and praise, dominion and splendour.
Therefore, we celebrate the festival,
as we voice our praise and sing.

*The community sings the acclamation.*

WITHOUT COMMUNION: If Communion will not be distributed, the Lord's Prayer and the Sign of Peace follow the Prayer of Praise (see pages 246-247).

A    Taught by our Saviour's command,
      and formed by the Word of God, we dare to say (sing):

B    With trust in our Father in heaven,
      we pray as Jesus taught us, saying (singing):

WITH COMMUNION: If Communion will be distributed, the Sign of Peace follows the Prayer of Praise (see page 255).

Let us seal our prayer with a sign of unity and reconciliation
as we offer one another a sign of peace.

## VII. PRAYER OF PRAISE (Romans 8, adapted)

The leader of prayer says:

Let us praise the Lord.

After a brief pause, the leader of prayer continues:

We praise you, ever-living God,
for in Christ you have called us according to your own kind purpose
and you have justified us
that we may be conformed to the image of your Son.

For you did not withhold your own Son from us
but gave him up for all:
Christ who died, indeed was raised;
Christ who sits at your right hand;
Christ who now intercedes for us.

For the wonders of our salvation,
we voice our praise and sing:

The community sings the acclamation.

The leader of prayer continues:

We thank you, mighty and eternal One.
For those who are in Christ there is no condemnation;
your Spirit has set us free!

By sending your Son in the likeness of sin,
you have defeated sin in our bodies
that we might live as children of adoption,
not according to the flesh,
but according to the Spirit.

For the wonders of our salvation,
we voice our praise and sing:

The community sings the acclamation.

The leader of prayer continues:

We glorify you, all-powerful Master,
that as you raised Christ from the dead
so you give life to our mortal bodies
through your Spirit who dwells in us.

In our weakness the Spirit helps us to pray
for when we have not words
your Spirit intercedes for us according to your will
that we may call out Abba

For the wonders of our salvation,
we voice our praise and sing:

The community sings the acclamation.

The leader of prayer continues:

We praise you, God of mercy,
for in Christ Jesus your life-giving Spirit has made us your children,
and given us a share in your inheritance.
If we are one with him in his suffering now,
then we shall also be glorified with him.

With eager longing all creation awaits the revelation of your children,
the glorious freedom you promise,
the redemption of our bodies, and the hope of future glory.

For the wonders of our salvation,
we voice our praise and sing:

The community sings the acclamation.

The leader of prayer continues:

We thank you, God of majesty,
that nothing can ever separate us from your love in Christ.
In hardship and distress, in persecution and death,
we are more than conquerors through Christ,
who loves us and brings us your salvation.

Through Christ and in the Spirit your glory is seen
and your righteousness is fulfilled
among those who live in the Spirit,
those who seek life and peace.

For the wonders of our salvation,
we voice our praise and sing:

The community sings the acclamation.

WITHOUT COMMUNION: If Communion will not be distributed, the Lord's Prayer and the Sign of Peace follow the Prayer of Praise (see pages 246-247).

A   Taught by our Saviour's command,
and formed by the Word of God, we dare to say (sing):

B   With trust in our Father in heaven,
we pray as Jesus taught us, saying (singing):

WITH COMMUNION: If Communion will be distributed, the Sign of Peace follows the Prayer of Praise (see page 255).

Let us seal our prayer with a sign of unity and reconciliation
as we offer one another a sign of peace.

## VIII. PRAYER OF PRAISE (Clement of Rome)*

The leader of prayer says:

Let us praise the Lord.

After a brief pause, the leader of prayer continues:

Creator of the universe,
you preserve your chosen ones in the whole world
through Jesus Christ, your beloved Son.
Through Christ you have called us from darkness to the light,
from ignorance to the full knowledge of your glory,
that we may hope in your name
for you are the source of all creation.

To you, most holy and glorious God,
we voice our praise and sing:

The community sings the acclamation.

The leader of prayer continues:

You have opened the eyes of our hearts
so that we may know you alone,
the Most High in the heavens
and the Holy One who dwells among the saints.

You humble the arrogance of the proud;
you defeat the plans of nations;
you exalt the lowly and subdue the powerful.
You enrich and make poor;
you bring to birth and redeem from death.
You alone are the Giver of life
and the God of all creation.

To you, most holy and glorious God,
we voice our praise and sing:

The community sings the acclamation.

---

*    Adapted from *The Great Prayer* of Clement of Rome in "Letter to the Corinthians" quoted in Lucien Deiss, *Come, Lord Jesus,* p. 244. WORLD LIBRARY PUBLICATIONS, a division of J.S. Paluch Company, Inc.

The leader of prayer continues:

Your gaze pierces the depth of the universe;
you survey the works of humans,
you are the helper of those who are in danger,
the Saviour of all in despair.
You are the Creator and Guardian of all life!

You multiply the people of the earth,
and through Jesus Christ, your beloved Son,
you call all who love you to be your own.
Through Christ you instruct, sanctify, and glorify us.

To you, most holy and glorious God,
we voice our praise and sing:

The community sings the acclamation.

The leader of prayer continues:

You ordered the universe in your wisdom and harmony
which is now revealed in all your works.
Faithful throughout all generations,
you are just in judgment
and wonderful in power and majesty.
Everything we see proclaims your goodness.

Steadfast in kindness and compassion,
you never fail those who put their trust in you.

To you, most holy and glorious God,
we voice our praise and sing:

The community sings the acclamation.

WITHOUT COMMUNION: If Communion will not be distributed, the Lord's Prayer and the Sign of Peace follow the Prayer of Praise (see pages 246-247).

**A**   Taught by our Saviour's command,
and formed by the Word of God, we dare to say (sing):

**B**   With trust in our Father in heaven,
we pray as Jesus taught us, saying (singing):

WITH COMMUNION: If Communion will be distributed, the Sign of Peace follows the Prayer of Praise (see page 255).

Let us seal our prayer with a sign of unity and reconciliation
as we offer one another a sign of peace.

## IX. PRAYER OF PRAISE (Based on Psalms 135 and 136)

The leader of prayer says:

Let us praise the Lord.

After a brief pause, he or she continues:

Blessed be God, who is merciful and kind,
whose steadfast love endures forever.
Sing praise, for the Lord is great!
Shout in joy, for the Lord is gracious!

Praise the name of the Lord
in the heavens and on earth.
Give thanks, for the Lord is good!
Together let us voice our praise and sing.

The community sings the acclamation.

The leader of prayer continues:

Blessed be the Lord, who has done marvellous deeds,
whose wisdom made the skies,
who fixed the earth firmly on the seas,
who made the sun, the moon and the stars.

Praise the Lord who summons the clouds from the ends of the earth,
who makes lightning produce the rains,
who releases the winds from the storehouse,
and who brings forth the fruit of the earth.
Give thanks, for the Lord is good!
Together let us voice our praise and sing.

The community sings the acclamation.

The leader of prayer continues:

Blessed be the Lord, who brought Israel out of slavery,
whose out-stretched arm worked signs and wonders,
who divided the Red Sea in two,
and who let Israel pass through its midst.

Praise the Lord who sent Jesus our Saviour,
whose Spirit anointed him as the Christ,
who remembered us in our distress,
and who snatched us away from the foe.
Give thanks, for the Lord is good!
Together let us voice our praise and sing.

The community sings the acclamation.

The leader of prayer continues:

Blessed be God, who has raised Jesus from the dead,
whose power exalted him on high,
who made us kings, prophets and priests,
and who anoints us with the Spirit of love.

Praise the Lord who loves us forever,
whose goodness fills all the earth,
who speaks the Word that guides our ways,
and who calls us to a kingdom of joy.
Give thanks, for the Lord is good!
Together let us voice our praise and sing.

The community sings the acclamation.

The leader of prayer concludes:

Blessed be the Lord, God of all creation,
who has given us life in his Son, Jesus Christ,
who has saved us from death
and who has renewed us in the new life of grace.

Praise the Lord who assembles us in love,
whose Spirit sends us out to the world,
who makes us servants and witnesses to the Word.
Give thanks, for the Lord is good!
Together let us voice our praise and sing.

The community sings the acclamation.

WITHOUT COMMUNION: If Communion will not be distributed, the Lord's Prayer and the Sign of Peace follow the Prayer of Praise (see pages 246-247).

A  Taught by our Saviour's command,
   and formed by the Word of God, we dare to say (sing):

B  With trust in our Father in heaven,
   we pray as Jesus taught us, saying (singing):

WITH COMMUNION: If Communion will be distributed, the Sign of Peace follows the Prayer of Praise (see page 255).

Let us seal our prayer with a sign of unity and reconciliation
as we offer one another a sign of peace.

## X. PRAYER OF PRAISE

The leader of prayer says:

Let us praise the Lord.

After a brief pause, he or she continues:

We give you thanks, almighty God and Father,
for your goodness and love in all creation,
by which you continually nourish and sustain us.

To you, most holy and glorious God,
we voice our praise and sing:

The community sings the acclamation.

The leader of prayer continues:

We give you thanks, Lord our God,
for revealing yourself throughout history,
and forming a covenant of salvation with your people.

To you, most holy and glorious God,
we voice our praise and sing:

The community sings the acclamation.

The leader of prayer continues:

We give you thanks, gracious God,
for speaking words of life through the prophets
and especially in the Word made flesh.

To you, most holy and glorious God,
we voice our praise and sing:

The community sings the acclamation.

The leader of prayer continues:

We give you thanks, God of mercy and love,
for sending your Son, Jesus Christ,
who freed us from slavery to sin
and anointed us as your beloved children.

To you, most holy and glorious God,
we voice our praise and sing:

The community sings the acclamation.

*The leader of prayer continues:*

We thank you, Lord of heaven and earth,
for the Spirit of adoption,
who consecrates us to proclaim the good news of salvation
and unites us in your eternal kingdom.

To you, most holy and glorious God,
we voice our praise and sing:

*The community sings the acclamation.*

WITHOUT COMMUNION: If Communion will not be distributed, the Lord's Prayer and the Sign of Peace follow the Prayer of Praise (see pages 246-247).

A   Taught by our Saviour's command,
and formed by the Word of God, we dare to say (sing):

B   With trust in our Father in heaven,
we pray as Jesus taught us, saying (singing):

WITH COMMUNION: If Communion will be distributed, the Sign of Peace follows the Prayer of Praise (see page 255).

Let us seal our prayer with a sign of unity and reconciliation
as we offer one another a sign of peace.

## XI. LITANY OF PRAISE

Since a litany demands a short response without a musical lead-in, the inflection of the leader of prayer's voice is important to provide the proper invitation to the community's response. An alternative method, using the music of CBW II, 223 or CBW III, 108, is for a cantor to provide a musical introduction as suggested in the text. This musical introduction is optional, or may be recited as an introduction to the sung acclamation.

The leader of prayer says:

Let us praise our God.

After a brief pause, the leader continues:

Blessed are you, O God, the Creator of all life.
who made the universe and sustains all creatures.

[Cantor:] You are blest, Lord God for ever.

*R.* To you glory and praise for evermore.

Blessed are you, O God, the Hope of all people,
who speaks the life-giving Word and brings forth the fruit of the earth.

[Cantor:] You are blest, Lord God for ever.

*R.* To you glory and praise for evermore.

Blessed are you, O God, the Father of our Lord Jesus Christ,
who enriches our lives with love and surrounds our days with joy.

[Cantor:] You are blest, Lord God for ever.

*R.* To you glory and praise for evermore.

Blessed are you, O God, the all holy One,
who chose us in Christ and anoints us with the Spirit of adoption.

[Cantor:] You are blest, Lord God for ever.

*R.* To you glory and praise for evermore.

Blessed are you, O God, the Rock of our salvation,
who inspires our hymns and renews our youth.

[Cantor:] You are blest, Lord God for ever.

*R.* To you glory and praise for evermore.

The leader of prayer says:
Blessed are you, O God, the Revelation of love,
who makes us one in Christ and gives us the crown of victory.

[Cantor:] You are blest, Lord God for ever.

*R.* To you glory and praise for evermore.

The leader of prayer says:

Blessed are you, O God, the Healer of hearts,
who forgives our sins and binds up our wounds.

[Cantor:] You are blest, Lord God for ever.

*R.* To you glory and praise for evermore.

The leader of prayer says:

Blessed are you, O God, the Guardian of your chosen ones,
who lives among us and leads us in all our ways.

[Cantor:] You are blest, Lord God for ever.

*R.* To you glory and praise for evermore.

The leader of prayer says:

Blessed are you, O God, the Source of eternal light,
who calls us from darkness and clothes us with glory.

[Cantor:] You are blest, Lord God for ever.

*R.* To you glory and praise for evermore.

The leader of prayer says:

Blessed are you, O God, the Provider of good gifts,
who raised us from death and crowns us with life.

[Cantor:] You are blest, Lord God for ever.

*R.* To you glory and praise for evermore.

WITHOUT COMMUNION: If Communion will not be distributed, the Lord's Prayer and the Sign of Peace follow the Prayer of Praise (see pages 246-247).

**A** Taught by our Saviour's command,
and formed by the Word of God, we dare to say (sing):

**B** With trust in our Father in heaven,
we pray as Jesus taught us, saying (singing):

WITH COMMUNION: If Communion will be distributed, the Sign of Peace follows the Prayer of Praise (see page 255).

Let us seal our prayer with a sign of unity and reconciliation
as we offer one another a sign of peace.

## XII. SONG or PSALM OF PRAISE

An appropriate song of praise addressed to God or a psalm of praise, which is sung by the whole community, may be used. It should be carefully selected, sufficiently long to establish an atmosphere of praise, and not specifically eucharistic. Such songs and psalms of praise include:

"Bless the Lord" (CBW II, 626; CBW III, 684)

"We praise thee, O God, our Redeemer" (CBW II, 648)

"We praise you, Lord, for Jesus Christ" (CBW III, 617)

"We praise, you, O Lord" (CBW III, 633)

"Praise the Lord, ye heav'ns, adore Him" (CBW II, 656; CBW III, 567)

"Praise my soul, the King of heaven" (CBW II, 650; CBW III, 565)

Psalm 66: "Let all the earth cry out to God with joy." (CBW III, 103, 589)

Psalm 96: "O Sing a New Song unto the Lord" (CBW II, 423; but not 660; CBW III, 117, 196)

Psalm 100: "Cry out with joy" (CBW II, 425, 426)

The leader of prayer says:

**In praise and thanksgiving we sing to the Lord**
**hymn number . . . . . from . . . . . (hymnal name), . . . . (hymn title).**

The song of praise is sung.

WITHOUT COMMUNION: If Communion will not be distributed, the Lord's Prayer and the Sign of Peace follow the Prayer of Praise (see below).

WITH COMMUNION: If Communion will be distributed, the Sign of Peace follows the Prayer of Praise (see page 255).

**Let us seal our prayer with a sign of unity and reconciliation**
**as we offer one another a sign of peace.**

## THE LORD'S PRAYER

At the end of the proclamation of praise, the leader introduces the Lord's Prayer. Either of two forms (Version A or Version B) may be used; each has an introduction particular to it. The Lord's Prayer is always concluded with its doxology.

# A

Taught by our Saviour's command,
and formed by the Word of God,
we dare to say [sing]:

The leader of prayer and the people say together:

Our Father,
who art in heaven,
hallowed be thy name;
thy kingdom come;
thy will be done,
on earth as it is in heaven.
Give us this day our daily bread;
and forgive us our trespasses
as we forgive those who trespass against us;
and lead us not into temptation
but deliver us from evil.

For the kingdom, the power, and the glory are yours
now and for ever. Amen.

Sung forms of this version are found in CBW II, 396 to 400; CBW III, 287)

# B

The leader of prayer says:

With trust in our Father in heaven,
we pray as Jesus taught us, saying [singing]:

The leader of prayer and the people say together:

Our Father in heaven,
hallowed be your name;
your kingdom come;
your will be done,
on earth as in heaven.
Give us today our daily bread.
Forgive us our sins
as we forgive those who sin against us.
Save us from the time of trial
and deliver us from evil.

For the kingdom, the power, and the glory are yours
now and forever. Amen.

Sung forms of this version are found in CBW II, 70; CBW III, 14L, 286.

## SIGN OF PEACE

Following the Lord's Prayer, the leader says in these or similar words:

Let us seal our prayer with a sign of fellowship
as we offer one another a sign of peace.

or

In the name of Christ,
let us offer each other a sign of peace.

or

Let us exchange with each other a sign of Christ's peace.

or

Let us share with our neighbour
a sign of the peace of Christ.

or

As children of God,
let us offer one another
a sign of reconciliation and peace.

The leader of prayer exchanges a sign of peace with those nearby. Members of the community exchange the sign of peace with each other.

# CONCLUDING RITE

## ANNOUNCEMENTS

Any announcements may be made briefly at this time by another member of the assembly, or by the leader of prayer.

## COLLECTION

Following the announcements, a collection may be taken up for the needs of the Church and the poor.

MUSIC: This is not an appropriate time for a congregational hymn, but instrumental music may be used, or the choir may sing a selection. The collection, including any music, should avoid any appearance of the presentation of the gifts at Mass, and music that would be used in the Eucharist should not be used here.

The collection begins without any introduction.

The collection may be brought forward by the collectors, and placed in a suitable place, but not on or near the altar; neither should it be received by the leader of prayer.

## BLESSING

After the collection all stand and the blessing follows. One of the forms below is used. At the appropriate time during the blessing, the leader of prayer signs himself or herself with the sign of the cross.

The leader of prayer says:

May the God of hope fill us with every joy in believing.
May the peace of Christ abound in our hearts.
May the Holy Spirit enrich us with his gifts,
✠ now and for ever.

or

May the Lord bless us,
protect us from all evil,
✠ and bring us to everlasting life.

or

May God the Father,
with the Son and the Holy Spirit,
who has shown us such great mercy,
be praised and ✠ blessed for ever and ever.

or

May God, who is blessed above all,
✠ bless us in all things through Christ,
so that whatever happens in our lives
will work together for our good,
now and for ever.

or

The blessing of the God of Sarah and Abraham,
the blessing of Jesus Christ, born of Mary,
the blessing of the Holy Spirit
who cares for us as a mother for her children,
✠ be with us now and for ever.

> or

God, the Father of mercies, has sent his Son into the world.
Through the Holy Spirit, who will teach us all truth,
may he make us messengers of the Gospel
✠ and witnesses of his love to the world
now and for ever.

> or

May God, the source of every good,
bless us and give success to our work,
so that we may rejoice in the gifts we have received
✠ and praise God's name now and for ever.

> All respond: Amen.

---

A deacon says:

The Lord be with you.

> All respond: And also with you.

Then he says:

May almighty God bless you,
the Father, and the Son
✠ and the Holy Spirit.

> or

May the blessing of almighty God,
the Father, and the Son,
✠ and the Holy Spirit,
descend upon you and remain for ever.

> All respond: Amen.

## Dismissal

Following the blessing, the leader of prayer dismisses the assembly in these or similar words:

Let us go forth in the name of Christ.

or

Let us go in peace to love and serve the Lord.

or

Go in the peace of Christ.

or

Let us go forth,
rejoicing in the power of the Spirit.

All answer: Thanks be to God.

---

During the Octave of Easter and on Pentecost Sunday the leader of prayer adds a double *Alleluia* to the dismissal.

The leader of prayer says or sings:

Go in the peace of Christ, alleluia, alleluia.

All respond: Thanks be to God, alleluia, alleluia.

---

RECESSIONAL MUSIC: As the community is leaving, music may be played or the choir may sing a suitable selection, but a congregational hymn is less appropriate.

# RITE OF DISTRIBUTION
# OF COMMUNION
# OUTSIDE THE EUCHARIST

# RITE OF DISTRIBUTION OF COMMUNION OUTSIDE THE EUCHARIST

## OUTLINE

**INTRODUCTORY RITE**

See page 203


**LITURGY OF THE WORD**

See page 217

Proclamation of Praise
Sign of Peace


**COMMUNION RITE**

Lord's Prayer
Invitation to Communion
Communion
Prayer after Communion


**CONCLUDING RITE**

Announcements
Collection
Blessing
Dismissal

The Celebration of the Liturgy of the Word is found on pages 203-246.

## SIGN OF PEACE

Following the Proclamation of Praise, the leader of prayer invites all to offer each other a sign of peace in these or similar words:

Let us seal our prayer with a sign of fellowship
as we offer one another a sign of peace.

or

In the name of Christ,
let us offer each other a sign of peace.

or

Let us exchange with each other a sign of Christ's peace.

or

Let us share with our neighbour
a sign of the peace of Christ.

or

As children of God,
let us offer one another
a sign of reconciliation and peace.

The leader of prayer exchanges a sign of peace with those nearby. Members of the community exchange the sign of peace with each other.

# RITE OF DISTRIBUTION OF COMMUNION

## BRINGING OF THE BLESSED SACRAMENT TO THE ALTAR

When the sign of peace is completed, and a short silent interval has taken place, the community remains standing. The communion ministers go to the tabernacle to bring the Blessed Sacrament to the altar in the vessels needed for communion. At the tabernacle the hosts are transferred to one or more vessels for distribution of communion by the ministers, if this was not done before the celebration began. The vessels are then brought to the altar. This should be done with simple dignity. The ministers may be accompanied by servers bearing candles; these can be placed on or near the altar. The cross or incense should not be used, nor is music appropriate here. After placing the vessels on the altar, they genuflect. The communion ministers remain at or near the altar, but slightly back from it, ready for the distribution of communion.

Where there is no tabernacle, the Blessed Sacrament should have been properly reserved before the liturgy in the sacristy or in another suitable place clearly distinct from the altar or lectern area. When all is prepared, the leader of prayer or the communion minister who is to lead the Rite of Communion comes to the altar and stands alone at it, facing the assembly.

## THE LORD'S PRAYER

After the Blessed Sacrament is placed on the altar, the minister introduces the Lord's Prayer which is recited or sung by the community.

Either of two forms (Version A or Version B) may be used. The Lord's Prayer is always concluded with its doxology.

### A

The minister says:

Taught by our Saviour's command,
and formed by the Word of God,
we dare to say [sing]:

The minister and the people say together:

Our Father,
who art in heaven,
hallowed be thy name;
thy kingdom come;
thy will be done,
on earth as it is in heaven.
Give us this day our daily bread;
and forgive us our trespasses
as we forgive those who trespass against us;
and lead us not into temptation
but deliver us from evil.

For the kingdom, the power, and the glory are yours
now and forever. Amen

Sung forms of this version are found in CBW II, 396 to 400; CBW III, 287)

## B

The minister says:

With trust in our Father in heaven,
we pray as Jesus taught us, saying [singing]:

The minister and the people say together:

Our Father in heaven,
hallowed be your name;
your kingdom come;
your will be done,
on earth as in heaven.
Give us today our daily bread.
Forgive us our sins
as we forgive those who sin against us.
Save us from the time of trial
and deliver us from evil.

For the kingdom, the power, and the glory are yours
now and forever. Amen

Sung forms of this version are found in CBW II, 70; CBW III, 14L, 286.

## INVITATION TO COMMUNION

After the Lord's Prayer, the minister genuflects, and taking a host from the ciborium raises it slightly.

The bread is never broken, and the accompanying chant, "Lamb of God . . ." is never sung nor recited.

The minister says aloud:

God's holy gifts for God's holy people:
draw near to receive them with praise and thanksgiving.

or

Behold the Lamb of God,
who takes away the sin of the world.
Blessed are those called to the banquet of the Lamb.

The minister and the people say together:

Lord I am not worthy to receive you,
but only say the word and I shall be healed.

The communion hymn then begins.

The minister receives communion, saying quietly: "May the body of Christ bring me everlasting life."

The minister then gives communion to the other communion ministers. They then go to their stations.

Communion ministers hold up the host before each communicant and say:

The Body of Christ.

The communicant answers: Amen.

## REPOSITION OF THE BLESSED SACRAMENT

After communion the communion ministers return the Blessed Sacrament to the tabernacle. If servers placed candles on the altar at the beginning of the communion rite, they now remove them. The candles may be placed on the side table or be placed near the cross.

Any empty communion vessels are brought to a side table, and may be reverently purified after the celebration.

The ministers then sit.

## Period of Silence

It is appropriate to have a period of silent prayer. While a psalm or hymn of praise is permitted, it is preferable to respect the silent prayer of the community.

## Prayer After Communion

The Rite of Communion concludes with the Prayer after Communion, which follows immediately, before any announcements. Since it is a part of the Communion Rite, it is appropriately led by the minister who led the Rite of Communion.

INVITATION: Standing at the altar, or at the usual place of the presiding, the minister says:

Let us pray.

SILENT PRAYER: All briefly pray in silence, and then the minister continues with the prayer after communion. This is taken from the Prayers after Communion, pages 260-267.

At the end the people give their assent: Amen.

If the communion minister led the prayer, he or she returns to his or her place after the Prayer.

# PRAYERS AFTER COMMUNION

## ADVENT

Lord our God,
grant that in our journey through this passing world
we may learn from this sacrament
to cherish even now the things of heaven
and to cling to the treasures that never pass away.
We ask this in the name of Jesus, the Lord.

or

In this communion, almighty God,
you have given us the pledge of eternal redemption.
Grant that the closer we come to the feast of Christmas,
the more eagerly we may prepare to celebrate
the saving mystery of your Son's birth.
We ask this through Jesus Christ our Lord.

## CHRISTMAS

Lord our God,
we celebrate with joy the birth of our Redeemer.
Grant that through worthy and holy lives
we may be welcomed into his glorious company for ever.
We ask this through Jesus Christ our Lord.

or

Merciful God,
grant that the Saviour of the world,
who was born this day
to bring us new and divine life,
may bestow upon us the gift of life everlasting.
We ask this in the name of Jesus, the Lord.

### Holy Family

Merciful Father,
you have refreshed us with this heavenly sacrament.
Grant us the grace to follow closely
the example of the Holy Family,
that, after the trials of this present life,
we may be welcomed into their company for ever.
We ask this through Jesus Christ our Lord.

**Mary, Mother of God**

> Lord,
> as we joyfully proclaim the Virgin Mary
> to be Mother of your Son and Mother of the Church,
> we ask that this heavenly sacrament
> by which we have been nourished
> may bring us to life everlasting.
> Grant this in the name of Jesus, the Lord.

**Epiphany and Baptism of the Lord**

> Refreshed by these holy gifts, Lord God,
> we seek your mercy,
> so that, by listening faithfully to your only Son,
> we may be your children in name and in truth.
> We ask this in the name of Jesus, the Lord.

# LENT

Lord,
may the sacrament we have received in faith
sustain and strengthen us,
so that our Lenten fast may win favour in your sight
and help to remedy our human weakness.
Grant this in the name of Jesus, the Lord.

> or

Lord,
you have renewed us with the heavenly bread
that enlivens our faith, inspires our hope, and strengthens our charity.
Teach us to hunger for Christ, the true and living bread,
and to live by every word that proceeds from your mouth.
We ask this through Jesus Christ our Lord.

> or

God of majesty,
you enlighten everyone who comes into this world;
fill our hearts with the light of your grace,
that our thoughts may always be pleasing to you
and our love for you always sincere.
We ask this through Jesus Christ our Lord.

# EASTER

Lord, remain close to your people,
whom you have enriched with the grace of this sacrament,
that we may pass from our old life of frailty
to new life in the risen Christ.
We make our prayer in the name of Jesus, the Lord.

or

All-powerful and ever-living God,
in the resurrection of Christ you restore us to eternal life.
Increase within us the effects of this sacrament
and pour out in our hearts the strength of this saving food.
We ask this through Jesus Christ our Lord.

**Pentecost**

God of mercy,
pour forth upon us your spirit of love,
that we who have been nourished
by the one bread from heaven
may be one in mind and heart.
Grant this through Jesus Christ our Lord.

# ORDINARY TIME

God of mercy,
pour forth upon us your spirit of love,
that we who have been nourished
by the one bread from heaven
may be one in mind and heart.
Grant this through Jesus Christ our Lord.

or

Nourished with the sacrament of our redemption,
we ask you, Lord, that by its saving power
true faith may always grow and prosper.
Grant this through Jesus Christ our Lord.

or

Having tasted the bread of heaven,
we beg you, Lord,
that we may always hunger for that food
by which we truly live.
Grant this through Jesus Christ our Lord.

or

Lord,
as the communion we have received
prefigures the union of all the faithful in you,
so may its power
bring unity and peace to your Church.
We ask this through Jesus Christ our Lord.

or

Merciful God,
let our sharing in this sacrament
deliver us from evil
and make us stand firm in the light of your truth.
We ask this in the name of Jesus, the Lord.

or

Complete within us, Lord,
the healing work of your mercy,
and by your grace transform and strengthen us,
that we may please you in all that we do.
Grant this through Jesus Christ our Lord.

or

God of blessings,
we have been fed at this table
with the bread of heaven.
Give us this food always,
that it may strengthen your love in our hearts
and inspire us to serve you in our brothers and sisters.
Grant this in the name of Jesus, the Lord.

# SOLEMNITIES OF THE LORD

**Christ the King**

Nourished by the food of immortal life,
we beg you, Lord,
that we who glory in our obedience to Christ,
the king of all creation,
may live with him always in the kingdom of heaven.
Grant this through Jesus Christ our Lord.

### Holy Trinity

Lord God,
we worship you,
a Trinity of persons, one eternal God.
Grant that the sacrament we have received
and the faith we profess
may bring us wholeness of mind and body.
We ask this through Jesus Christ our Lord.

### Body and Blood

Lord Jesus Christ,
bring us one day
to that eternal union with your Godhead,
which is prefigured here on earth
by our sharing in your sacred body.
You live and reign for ever and ever.

### Sacred Heart

Lord our God,
may this sacrament of charity
enkindle in our hearts the flame of your love,
so that, drawn to the person of Christ your Son,
we may learn to recognize him in our brothers and sisters.
Grant this in the name of Jesus, the Lord.

# FEASTS OF THE LORD

### Presentation of the Lord (2 February)

Through this holy banquet, O God,
make your grace perfect in us,
and as you satisfied the longing of Simeon
that he would not see death
before he had welcomed the Messiah,
grant that we, going forth to meet the Lord,
may also embrace the gift of eternal life.
We ask this through Jesus Christ our Lord.

### Annunciation of the Lord (25 March)

Lord God,
we profess as truly God and truly human
the child conceived by the Virgin Mary.
Seal in our hearts the mysteries of true faith,
and through the saving power of the resurrection
guide us to eternal happiness.
We ask this in the name of Jesus, the Lord.

### Transfiguration (6 August)

Grant, Lord God,
that the bread from heaven which we have received
may transform us into the likeness of Christ,
whose splendour you revealed
when he was transfigured in glory.
We ask this in the name of Jesus, the Lord.

### Holy Cross (14 September)

Nourished at this heavenly table,
we ask you, Lord Jesus Christ,
to lead to the glory of the resurrection
all whose salvation you purchased
by the life-giving wood of the cross.
You live and reign for ever and ever.

### Dedication of a Church (9 November)

O God,
you chose to foreshadow in your Church on earth
the new and heavenly Jerusalem.
Through our sharing in these sacred mysteries,
fashion us into a temple of your grace
and lead us one day to the place where your glory dwells.
We ask this through Jesus Christ our Lord.

# BLESSED VIRGIN MARY

### General and Mary, Mother of God (January)

Lord,
as we joyfully proclaim the Virgin Mary
to be Mother of your Son and Mother of the Church,
we ask that this heavenly sacrament
by which we have been nourished
may bring us to life everlasting.
Grant this in the name of Jesus, the Lord.

### Assumption (15 August)

Lord God,
you have raised the Virgin Mary to the glory of heaven;
through her intercession
grant that we who have shared this saving sacrament
may be brought to the glory of the resurrection.
We ask this in the name of Jesus, the Lord.

### Immaculate Conception (8 December)

Lord our God,
let the sacrament we have received
heal in us the wounds of that sin
from which you preserved the Virgin Mary
through the singular grace of her immaculate conception.
Grant this through Jesus Christ our Lord.

# SAINT JOSEPH

Lord God,
on this joyous feast of blessed Joseph
watch over your household, the Church,
which you have nourished at the altar of life,
and safeguard the gifts
you have graciously bestowed upon us.
We ask this in the name of Jesus, the Lord.

# SAINT JOHN THE BAPTIST

Lord God,
your Church has been renewed at the table of the Lamb.
As we rejoice at the birth of John the Baptist,
grant that we may acknowledge as author of our rebirth
the Christ whose coming John foretold.
We ask this in the name of Jesus, the Lord.

# APOSTLES

Lord God,
by the power of these heavenly sacraments
confirm in truth your faithful people,
whom you have enlightened by the teaching of the apostles.
We ask this through Jesus Christ our Lord.

# SAINTS

We adore you, Lord God,
for you are the holy one
and are glorified in all your saints.
We implore your grace,
that we may reach the full measure of holiness and love
and pass from this table where we gather as a pilgrim people
to the banquet prepared for us in heaven.
Grant this in the name of Jesus, the Lord.

# ALL SOULS

Lord,
we have received the sacrament of your only Son,
who was sacrificed for us and rose in glory.
We humbly pray for the faithful departed,
that they may share in the glory of the final resurrection.
Grant this through Jesus Christ our Lord.

# CONCLUDING RITE

## ANNOUNCEMENTS

Any announcements may be made briefly at this time by another member of the assembly, or by the leader of prayer.

## COLLECTION

Following the announcements a collection may be taken up for the needs of the Church and the poor.

MUSIC: This is not an appropriate time for a congregational hymn, but instrumental music may be played, or the choir may sing a selection. The collection, including any music, should avoid any appearance of the presentation of the gifts at Mass, and music that would be used in the Eucharist should not be used here.

The collection may be brought forward by the collectors, and placed in a suitable place, but not on or near the altar; neither should it be received by the leader of prayer.

## BLESSING

After the collection all stand and the blessing follows. One of the forms below is used. At the appropriate time during the blessing, the leader of prayer signs himself or herself with the sign of the Cross.

The leader of prayer says:

May the God of hope fill us with every joy in believing.
May the peace of Christ abound in our hearts.
May the Holy Spirit enrich us with his gifts,
✠ now and for ever.

or

May the Lord bless us,
protect us from all evil,
✠ and bring us to everlasting life.

or

May God the Father,
with the Son and the Holy Spirit,
who has shown us such great mercy,
be praised and ✠ blessed for ever and ever.

or

May God, who is blessed above all,
✠ bless us in all things through Christ,
so that whatever happens in our lives
will work together for our good,
now and for ever.

or

The blessing of the God of Sarah and Abraham,
the blessing of Jesus Christ, born of Mary,
the blessing of the Holy Spirit
who cares for us as a mother for her children,
✠ be with us now and for ever.

> or

God, the Father of mercies, has sent his Son into the world.
Through the Holy Spirit, who will teach us all truth,
may he make us messengers of the Gospel
✠ and witnesses of his love to the world
now and for ever.

> or

May God, the source of every good,
bless us and give success to our work,
so that we may rejoice in the gifts we have received
✠ and praise God's name now and for ever.

> All respond: **Amen.**

---

> A deacon says:

The Lord be with you.

> All respond: **And also with you.**

> He then says:

May almighty God bless you,
the Father, and the Son
✠ and the Holy Spirit.

> or

May the blessing of almighty God,
the Father, and the Son,
✠ and the Holy Spirit,
descend upon you and remain for ever.

> All respond: **Amen.**

## DISMISSAL

Following the blessing, the leader of prayer dismisses the assembly in these or similar words:

Let us go forth in the name of Christ.

or

Let us go in peace to love and serve the Lord.

or

Go in the peace of Christ.

or

Let us go forth,
rejoicing in the power of the Spirit.

All respond: Thanks be to God.

During the Octave of Easter and on Pentecost Sunday the leader of prayer adds a double *Alleluia* to the dismissal.

The leader of prayer says or sings:

Go in the peace of Christ, alleluia, alleluia.

All respond: Thanks be to God, alleluia, alleluia.

RECESSIONAL MUSIC: As the community is leaving, music may be played or the choir may sing a suitable selection, but a congregational hymn is less appropriate.

# SUNDAY
## CELEBRATION
## OF THE HOURS:
## MORNING PRAYER

# MORNING PRAYER

# OUTLINE

**INTRODUCTORY RITES**

Gathering of the Community
Introductory Remarks
Invitation to Prayer
Morning Hymn

**PSALMS**

Morning Psalm
Psalm Prayer
Second Psalm
Psalm Prayer
Canticle

**WORD OF GOD**

Reading
Homily (Reflection)

**PRAISE AND INTERCESSION**

Gospel Canticle (Canticle of Zechariah or Gloria)
Intercessions
The Lord's Prayer
Concluding Prayer

**CONCLUDING RITE**

Announcements
Collection
Blessing
Sign of Peace

# INTRODUCTORY RITES

## GATHERING OF THE COMMUNITY

As the community gathers the members welcome one another. Some members may be chosen to greet and welcome others as they enter the church. The ministers may take their places without any liturgical form of entrance. The leader of prayer takes his or her place with the community (see Liturgical Notes, no. 174, page xxxv).

The usual presidential chair, a sign of the office of the bishop or presbyter (*A Book of Blessings*, no. 881), remains empty. If a deacon presides, a special chair is placed to the right of the presidential chair. If a lay person leads the prayer of the community, a chair is placed in another suitable place, preferably in the sanctuary.

The leader of prayer goes to the place from which he or she will preside. The altar or ambo (lectern) is never used for this purpose.

## INTRODUCTORY REMARKS

When the Eucharist will not be celebrated in the parish, the leader of prayer may introduce the celebration in these or similar words. The words should be suited to the particular occasion, and should call to mind the unity of this assembly with Sunday celebrations of the Eucharist taking place elsewhere.

At the beginning of a new day,
a day for ever made holy by the Lord Jesus Christ,
we, the people of God, gather to give praise and thanks.
We look forward to that day
when we will again celebrate the Eucharist,
as Christ commanded us to do in his memory.
Our community offers this morning praise
in union with the Church throughout the world,
with *N.* our Pope,
*N.*, our bishop,
[our pastor, Father *N.*,
who is unable to be with us,]
and with our brothers and sisters in neighbouring parishes
who keep holy the Lord's day
in the celebration of his sacrifice and supper.

or

On a weekday, the following, or similar, may be said instead:

At the beginning of a new day,
we gather to voice our praise and thanks.
We join our morning praise
to the prayers of the Church throughout the world,
in union with *N.* our Pope,
*N.* our bishop,
and all those who minister to us.

➤

With the people of every race and nation,
we rejoice this day in the mighty works of God,
who, by raising Jesus from death to life,
began a day that will have no end.

## PROCESSION

> When the community has assembled, a server carrying the thurible into which incense has just
> been placed leads the procession, followed by a minister carrying a vessel of holy water, if it is used
> during the morning psalm, a reader carrying the Lectionary and the leader of prayer. When the
> procession reaches the sanctuary, the Lectionary is placed upon the lectern. The ministers
> carrying the incense and/or the vessel of water place these in an appropriate place until they are
> needed. (See Liturgical Notes, no. 174, page xxxv).

> It is not appropriate to sing a hymn at this time. Instrumental music may accompany the
> procession, otherwise the ministers enter in silence.

## INVITATION TO PRAYER

> The leader of prayer goes to the place from which he or she will preside, and sings or says the
> invitation to prayer according to the two forms that follows.

> All trace the sign of the cross on their lips, while the leader of prayer sings or says:

### Lord, ✠ open our lips.

> All respond: And we shall proclaim your praise.

> The leader of prayer sings or says:

### Glory to God in the highest.

> All respond: And peace to God's people on earth.

> or

### 13A

Presider
Lord, + o - pen our lips.

All
And we shall pro - claim your praise.

Presider
Glory to God in the highest.

All
And peace to God's people on earth.

or

*Presider*

O Lord, o - pen our lips,

*All*

and we shall pro - claim your praise.

## MORNING HYMN

The morning hymn begins at once, and is sung by the whole assembly. It may be led by a cantor or by the choir. Suitable hymns are found in the *Catholic Book of Worship*. A hymn suitable for morning use or one appropriate to the liturgical season may be selected.

The community remains standing for the morning hymn.

# PSALMS

## MORNING PSALM

PSALM: After the hymn, the morning psalm is sung by the assembly. The whole psalm may be sung by all, or verses may be alternated between the choir and the rest of the assembly, or between one side of the assembly and the other. If the psalm chosen has a musical refrain, it may be sung responsorially. For this psalm the assembly remains standing, especially if the assembly is sprinkled with holy water during the singing of Psalm 63.

HOLY WATER: If Psalm 63 is used, the assembly may be sprinkled with holy water during the singing of the psalm. If the community is small enough, the members may come forward to dip their hands in a vessel of holy water and make the sign of the cross.

CATHOLIC BOOK OF WORSHIP II: "In the Shadow of Your Wings" (Psalm 63, CBW 75) is recommended. However, another suitable psalm may be chosen instead. Psalm 118 (CBW 199, and CBW 204-6), Psalm 100 (CBW 425-6) and Psalm 8 (CBW 409) are very appropriate.

CATHOLIC BOOK OF WORSHIP III: "Your love is finer than life" (Psalm 63, CBW 13D); "In the shadow of your wings I rejoice" (CBW 656); "As morning breaks" (CBW 657); or "God, my God, you I crave" (CBW 658).

PSALM PRAYER: A period of silent reflection follows the psalm. The leader of prayer may introduce the period of silent reflection by saying: *Let us pray*, or it may be omitted. Other forms of the psalm prayer are found in the Appendix, pages 331-333. Then the leader of prayer, with hands extended, prays in these or similar words:

### For Psalm 63

Lord our God,
Fountain of refreshing love,
in morning light we seek your presence and strength,
for your love is better than life itself.

Accept our prayers with uplifted hands
as we proclaim your praise in songs of joy.
Satisfy our longing hearts and renew our thirsting spirits
that our worship may give you glory
and our lives be poured out in loving service.

Glory and praise to you, loving God,
through our Lord Jesus Christ, your Son,
who lives and reigns with you in the unity of the Holy Spirit,
God for ever and ever.

All respond: **Amen.**

**If holy water was used**

O Lord, our God,
you have refreshed our thirsting souls,
with the gift of the Spirit in the waters of adoption.

Accept our praise as a morning offering
for the wonders of your saving deeds in our midst.
Renew your Church each day with the Spirit given us in baptism,
that through the death and resurrection of your Son,
we may live the new life of grace.

Glory and praise to you, God of splendour and love,
through our Lord Jesus Christ, your Son,
who lives and reigns with you in the unity of the Holy Spirit,
God for ever and ever.

**For a psalm of praise**

All praise and glory are yours, Lord our God,
maker of heaven and earth,
for you have called us to be your people of praise.
We proclaim the marvels of your love
and rejoice in the gift of creation.
Accept our worship as a holy offering
and our work for the glory of your name.

Glory and praise to you, loving God,
through our Lord Jesus Christ, your Son,
who lives and reigns with you in the unity of the Holy Spirit,
God for ever and ever.

**Sundays**

God of our salvation,
you have given us this great day of rejoicing:
Jesus Christ, the stone rejected by the builders,
has become the cornerstone of the Church, our home.
Enlightened by the rays of your glory
may your Church echo with sounds of joy
that your praise may ring forth to the ends of the earth.
We make our prayer through Christ our Lord.

All respond: **Amen.**

The community sits for the second psalm.

## Second Psalm

PSALM: After a brief pause, a second psalm is sung. It may be sung responsorially, with a cantor singing the verses, and the whole assembly singing the refrain. A psalm suited to the liturgical season is particularly appropriate. The cantor leads the psalm from the lectern. If necessary, the psalm may be recited, with one section of the community alternating with the other. The assembly sits during this psalm.

PSALM PRAYER: A period of silent reflection follows the psalm. The leader of prayer may introduce the period of silence by saying *Let us pray*. Other forms of the psalm prayer are found in the Appendix, pages 331-333. The assembly stands for the prayer. The leader prays in these or similar words:

Father of light,
yours is the morning and yours is the evening.
Make Christ, the Sun of righteousness,
shine for ever in our hearts
and draw us to that light of that new and eternal day
where you live in radiant glory.
We make our prayer through Christ our Lord.

or

To enlighten the world, O Lord,
you sent to us your Word
as the Sun of truth and justice.

Give light to our eyes
that throughout this day
we may discover your presence
in the many works of your hand.
May we continually praise you for your saving deeds
that reveal your glory and love.

We ask this through Christ our Lord.

All respond: Amen.

## Canticle or Psalm of Praise

CANTICLE: If desired a canticle of praise or a psalm of praise may be sung. All stand for the canticle or psalm of praise. A period of silence follows, but a psalm prayer is not prayed.

The cantor returns to the seat for the reading, and all are seated.

# WORD OF GOD

## READING

During the reading of God's word there are proper times for silence, for example, after the reading and after the homily or reflection.

The community sits. Following a brief period of silence, the first reader proclaims the Word of God from the Lectionary in the usual way. It is always followed by a period of silence. At the end of the period of silence, the reader returns to his or her seat.

The reading may be chosen from the First or Second Reading of the Sunday, found in the Lectionary. It is recommended that the second reading should be read on the Sundays of Advent, Christmas, Lent, and Easter times, and on Solemnities (e.g. Pentecost, Corpus Christi, All Saints, Christmas, etc.). Since the Canticle of Zechariah is taken from the gospels and is the climax of Morning Prayer, a gospel reading is not chosen.

## HOMILY (REFLECTION)

A person authorized to preach by the bishop may then give a reflection on the reading. If no one is so authorized, another person, not a reader who has read the reading, reads the homily for the day provided by the diocese or by the pastor. This may be done by the leader of prayer. The reflection or homily is given from the lectern. Following it, the person who gives it returns to his or her seat.

After the homily, there follows a period of silence so that the community may further reflect on God's Word.

If there is no homily, there is a longer period of silent reflection.

# PRAISE AND INTERCESSION

## GOSPEL CANTICLE

The community stands. The gospel canticle, either the Canticle of Zechariah *(Benedictus)* or the Hymn of Praise *(Gloria)* is sung as a hymn of praise. The recommended forms are in the *Catholic Book of Worship.* Other forms of these canticles may be used, but it is always sung. The canticle is to be sung by the whole community together, or with the community singing alternating verses with the choir, or with one side of the community alternating with the other.

The leader of prayer may introduce the gospel canticle as follows:

### Canticle of Zechariah

Let us sing the praise of the God who saves us,
whose great deeds never cease:

The *Benedictus* is sung. All make the sign of the Cross at the beginning.

### Hymn of Praise

Let us sing the praises of the Lord, the God who made us,
whose glory is from age to age.

or

With people everywhere, let us glorify our God in joyful song:

or

With all the voices of heaven,
let us sing praise and honour and glory to God:

The *Gloria* is then sung.

INCENSE: During the singing of the canticle, the altar may be incensed as a symbol of Christ, through whom our prayers are raised to God. When the canticle begins, a server brings the thurible to the leader of prayer, who places some incense in it. The server then goes to the altar, and walks slowly around it while incensing it. The leader of prayer and the people may be incensed after the incensation of the altar as a sign of respect for the presence of Christ among those gathered in his name.

# INTERCESSIONS

INVITATION TO PRAYER: Following the canticle, the community joins in prayer for the Church and the world through the singing of the intercessions. The leader of prayer introduces the intercessions in these or similar words:

Like incense,
we let our prayers rise in the sight of God
as we remember the needs of the Church and the world:

or

As we begin a new day,
we acknowledge God's saving power,
and pray for the needs of the Church and the world:

INTERCESSIONS: The singing of the intercessions is led by a cantor from the stand or from the lectern.

The intentions should be adapted or added to so as to reflect the needs of the particular community at this time. When there is no Sunday Eucharist, for example, there should always be a prayer for vocations to the priesthood. The sick and the dead can appropriately be prayed for. One petition should be (in these or similar words): "Lord Jesus Christ, hear our particular needs/ . . . [Pause to give time for thought of personal intentions] . . . and bless us on this day." Normally the order of prayers is:

a) for the Church community and its ministers;

b) for civil authorities and the pressing needs of the world;

c) for the suffering and the oppressed;

d) for the local community.

A form of the intercessions is given in the *Catholic Book of Worship*. Other similar forms of sung intercessions can be used. If necessary the intercessions may be recited. Sample intercessions are found in the Appendix, pages 307-313.

PRAYER OF THE ASSEMBLY: The whole community prays by singing a refrain. The forms given in *Catholic Book of Worship* are recommended.

# THE LORD'S PRAYER

Following the intercessions, the leader of prayer introduces the Lord's Prayer, which is recited or sung by all. The cantor remains at the lectern or stand until the closing prayer.

Either of two forms (Version A or Version B) may be used; each has an introduction particular to it. The doxology is omitted when the concluding prayer follows immediately after the Lord's Prayer.

The leader of prayer says:

## A

Taught by our Saviour's command,
and formed by the Word of God,
we dare to say [sing]:

The leader of prayer and the people say together:

Our Father,
who art in heaven,
hallowed be thy name;
thy kingdom come;
thy will be done,
on earth as it is in heaven.
Give us this day our daily bread;
and forgive us our trespasses
as we forgive those who trespass against us;
and lead us not into temptation
but deliver us from evil.

## B

With trust in our Father in heaven,
we pray as Jesus taught us, saying [singing]:

The leader of prayer and the people say together:

Our Father in heaven,
hallowed be your name;
your kingdom come;
your will be done,
on earth as in heaven.
Give us today our daily bread.
Forgive us our sins
as we forgive those who sin against us.
Save us from the time of trial
and deliver us from evil.

The sung forms are found in the *Catholic Book of Worship*.

---

## Concluding Prayer

The leader of prayer continues with the prayer proper to the Sunday. This prayer is chosen from the Proper of Seasons. On a weekday one the following prayers may be said.

Almighty God,
all justice and goodness come from you;
you hate evil and abhor deceit.
Lead us, your servants,
in the path of your justice,
so that all who hope in you
may rejoice with the Church and in Christ.

We ask this grace through Christ our Lord.

or

Almighty God,
whose never-failing providence rules all things
both in heaven and on earth,
listen to the cry of your people
and govern in peace the course of our days.

We make our prayer through Christ our Lord.

or

Ever-living God,
we praise you for giving us new life in Jesus your Son
and for bringing us to the light of this new day.
Fill us with the splendour of holiness
that our lives may bear witness
to the power of his resurrection.

We ask this through Christ our Lord.

All respond: Amen.

# CONCLUDING RITE

## ANNOUNCEMENTS

After the intercessions any announcements may be made briefly by another member of the assembly, or by the leader of prayer.

## COLLECTION

Following the announcements a collection may be taken up for the needs of the Church and the poor. The collection begins without any introduction.

MUSIC: This is not an appropriate time for a congregational hymn, but instrumental music may be played, or the choir may sing a selection. The collection, including any music, should avoid any appearance of the presentation of the gifts at Mass.

The collection may be brought forward by the collectors, and placed in a suitable place, but not on or near the altar; neither should it be received by the leader of prayer.

## BLESSING

After the collection the blessing follows. One of the forms below is used. At the appropriate time during the blessing, the leader of prayer signs himself or herself with the sign of the Cross.

The leader of prayer says:

May the Lord bless us,
protect us from all evil,
✠ and bring us to everlasting life.

or

May God, who is blessed above all,
✠ bless us in all things through Christ,
so that whatever happens in our lives
will work together for our good,
now and for ever.

or

May God the Father,
with the Son and the Holy Spirit,
who has shown us such great mercy,
be praised and ✠ blessed for ever and ever.

or

May God, the source of every good,
bless us and give success to our work,
so that we may rejoice in the gifts we have received
✠ and praise God's name now and for ever.

> or

May the Lord almighty
✠ order our days and our deeds in his peace.

> or

May God the Father almighty bless and keep us.
May Jesus Christ, his only Son, our Lord, graciously smile upon us.
✠ May the Holy Spirit, the Lord and giver of life, grant us peace.

> All respond: Amen.

> or

**131**

*Presider*

May the Lord almighty + order our days and our

deeds in his peace.

*All*

A - men.

## SIGN OF PEACE

Following the blessing, the leader of prayer says in these or similar words:

As we go forth in the name of Christ,
let us offer each other a sign of peace.

or

As we go in peace to love and serve the Lord,
let us exchange with each other a sign of peace.

or

As we go in the peace of Christ,
let us exchange with our neighbour
a sign of that peace.

or

As we go forth,
children of the God of peace,
let us offer one another
a sign of reconciliation and peace.

The leader of prayer exchanges a sign of peace with those nearby. Members of the community exchange the sign of peace and leave informally, as do the leader of prayer and other ministers.

MUSIC: As the community is leaving, music may be played or the choir may sing a suitable selection, but a congregational hymn is not appropriate.

# SUNDAY
# CELEBRATION
# OF THE HOURS:
# EVENING PRAYER

# EVENING PRAYER

## OUTLINE

**SERVICE OF LIGHT**

Gathering of the Community
Introductory Remarks
Procession
Opening Verse
Thanksgiving for the Light
[Invitation to Prayer]
Evening Hymn

**PSALMS**

Evening Psalm
Psalm Prayer
Second Psalm
Psalm Prayer
Canticle

**WORD OF GOD**

Reading
Homily (Reflection)

**PRAISE AND INTERCESSION**

Gospel Canticle (Canticle of Mary or Simeon)
Intercessions
The Lord's Prayer
Concluding Prayer

**CONCLUDING RITE**

Announcements
Collection
Blessing
Sign of Peace

# INTRODUCTORY RITE

## GATHERING OF THE COMMUNITY

As the community gathers the members welcome one another. Some members may be chosen to greet and welcome others as they enter the church. The lights of the church are dimmed in advance. The community, except the ministers who will take part in the procession, take their places without any liturgical form of entrance (see Liturgical Notes, no. 175 page xxxv). The members of the community may be given candles as they enter the church.

The usual presidential chair, a sign of the office of the bishop or presbyter (*A Book of Blessings*, no. 881), remains empty. If a deacon presides, a special chair is placed to the right of the presidential chair. If a lay person leads the prayer of the community, a chair is placed in another suitable place, preferably in the sanctuary.

The leader of prayer goes to the place from which he or she will preside. The altar or ambo (lectern) is never used for this purpose.

## INTRODUCTORY REMARKS

When the Eucharist is not celebrated in the parish, a minister may introduce the celebration in these or similar words. The words should be suited to the particular occasion, and should call to mind the unity of this assembly with Sunday celebrations of the Eucharist taking place elsewhere.

As this day draws to a close,
we, the people of God, gather
to offer an evening sacrifice of praise
for God's marvellous works.
We look forward to a new day
when we will once again celebrate the Eucharist
as Christ commanded us to do in his memory,
and share the sacrament of his body and blood.
We join our evening praise
to that of the Church throughout the world,
in union with *N.* our Pope,
*N.*, our bishop,
the priests who serve our needs,
and our brothers and sisters in neighbouring parishes
who keep holy this day
in the celebration of the Lord's sacrifice and supper.

On a weekday, the following, or similar, may be said:

As this day draws to a close,
we offer thanks and praise for God's marvellous works.
This, our evening sacrifice,
we join to the praise of the Church throughout the world,
in union with *N.* our Pope,
*N.* our bishop,
and all those who minister to us.

➤

As evening shadows lengthen,
we give praise above all for that Sun which never sets,
Jesus Christ, the light of the world,
and the life of those who believe in his name.

## PROCESSION

When the community has assembled, the procession begins in silence. The assembly stands. The procession is led by a server carrying the thurible into which incense has just been placed, then a minister carrying a large lighted candle, a reader carrying the Lectionary and the leader of prayer. When the procession reaches the sanctuary, the candle is put in a prominent place, and the Lectionary is placed upon the lectern. (See Liturgical Notes, no. 175, page xxxv).

It is not appropriate to sing a hymn at this time. Instrumental music may accompany the procession, but it is more appropriate for the ministers to enter the darkened church in silence.

# SERVICE OF LIGHT

If the service of Light is not part of Evening Prayer, the celebration begins with the Invitation to Prayer on page 294.

## OPENING VERSE

The leader of prayer, the cantor and ministers who holds ritual book and the incense stand near the candle. The leader or the cantor sings or says the opening verse, according to one of the forms that follow.

The leader of prayer sings or says:

Light and peace, in Jesus Christ our Lord.

All respond: Thanks be to God.

or

Jesus Christ is the light of the world.

All respond: A light no darkness can extinguish.

or

**14A**

Light and peace, in Je - sus Christ our Lord.

Thanks be to God.

or

**14B**

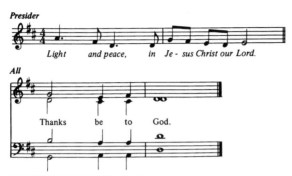

*Presider*

Light and peace, in Je - sus Christ our Lord.

*All*

Thanks be to God.

or

**14C**

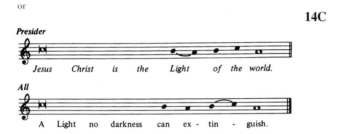

*Presider*

Jesus Christ is the Light of the world.

*All*

A Light no darkness can ex - tin - guish.

or

**14D**

*Presider*

Light and peace, in Je - sus Christ our Lord.

*All*

Thanks be to God.

## THANKSGIVING FOR THE LIGHT

On Sundays and Solemnities it is fitting to begin evening prayer with a celebration of light (lucernarium). Other forms of the thanksgiving are found in the Appendix, pages 314-330. The candles of the people and the candles on or near the altar, or near the lectern or cross are lighted from the candle carried in procession. The leader of prayer, or a cantor, invites the assembly to give thanks to God, and sings the following.

The leader of prayer may remain near the candle or at the place of presiding for the evening thanksgiving and hymn.

**14E**

*Assistant*
Let us give thanks to God the Fa - ther,
al - ways and for ev - 'ry - thing.

*All*
In the name of our Lord Je - sus Christ.

*Assistant*
God our Fa - ther, we give you thanks
for all your gifts so free - ly be - stowed up - on us:
for the beau - ty and won - der of your cre - a - tion,
in earth and sky and sea; for all that is gra - cious
in the lives of men and wom - en,
re - veal - ing the light of Christ;

for minds to muse and hearts to love and hands to serve;

for health and strength to work,

for lei - sure to rest and play;

for com - mun - ion with your saints,

in all times and plac - es;

and a - bove all, for the great prom - is - es and mer - cies

giv - en to us in Christ Je - sus our Lord.

To him be praise and glo - ry,

with you and the Ho - ly Spir - it,

*All*

now and for ev - er. A - men.

At the conclusion of the thanksgiving (or after the hymn), the people may extinguish their candles and join in the hymn.

## INVITATION TO PRAYER

When the celebration of Light does not take place, the following invitation to prayer may be used. All make the sign of the cross.

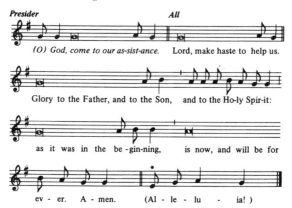

**Presider**
(O) God, come to our as-sist-ance.

**All**
Lord, make haste to help us.

Glory to the Father, and to the Son,      and to the Ho-ly Spir-it:

as it was in the be-gin-ning,      is now, and will be for

ev - er.   A - men.      (Al - le - lu - ia! )

Setting: Howard Hughes; Copyright © 1976, 1978, ICEL; from *New Musical Settings for the Liturgy of the Hours*.
\* *Omit during Lent.*

## EVENING HYMN

The evening hymn begins at once, and is sung by the whole assembly. It may be led by a cantor or by the choir. During the evening hymn the lights of the church may be turned on gradually.

A suitable hymn is "O Radiant Light" and is found in the *Catholic Book of Worship*, which may be used with a number of musical settings. Suitable hymns of praise may be substituted. A hymn suitable for evening use, one which has light as its theme (see index in CBW), or one appropriate to the liturgical season may be selected.

INCENSE; During the hymn, the candle may be incensed. The community remains standing.

# PSALMS

## EVENING PSALM

PSALM: After the hymn, the evening psalm is sung by the assembly. The whole psalm may be sung by all, or verses may be alternated between the choir and the rest of the assembly, or between one side of the assembly and the other. If the psalm chosen has a musical refrain, it may be sung responsorially. For this psalm the assembly remains standing, especially if the assembly is incensed during the singing of Psalm 141.

CATHOLIC BOOK OF WORSHIP II: "I call on you, O Lord" (Psalm 141, CBW, 65) or another suitable psalm may be chosen. Psalm 27 (CBW 412, and CBW, 142) and Psalm 43 (CBW, 418) are very appropriate.

CATHOLIC BOOK OF WORSHIP III: "O let my prayer rise before you" (Psalm 141, CBW, 14H) "Be gracious, O Lord" (CBW, 670); "My prayer rises like incenses" (CBW, 671); "My prayers rise like incense" (CBW, 672); or "Like burning Incense, Lord" (CBW, 673) may be chosen.

INCENSE: During the singing of the psalm, incense may be placed in the thurible or in a brazier which has been placed in the midst of the assembly. It is also possible to incense the assembly during the singing of the psalm as a sign of respect for Christ's presence among those gathered in his name. In this case a server brings the thurible to the leader of prayer, who puts in it some incense. The server first incenses the leader of prayer, then goes throughout the assembly to incense the whole community.

PSALM PRAYER: A period of silence follows the psalm. The leader of prayer may introduce a period of silent reflection, by saying: "Let us pray," or it may be omitted. Other forms of the psalm payer are found in the Appendix, pages 334-335. After a time of silent prayer, the leader of prayer may pray in these or similar words:

## For Psalm 141

Almighty and ever-living God,
you raised your Son, Jesus Christ, from death
and exalted him at your right hand in glory.
Grant that our prayers may rise like incense before you,
and our hands like an evening offering.
Accept our lives as a sacrifice of praise
that our deeds may proclaim your love
and our words sing your mighty deeds.

Glory and praise to you, God of our salvation,
through our Lord Jesus Christ, your Son,
who lives and reigns with you in the unity of the Holy Spirit,
God for ever and ever.

or

Loving God,
creator of light and life,
may our prayers ascend to you
like the fragrance of incense.
Purify our hearts to sing your praise
in the company of your saints in glory.
We ask this through Christ our Lord.

Lord our God,
maker of heaven and earth,
you have formed us in your own image
and set us over the earth.
We proclaim the marvels of your love
and rejoice in your gift of creation.
Accept our worship as a holy offering,
and bless your people as we gather at the end of this day.
Cleanse our hearts that we may continue to praise you
and work for the salvation of the world.
We make our prayer through Christ our Lord.

or

Almighty God, our Father,
the radiance of your Son illumines this night
and brings warmth to the hearts of all who serve you.
May our praise, inspired by the Spirit of love,
fill this night with the glory of your presence.
We offer our praise through Jesus Christ, your Son,
who lives and reigns with you in the unity of the Holy Spirit,
God for ever and ever.

All respond: Amen.

## SECOND PSALM

PSALM: After a brief pause, a second psalm is sung. It may be sung responsorially, with a cantor singing the verses, and the whole assembly singing the refrain. If necessary the community may recite the psalm, alternating between one part and another. A psalm suited to the liturgical season is particularly appropriate. The cantor leads the psalm from the lectern. The assembly sits during this psalm.

PSALM PRAYER: A period of silent reflection follows the psalm. The leader of prayer may introduce the period of silence by saying *Let us pray*. The assembly stands for the prayer. Other forms are found in the Appendix, pages 334-335. The leader of prayer may pray in these or similar words:

O God, our creator and redeemer,
the light of your glory
shines in the darkness of our lives
and enkindles our hearts with praise.
Attentive to your presence,
we rejoice in the gifts of your love
and ever seek to follow in the steps
of the one who is our true light,
Jesus Christ, your Son,
who lives for ever and ever.

or

Lord our God,
in fulfillment of your will
your Son became our paschal sacrifice.
Accept the praise of your Church
for the light and salvation
you have given to your people.
May we rejoice one day in the kingdom of your splendour.
We ask this through Christ our Lord.

All respond: Amen.

## CANTICLE OR PSALM OF PRAISE

CANTICLE: If desired a canticle of praise or a psalm of praise may be sung. All stand for the canticle or psalm of praise. A period of silence follows, but a psalm prayer is not prayed.

The cantor returns to the seat for the reading, and all are seated.

# WORD OF GOD

## READING

The reading may be chosen from the First or Second Reading of the Sunday, found in the Lectionary. It is recommended that the second reading be read on the Sundays of Advent, Christmas, Lent, and Easter times, and on Solemnities (e.g. Pentecost, Corpus Christi, All Saints, Christmas, etc.). Since the Canticle of Mary or Simeon is taken from the gospels and is the climax of Morning Prayer, a gospel reading is not chosen.

When the community is seated, and following a brief period of silence, the reader proclaims the Word of God from the Lectionary in the usual way. It is always followed by a period of silence. At the end of the period of silence, the reader returns to his or her seat.

## HOMILY (REFLECTION)

A person authorized to preach by the bishop may then give a reflection on the reading. If no one is so authorized, another person, not a reader who has read the readings, reads the homily for the day provided by the diocese or by the pastor. This may be done by the leader of prayer. The reflection or homily is given from the ambo (lectern). Following it, the person who gives it returns to his or her seat.

After the homily, there follows a period of silence so that the community may further reflect on God's Word.

If there is no homily, there is a longer period of silent reflection.

# PRAISE AND INTERCESSION

## GOSPEL CANTICLE

The community stands. The gospel canticle, either the Canticle of Mary *(Magnificat)* or the Canticle of Simeon *(Nunc Dimittis)* are sung as a hymn of praise. The recommended forms are found in the *Catholic Book of Worship*. Other forms of these canticles may be used, but it is always sung. The canticle is to be sung by the whole community together, or with the community singing alternating verses with the choir, or with one side of the community alternating with the other.

The Canticle of Simeon is appropriately used at a late evening celebration, otherwise the Canticle of Mary is used.

The leader of prayer may introduce the gospel canticle as follows:

### Canticle of Mary

Let us sing the praises of the Lord our God,
who has saved and exalted us:

The *Magnificat* is sung. All make the sign of the cross at the beginning.

### Canticle of Simeon

Let us sing the praises of our God,
whose glory is revealed in our Saviour.

The Canticle of Simeon is sung. All make the sign of the cross at the beginning.

INCENSE: During the singing of the canticle, the altar may be incensed as a symbol of Christ, in whom our prayers are raised to God. In this case, when the canticle begins, a server brings the thurible to the leader of prayer, who places some incense in it. The server then goes to the altar, and walks slowly around it while incensing it. If they have not been incensed earlier, the leader of prayer and the people may be incensed after the incensation of the altar as a sign of respect for the presence of Christ among those gathered in his name.

# INTERCESSIONS

**INVITATION TO PRAYER** Following the canticle, the community joins in prayer for the Church and the world through the singing of the intercessions. The leader of prayer introduces the intercessions in these or similar words:

Like incense,
we let our prayers rise to God
as we remember the needs of the Church and the world:

or

As evening falls,
we ask God's protection and peace for ourselves,
and pray for the needs of the Church and the world:

INTERCESSIONS: The singing of the intercessions is led by a cantor from the stand or from the lectern.

The intentions should be adapted or added to so as to reflect the needs of the particular community at this time as well as the concerns of the universal Church. When there is no Sunday Eucharist, for example, there should always be a prayer for vocations to the priesthood. The sick and the dead can appropriately be prayed for. One petition should be (in these or similar words): "For other intentions we have today . . . [Pause to give time for thought of personal intentions] . . . let us pray to the Lord."

Normally the order of prayers would be:

a) for the Church community and its ministers;
b) for civil authorities and the pressing needs of the world;
c) for the suffering and the oppressed;
d) for the local community.
e) for the dead.

The cantor may conclude the intercessions by singing: "Rejoicing in the fellowship of the Blessed Virgin Mary, (of Saint N. [insert the name of the patron saint]), and of all the saints, let us commend ourselves, one another, and our whole life to Christ our Lord." The assembly responds by singing: "To you, O Lord."

A form of the intercessions is given in the *Catholic Book of Worship*. Other similar forms of sung intercessions can be used. If necessary the intercessions can be recited. Sample intercessions are found in the Appendix, pages 307-313

PRAYER OF THE ASSEMBLY: The whole community sings the response "Lord, have mercy." or similar refrain. The form given in *Catholic Book of Worship* is recommended.

# THE LORD'S PRAYER

Following the intercessions, the leader of prayer introduces the Lord's Prayer, which is recited or sung by all. the cantor remains at the lectern or stand until the closing prayer.

Either of two forms (Version A or Version B) may be used; each has an introduction particular to it. The doxology is omitted when the concluding prayer follows immediately after the Lord's Prayer.

The leader of prayer says:

### A

Taught by our Saviour's command,
and formed by the Word of God,
we dare to say [sing]:

The leader of prayer and the people say together:

Our Father,
who art in heaven,
hallowed be thy name;
thy kingdom come;
thy will be done,
on earth as it is in heaven.
Give us this day our daily bread;
and forgive us our trespasses
as we forgive those who trespass against us;
and lead us not into temptation
but deliver us from evil.

### B

With trust in our Father in heaven,
we pray as Jesus taught us, saying [singing]:

The leader of prayer and the people say together:

Our Father in heaven,
hallowed be your name;
your kingdom come;
your will be done,
on earth as in heaven.
Give us today our daily bread.
Forgive us our sins
as we forgive those who sin against us.
Save us from the time of trial
and deliver us from evil.

Sung forms of this version are found in CBW II, 70; CBW III, 14L, 286.

## Concluding Prayer

The leader of prayer continues with the prayer proper to the Sunday. This prayer is chosen from the Proper of Seasons. On a weekday one of the following prayers may be said.

Blessed are you, Father of light,
Lord of all the universe,
in the name of Jesus our Lord we pray for your world.
Grant peace to your people,
strength to the weak,
courage to the downhearted,
and guidance to all in despair.
Send your Spirit to conquer evil,
and make your kingdom come among us.

We ask this grace through Christ our Lord.

*or*

Creator of the universe,
watch over us
and keep us in the light of your presence.
May our praise continually blend with that of all creation,
until we come together to the eternal joys
which you promise in your love.

We ask this through Christ our Lord.

*or*

Blessed are you Source of light.
As the daylight fails, we turn to you.
Scatter the darkness that surrounds us
with the light of your presence.
Grant peace to all who hope in you.

We ask this through Christ our Lord.

All respond: **Amen.**

# CONCLUDING RITE

## ANNOUNCEMENTS

After the intercessions any announcements may be made briefly by another member of the assembly, or by the leader of prayer.

## COLLECTION

Following the announcements, a collection may be taken up for the needs of the Church and the poor. The collection begins without any introduction.

MUSIC: This is not an appropriate time for a congregational hymn, but instrumental music may be used, or the choir may sing a selection. The collection, including any music, should avoid any appearance of the presentation of the gifts at Mass.

The collection may be brought forward by the collectors, and placed in a suitable place, but not on or near the altar; neither should it be received by the leader of prayer.

## BLESSING

After the collection all stand and the blessing follows. One of the forms below is used.

At the appropriate time during the blessing, the leader of prayer signs himself or herself with the sign of the cross.

The leader of prayer says:

May the Lord bless us,
protect us from all evil,
✠ and bring us to everlasting life.

> or

May God, who is blessed above all,
✠ bless us in all things through Christ,
so that whatever happens in our lives
will work together for our good,
now and for ever.

> or

May God the Father,
with the Son and the Holy Spirit,
who has shown us such great mercy,
be praised and ✠ blessed for ever and ever.

> or

May God, the source of every good,
bless us and give success to our work,
so that we may rejoice in the gifts we have received
✠ and praise God's name now and for ever.

> or

May the Lord almighty
✠ order our days and our deeds in his peace.

> or

May God the Father almighty bless and keep us.
May Jesus Christ, his only Son, our Lord, graciously smile upon us.
✠ May the Holy Spirit, the Lord and giver of life, grant us peace.

All respond: Amen.

> or

**14M**

*Cantor*

Let us bow our heads to the Lord.

*Presider*

May God the Father almighty bless us and keep us.

*All*

A men, a men.

(DCI)

*Presider*

May Jesus Christ, his only Son, our Lord, graciously smile up-on us.

*All*
Amen, amen.

*Presider*

May the Ho-ly Spirit, the Lord and giver of life, grant us peace.

*All*
**Amen, amen.**

## SIGN OF PEACE

Following the blessing, the leader of prayer says in these or similar words:

As we go forth in the name of Christ,
let us offer each other a sign of peace.

or

As we go in peace to love and serve the Lord,
let us exchange with each other a sign of peace.

or

As we go in the peace of Christ,
let us exchange with our neighbour
a sign of that peace.

or

As we go forth,
children of the God of peace,
let us offer one another
a sign of reconciliation and peace.

The leader of prayer exchanges a sign of peace with those nearby. Members of the community exchange the sign of peace and leave informally, as do the leader of prayer and other ministers.

MUSIC: As the community is leaving, music may be played or the choir may sing a suitable selection, but a congregational hymn is not appropriate.

# APPENDICES
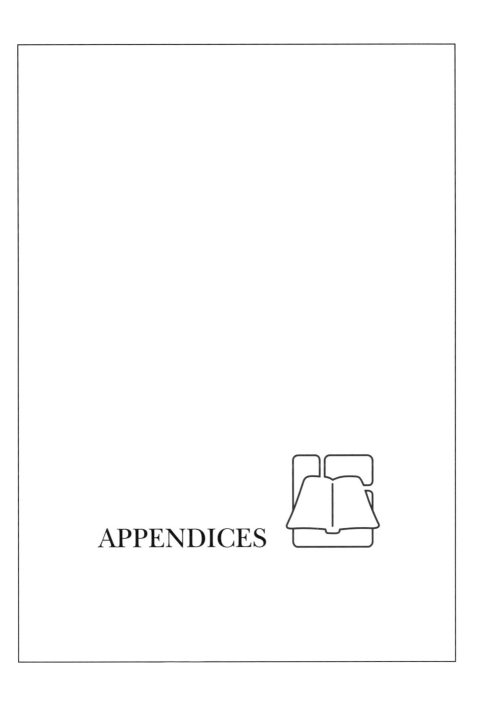

# APPENDICES

# CONTENTS

# MODEL INTERCESSIONS

## ADVENT

*Leader:*

My sisters and brothers,
let us entrust our needs to the Lord
who comforts us with the promise of salvation.

*Reader:*

For the church and all its ministers, called, as Mary was,
to hear God's word and bring it to birth.
We pray to the Lord.

For leaders of nations and peoples,
as they must respond to the new economic and political challenges of our times.
We pray to the Lord.

For harmony and reconciliation among all people and nations;
for all whose peace has been shattered;
and for all who are persecuted.
We pray to the Lord.

Or: For peace in our broken world;
for victims of war and violence far away and in our midst;
and for all peace-makers.
We pray to the Lord.

For those who are poor and homeless;
for those among us who are lonely, ill or unemployed;
and for the safety of all who work to establish justice and peace.
We pray to the Lord.

Or: For those who hunger for food and dignity;
for prisoners;
for those who are sick and dying.
We pray to the Lord.

For us gathered here, the work of God's hand,
called to keep awake until the Lord's return.
We pray to the Lord.

For the faithful departed:
and for all who have died;
for all who mourn them.
We pray to the Lord.

# CHRISTMAS

*Leader:*
My sisters and brothers,
our God has drawn near to us in a tiny child,
Emmanuel: God-with-us.
United as members of his body,
let us place our prayers before the Lord of the universe.

*Reader:*
For the Church and all communities,
who join with the shepherds and angels to witness
to the mystery of God's birth in human flesh.
We pray to the Lord.

For Pope N., and for N, our bishop;
for those entrusted with the care of this parish;
and for men and women who, by their ministry,
are called to announce good news of great joy to all people.
We pray to the Lord.

For peace:
for its dawning in lands shattered by war's darkness;
for its healing in hearts broken by strife, turmoil and despair.
We pray to the Lord.

For men, women and children whose human dignity is violated or destroyed,
and for those who fail to honour the dignity of each human person.
We pray to the Lord.

Or:  For all who, on this day [night] of feasting,
      lack food, work, shelter, warmth, friendship, and love.
      We pray to the Lord.

For all families and parents;
for the safety of travellers and the healing of the sick.
We pray to the Lord.

For those called to the glory of eternal life:
for all who have died,
and for all who must mourn in this season of joy.
We pray to the Lord.

# LENT

*Leader:*

My brothers and sisters,
let us place before the God of all life
our own needs and those of the whole world.

*Reader:*

For the church, herald of God's compassion and peace;
and for the renewal of its baptismal mission.
We pray to the Lord.

For the leaders of nations;
for all who work to implement justice and peace for their peoples.
We pray to the Lord.

Or:  For peace in our world,
and for the safety of all who work to establish justice and peace.
We pray to the Lord.

For all who stand firm in the face of power, tyranny and oppression.
We pray to the Lord.

For the elect of the church,
called to holiness and new life in the waters of baptism.
We pray to the Lord.

For all who suffer the inequalities of our world's structures;
for those imprisoned or tortured for the sake of truth and justice.
We pray to the Lord.

For those among us who are homeless or without food,
unemployed or lonely, sick or dying,
and for all who minister to them.
We pray to the Lord.

For us, God's people,
as we prepare to celebrate the paschal feast
of the Lord's death and resurrection.
We pray to the Lord.

For those who have died:
and all who mourn them.
We pray to the Lord.

# EASTER

*Leader:*

My brothers and sisters,
Let us entrust to the God who raised Jesus from the dead
our own needs and those of all humanity.

*Reader:*

For the church, steward of the mystery of God
and witness to Christ's resurrection.
We pray to the Lord.

For all who announce, in word and in action,
the good news of the resurrection:
for the Pope and all bishops, priests and deacons,
and all women and men who are ministers of the gospel.
We pray to the Lord.

For peace, where conflict ravages;
love, where hatred reigns;
joy, where sorrow lingers;
feasting, where famine stalks;
healing, where brokenness crushes.
We pray to the Lord.

For all those who have joined us at the Lord's table
through profession of faith and sacraments of initiation.
We pray to the Lord.

For married couples, sacraments of God's love and fidelity;
for those preparing for marriage;
and for all God's people,
called to lead lives marked by service, love and faith.
We pray to the Lord.

Or: For us, God's holy people,
baptized into the Lord's death and rising,
and called to live this dignity each day.
We pray to the Lord.

For those who have shared in the death of Jesus:
and for their families and loved ones.
We pray to the Lord.

# ORDINARY TIME I

*Leader:*

My sisters and brothers,
Let us entrust to the Lord, who remembers us,
our own needs and those of all people.

*Reader:*

For the church, the body of Christ,
and for all who are called to leadership among us.
We pray to the Lord.

For all in positions of political leadership,
for those responsible for policies and actions
to ensure justice and well-being for all citizens.
We pray to the Lord.

For peace in our broken world,
and for the safety of all who work for the peace and healing of nations.
We pray to the Lord.

For those who are poor, lonely or hungry;
for those who struggle in difficult marriages
for those in prison; for the unemployed;
for the sick and the dying.
We pray to the Lord.

Or:  For those who are fearful or suffering;
      for all who cannot speak out against injustice;
      and for those unable to listen.
      We pray to the Lord.

For us, God's holy people,
called to journey together in gentleness and mutual support.
We pray to the Lord.

For those who died this week
and for all seek the light of faith.
We pray to the Lord.

# ORDINARY TIME 2

*Leader:*

My sisters and brothers,
Let us entrust to our God, whose love is eternal,
our own needs and those of all humanity.

*Reader:*

For the church, community of reconciled sinners,
entrusted with the good news of reconciliation.
We pray to the Lord.

For all who lead and serve the community of believers,
and for all leaders of nations and governments.
We pray to the Lord.

For peace in our broken world,
and for the safety of all who have dedicated their lives
for the service of others.
We pray to the Lord.

For the safety of travellers;
for those struggling with addictions;
for all who are poor, lonely and hungry;
and for those in any kind of trouble;
We pray to the Lord.

Or: For victims of war and hatred;
for those in prison and for those who seek work;
for those who are sick and dying;
and for all who minister to others.
We pray to the Lord.

For us, God's people gathered here,
called to see and serve with the eyes of faith.
We pray to the Lord.

For those who have died,
especially those who were models of faith to us;
and for all who mourn.
We pray to the Lord.

# ORDINARY TIME 3

*Leader:*

As we have gathered to give glory and honour to our God,
let us now intercede for salvation of the world
and the work of the Church.

*Reader:*

For the Church, sacrament of Christ's presence to the world;
and for all who minister in the name of Jesus.
We pray to the Lord.

For those who govern;
for compassion and generosity
in responding to the needs of those around us;
and for a just sharing of the fruits of the earth.
We pray to the Lord.

For ears to hear the cry of the poor;
for hearts to share in the pain of others;
and for hands to reach out in the name of Jesus.
We pray to the Lord.

For those in need;
for the sick and those who now experience weakness, testing and pain;
for orphans, widows and widowers;
and for all those who must face life alone.
We pray to the Lord.

For ourselves, God's holy people;
for the safety of all the members and families of our parish;
and for all who share their time, talent and treasure for our benefit.
We pray to the Lord.

For those who have died this week;
for the souls of all the faithful departed;
and for their loved ones.
We pray to the Lord.

# EVENING PRAYER
## PRAYERS OF THANKSGIVING FOR THE LIGHT

**ADVENT**

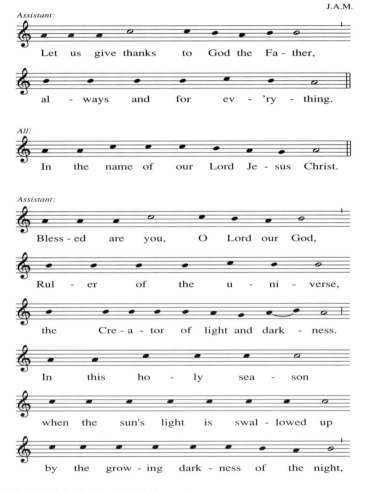

J.A.M.

*Assistant:*

Let us give thanks to God the Fa - ther,
al - ways and for ev - 'ry - thing.

*All:*

In the name of our Lord Je - sus Christ.

*Assistant:*

Bless - ed are you, O Lord our God,
Rul - er of the u - ni - verse,
the Cre - a - tor of light and dark - ness.
In this ho - ly sea - son
when the sun's light is swal - lowed up
by the grow - ing dark - ness of the night,

you re - new your prom-ise to re - veal a - mong us

the splen - dor of your glo - ry,

en - fleshed and vis - i - ble to us

in Je - sus Christ, your Son. Through the

proph-ets you teach us to hope for his reign of peace.

Through the out - pour - ing of his Spir - it,

you o - pen our blind - ness to the glo - ry

of his pres - ence. Strength-en us in our weak-ness.

Sup - port us in our stum - bling ef - forts

to do your will and free our tongues

to sing your praise. For to you all hon - our

*All:*

and bless - ing are due, now and for - ev - er. A - men.

# CHRISTMAS

J.A.M.

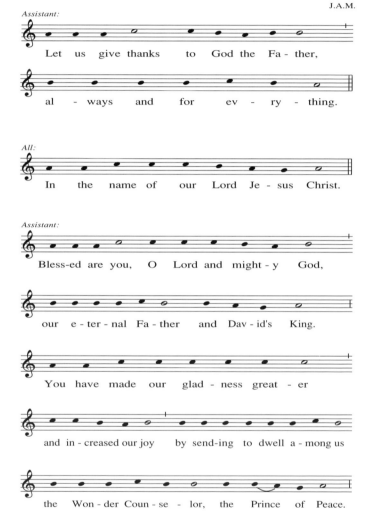

*Assistant:*

Let us give thanks to God the Fa - ther,

al - ways and for ev - ry - thing.

*All:*

In the name of our Lord Je - sus Christ.

*Assistant:*

Bless-ed are you, O Lord and might - y God,

our e - ter - nal Fa - ther and Dav - id's King.

You have made our glad - ness great - er

and in - creased our joy by send-ing to dwell a - mong us

the Won - der Coun - se - lor, the Prince of Peace.

Born of Mar - y, pro - claimed to the shep - herds
and ac - knowl-edged to the ends of the earth,
your un - con - quered Sun of Jus - tice
des - troys our dark - ness and es - tab - lish - es us in free - dom
and we are led forth from bond - age.
All glo - ry in the high - est be to you,
through Christ, the Son of your fav - our,
in the a - noint - ing love of his Spir - it
*All:*
this night and for ev - er and ev - er. A - men.

J.A.M.

*Assistant:*

Let us give thanks to God the Fa - ther,

al - ways and for ev - 'ry - thing.

*All:*

In the name of our Lord Je - sus Christ.

*Assistant:*

Bless - ed are you, O Lord our God,

the Shep - herd of Is - ra - el,

their pil - lar of cloud by day,

their pil - lar of fire by night.

In these for - ty days you lead us in - to

the des - ert of re - pen - tance that in this

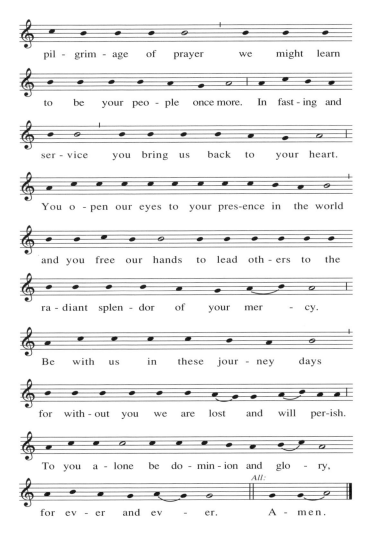

pil - grim - age of prayer we might learn to be your peo - ple once more. In fast - ing and ser - vice you bring us back to your heart. You o - pen our eyes to your pres-ence in the world and you free our hands to lead oth - ers to the ra - diant splen - dor of your mer - cy. Be with us in these jour - ney days for with - out you we are lost and will per-ish. To you a - lone be do - min - ion and glo - ry, for ev - er and ev - er. *All:* A - men.

Let us give thanks to God the Fa - ther,

al - ways and for ev - 'ry - thing.

*All:*

In the name of our Lord Je - sus Christ.

*Assistant:*

Bless - ed are you. O Lord Re - deem - er God.

You de - stroyed the bonds of death

and from the dark - ness of the tomb

drew forth the light of the world.

Led through the wa - ters of death.

we be - come the chil - dren of light

sing - ing our Al - le - lu - ia

and danc - ing to the mu - sic of new life.

Pour out your Spir - it up - on us

that dreams and vis - ions bring us ev - er clos - er to the

king-dom of Je - sus Christ, our Ris - en Sav - iour.

Through him and in the Ho - ly Spir - it

all glo - ry be to you, Al - might - y Fa - ther.

*All:*

this night and for ev - er and ev - er. A - men.

# ORDINARY TIME 2

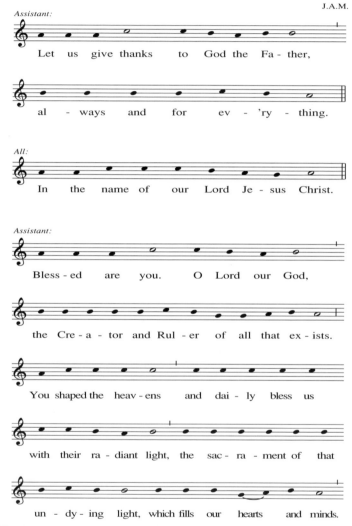

J.A.M.

*Assistant:*

Let us give thanks to God the Fa - ther,

al - ways and for ev - 'ry - thing.

*All:*

In the name of our Lord Je - sus Christ.

*Assistant:*

Bless - ed are you. O Lord our God,

the Cre - a - tor and Rul - er of all that ex - ists.

You shaped the heav - ens and dai - ly bless us

with their ra - diant light, the sac - ra - ment of that

un - dy - ing light, which fills our hearts and minds.

As night ap - roach-es, we thank you for the pow - er
to cre - ate the light which dis - pels the dark - ness
a - round us. Be with us still, en - light - en our hearts
with your glo - ry and lead us to the full - ness
of your splen - dor. All hon - or and bless - ing
be to you, through Je - sus Christ, the light
of the world, and in the Ho - ly Spir - it,
who en - a - bles us to sing your praise

*All:*

now and for ev - er, A - men.

J.A.M.
Jewish Berakah of the Evening

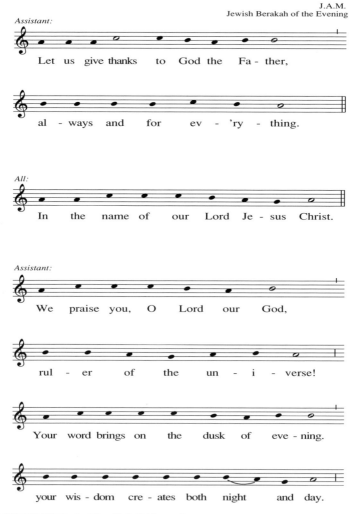

*Assistant:*
Let us give thanks to God the Fa - ther,

al - ways and for ev - 'ry - thing.

*All:*
In the name of our Lord Je - sus Christ.

*Assistant:*
We praise you, O Lord our God,

rul - er of the un - i - verse!

Your word brings on the dusk of eve - ning.

your wis - dom cre - ates both night and day.

# ORDINARY TIME 4

J.A.M.
Apostolic Tradition

*Assistant:*

Let us give thanks to God the Fa - ther,

al - ways and for ev - 'ry - thing.

*All:*

In the name of our Lord Je - sus Christ.

*Assistant:*

We praise and thank you, O God.

through your Son Je - sus Christ our Lord.

through whom you have en - light - ened us

by re - veal - ing the light that nev - er fades.

Joy to all crea - tures, hon - or, feast - ing and de - light.

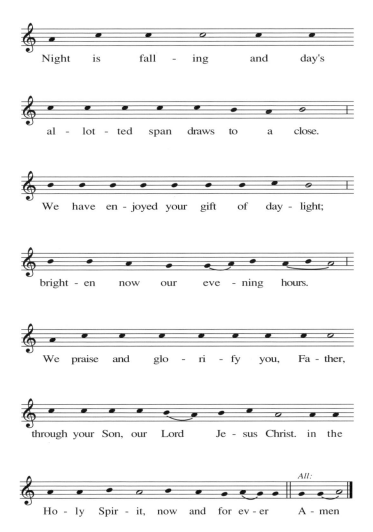

Night    is    fall - ing    and    day's

al - lot - ted    span    draws    to    a    close.

We    have    en - joyed    your    gift    of    day - light;

bright - en    now    our    eve - ning    hours.

We    praise    and    glo - ri - fy    you,    Fa - ther,

through your    Son,    our    Lord    Je - sus    Christ.    in    the

*All:*

Ho - ly    Spir - it,    now    and    for    ev - er    A - men

J.A.M.
Apostolic Constitutions

*Assistant:*

Let us give thanks to God the Fa - ther,

al - ways and for ev - 'ry - thing.

*All:*

In the name of our Lord Je - sus Christ.

*Assistant:*

We praise and thank you, O God,

for you are with - out be - gin - ning and with - out end.

Through Christ, you cre - at - ed the whole world;

through Christ, you pre - serve it.

You are his God and Fa - ther,

the Giv - er of the Spir - it,

the Rul - er of all that is seen and un - seen.

You made the day for the works of light

and the night for the re - fresh - ment

of our minds and our bod - ies. O lov - ing Lord

and source of all that is good, gra - cious - ly

ac - cept our eve - ning sac - ri - fice of praise.

You have con - duct - ed us through the day

and brought us to night's be - gin - ning.

Keep us now in Christ, grant us a peace - ful

eve - ning and a night free from sin,

and bring us at last to e - ter - nal life.

Through Christ and in the Ho - ly Spir - it,

we of - fer you all glo - ry, hon - or and

*All:*

wor - ship, now and for ev - er. A - men.

# PSALM PRAYERS
# FOR MORNING PRAYER

PSALM PRAYER: The leader of prayer may introduce a period of silent reflection, by saying *Let us pray*, or it may be omitted. Then the leader of prayer, with hands extended, may pray one of the following prayers.

**For Psalm 63**

God of life and love,
you are the fulfilment of all our desires.
As we long for your light and grace,
fill our hearts with your Word
that we may rejoice in your love
and offer thanksgiving for the gift of a new day.
May we pour out our love in the service of your kingdom.

Glory and praise to you, loving God,
through our Lord Jesus Christ, your Son,
who lives and reigns with you in the unity of the Holy Spirit,
God for ever and ever.

**For Psalm 51**

God of mercy and kindness,
our helper and consoler,
hear our morning prayer of repentance
as we acknowledge our sinfulness before you.
Cleanse us from our guilt
that we may rejoice in your mercy
and proclaim your goodness.
With the gift of the Spirit
we shall know the joy of your assistance
and live as witnesses of your steadfast love.

Glory and praise to you, loving God,
through our Lord Jesus Christ, your Son,
who lives and reigns with you in the unity of the Holy Spirit,
God for ever and ever.

**For Psalms of Praise**

Lord God,
you live in unapproachable light
yet in the beauty of creation
you have revealed your goodness and love.
Accept our morning prayer of praise
and fill our hearts with the beauty of your love
that our spirits may rejoice in your presence.

Glory and praise to you, loving God of power
through our Lord Jesus Christ, your Son,
who lives and reigns with you in the unity of the Holy Spirit,
God for ever and ever.

or

Almighty God,
author and giver of all good things,
through the coming of your Son,
you broken the tyranny of sin
and have given us the pledge of salvation.
We glorify you for the beauty of creation
and we praise you for saving us in Jesus Christ.
Accept our worship and bless our lives,
that we may work today for your honour and glory.

We praise you through your Son, Jesus Christ our Lord,
who lives and reigns and with you in the unity of the Holy Spirit
God forever and ever.

or

O God,
we hunger and thirst for you.
Fill our hearts with your love today.
May we praise you with joy
and serve you in our brothers and sisters.

We ask this through Christ our Lord.

or

Heavenly Father,
may everything we do
begin with your inspiration
and continue with your saving help.
Let our work always have its origin in you
and through you be brought to its completion.

We make our prayer through Christ our Lord.

or

God, creator of unfailing light,
give that same light to those who call upon you.
May our lips praise you,
our lives proclaim your goodness,
our work give you honour,
and our voices celebrate you for ever.

We ask this through Christ our Lord.

# PSALM PRAYERS FOR EVENING PRAYER

PSALM PRAYER: The leader of prayer may introduce a period of silent reflection, by saying *Let us pray,* or it may be omitted. Then the leader of prayer, with hands extended, may pray one of the following prayers.

**For Psalm 141**

Lord God of mercy and love,
from the rising of the sun to its setting
your name is worthy of all praise.
Make our prayer ascend like incense before you
and from our upraised hands
receive our evening sacrifice to your glory.

We ask this through Christ our Lord.

**For Psalms of Praise**

Blessed are you, Lord God,
for you watch over the family
redeemed by your Son and renewed in the Spirit.
You have gathered in your presence to proclaim your praise
for the wonders of creation and salvation.

Guide our way on the pilgrimage of life,
and keep our lives from evil,
that we may come to the table prepared for us by your Son
in your eternal home.

Glory and praise to you, O God,
through our Lord Jesus Christ, your Son,
who lives and reigns with you in the unity of the Holy Spirit,
for ever and ever.

> or

God of our salvation,
your Son has made us children of the light
and sealed us with the pledge of your love.

We proclaim the greatness of your love
and rejoice in your gift of salvation.
Accept our worship as a holy offering,
as we gather at the end of this day,
and grant that we may always walk in the light of your glory.

All praise and honour are yours, loving God,
through our Lord Jesus Christ, your Son,
who lives and reigns with you in the unity of the Holy Spirit,
God for ever and ever.

# PROFESSION OF FAITH
# FOR EASTER SUNDAY

## BAPTISMAL PROFESSION OF FAITH

The leader of prayer asks:

Do you believe in God, the Father Almighty,
Creator of heaven and earth?

The people answer: I do.

The leader of prayer asks:

Do you believe in Jesus Christ, his only Son, our Lord,
who was born of the Virgin Mary,
was crucified, died, and was buried,
rose from the dead,
and is now seated at the right hand of the Father?

The people answer: I do.

The leader of prayer asks:

Do you believe in the Holy Spirit,
the holy catholic Church, the communion of saints,
the forgiveness of sins, the resurrection of the body,
and the life everlasting?

The people answer: I do.

The leader of prayer continues:

This is our faith.
This is the faith of the Church.
We are proud to profess it
in Christ Jesus our Lord.

The community responds: Amen.

# PROFESSION OF FAITH FOR OCCASIONAL USE

## Apostles' Creed in Question Form

The leader of prayer asks:

Do you believe in God?

The community answers:

I believe in God, the Father Almighty,
Creator of heaven and earth.

The leader of prayer asks:

Do you believe in Jesus Christ?

The community answers:

I believe in Jesus Christ, God's only Son, our Lord.
He was conceived by the power of the Holy Spirit,
and born of the Virgin Mary.
He suffered under Pontius Pilate,
was crucified, died, and was buried.
He descended to the dead.
On the third day he rose again;
he ascended into heaven,
and is seated at the right hand of the Father.
He will come again to judge the living and the dead.

The leader of prayer asks:

Do you believe in the Holy Spirit?

The community answers:

I believe in the Holy Spirit,
the holy catholic Church,
the communion of saints,
the forgiveness of sins,
the resurrection of the body,
and the life everlasting. Amen.

# PSALMS FOR THE PROCLAMATION OF PRAISE

These psalms are provided for cantors or leaders of prayer in order to provide a fuller text than what may be available in the Catholic Book of Worship. A number of verses may be selected and a suitable refrain and psalm tone should be chosen from the Hymnal.

**Psalm 8**

Lord our God,
the whole world tells
the greatness of your name.
your glory reaches beyonds the stars.

Even the babble of infants
declares your strength,
your power to halt
the enemy and avenger.

I see your handiwork
in the heavens:
the moon and the stars
you set in place.

What is humankind
that you remember them,
the human race
that you care for them?

You treat them like gods,
dressing them in glory and splendour.
You give them charge of the earth,
laying all at their feet:

cattle and sheep,
wild beasts,
birds of the sky,
fish of the sea,
every swimming creature.

Lord our God,
the whole world tells
the greatness of your name.

**Psalm 100**

Shout with joy to the Lord, all earth,
serve the Lord with gladness,
enter God's presence with joy!

Know that the Lord is God,
our maker to whom we belong,
our shepherd, and we the flock.

Enter the temple gates,
the courtyard with thanks and praise;
give thanks and bless God's name.

Indeed the Lord is good!
God's love is forever,
faithful from age to age.

**Psalm 103**

My soul, bless the Lord,
bless God's holy name!
My soul, bless the Lord,
hold dear all God's gifts.

Bless God, who forgives your sin
and heals every illness,
who snatches you from death
and enfolds you with tender care,
who fills your life with richness
and gives you an eagle's strength.

The Lord, who works justice
and defends the oppressed,
teaches Moses and Israel
divine ways and deeds.

The Lord is tender and caring,
slow to anger, rich in love.
God will not accuse us long,
nor bring our sins to trial,
nor exact from us in kind
what our sins deserve.

As high as heaven above earth,
so great is God's love for believers.
As far as east from west,
so God removes our sins.

As tender as to child,
so gentle is God to believers.
The Lord knows how we are made,
remembers we are dust.

Our days pass by like grass,
our prime like a flower in bloom.
A wind comes, the flower goes,
empty now its place.

God's love is from all ages,
God's justice beyond all time
for believers of each generation:
those who keep the covenant,
who take care to live the law.

The Lord reigns from heaven,
rules over all there is.
Bless the Lord, you angels,
strong and quick to obey,
attending to God's word.

Bless the Lord, you powers,
eager to serve God's will.
Bless the Lord, you creatures,
everywhere under God's rule.

[My soul, bless the Lord!]

**Psalm 113**

[Hallelujah!]
Servants of the God, praise,
praise the name of the Lord.
Bless the Lord's name
now and always.

Praise the Lord's name
here and in every place,
from east to west.

The Lord towers above nations,
God's glory shines over the heavens.
Who compares to our God?
Who is enthroned so high?

The Lord bends down
to see heaven and earth,
to raise the weak from the dust
and lift the poor from the mire,
to seat them with princes
in the company of their leaders.

The childless, no longer alone,
rejoice now in many children.
[Hallelujah!]

## Psalm 118.1–4, 14–15, 17+19, 20–27

Give thanks, the Lord is good,
God's love is forever!
Now let Israel say,
"God's love is forever!"

Let the house of Aaron say,
"God's love is forever!"
Let all who revere the Lord say,
"God's love is forever!"

My strength, my song is the Lord,
who has become my saviour.
Glad songs of victory sound
within the tents of the just.

I shall not die but live
to tell the Lord's great deeds.
Open the gates of justice,
let me praise God within them.

This is the Lord's own gate,
only the just will enter.
I thank you for you answered me,
and you became my saviour.

The stone the builders rejected
has become the cornerstone.
This is the work of the Lord,
how wonderful in our eyes.

This is the day the Lord has made,
let us rejoice and be glad.
Lord, give us the victory!
Lord, grant us success!

Blest is the one who comes,
who comes in the name of the Lord.
We bless you from the Lord's house.
The Lord God is our light:
adorn the altar with branches.

I will thanks you, my God,
I will praise you highly.
give thanks, the Lord is good,
God's love is forever!

## Psalm 136. 1–18, 21–26

Our God is good,  give thanks!
God's love is forever!
Our God of gods,  give thanks!
God's love is forever!
Our Lord of lords,  give thanks!
God's love is forever!

Alone the maker of worlds!
God's love is forever!
Architect for the skies!
God's love is forever!
Spread the land on the seas!
God's love is forever!

Set the great lights above!
God's love is forever!
The sun to rule the day!
God's love is forever!
The moon and stars, the night!
God's love is forever!

Struck down Egypt's firstborn
God's love is forever!
Guided Israel's escape!
God's love is forever!
Held out a mighty arm!
God's love is forever!

Split in two the Reed Sea!
God's love is forever!
Led Israel across!
God's love is forever!
Drowned Pharaoh and his troops!
God's love is forever!

Led the desert trek!
God's love is forever!
Gave Israel a land!
God's love is forever!
For God's servants to keep!
God's love is forever!

Remembered our distress!
God's love is forever!
God feeds all living things!
God's love is forever!
To the God in heaven, give thanks!
God's love is forever!

## Psalm 145

I will exalt you, God my king,
for ever bless your name.
I will bless you every day,
for ever praise your name.

Great is the Lord,
highly to be praised,
great beyond our reach.

Age to age proclaims your works,
recounts your mighty deeds.
I ponder your splendour and glory
and all your wonderful works.

They reveal your fearful power,
I tell of your great deeds.
They recall your ample goodness,
joyfully sing your justice.

Gracious and merciful is the Lord,
slow to anger, full of love.
The Lord is good in every way,
merciful to every creature.

Let your works praise you, Lord,
your faithful ones bless you.
Let them proclaim your glorious reign,
let them tell of your might.

Let them make known to all
your might and glorious reign.
Your dominion lasts for ever,
your rule for all generations!

The Lord is faithful in every word
and gracious in every work.
The Lord supports the fallen,
raises those bowed down.

The eyes of all look to you,
you give them food in due time.
You open wide your hand
to feed all living things.

The Lord is just in every way,
loving in every deed.
The Lord is near to those call,
who cry from their hearts.

God grants them their desires,
hears their cry and saves them.
Those who love God are kept alive;
the wicked, the Lord destroys.

I will sing the Lord's praise,
all flesh will bless God's Name,
holy, both now and for ever.

## Psalm 148

Praise the Lord!
Across the heavens,
from the heights,
all you angels, heavenly beings,
sing praise, sing praise.

Sun and moon, glittering stars,
sing praise, sing praise.
Highest heavens, rain clouds,
sing praise, sing praise.

Praise God's name,
whose word called you forth
and fixed you in place for ever
by eternal decree.

Let there be praise:
from depths of the earth,
from creatures of the deep.

Fire and hail, snow and mist,
storms, winds, mountains, hills,
fruit trees and cedars,
wild beasts and tame, snakes and birds,

princes, judges, rulers, subjects,
men, women, old and young,
praise, praise the holy name,
this name beyond all names.

God's splendour above the earth,
above the heavens,
gives strength to the nation,
glory to the faithful,
a people close to the Lord.
Israel, let there be praise!

## Psalm 149

Sing a new song, you faithful,
praise God in the assembly.
Israel, rejoice in your maker,
Zion, in your king.
Dance in the Lord's name,
sounding harp and tambourine.

The Lord delights
in saving a helpless people.
Revel in God's glory,
join in clan by clan.
Shout praise from your throat,
sword flashing in hand

to discipline nations
and punish the wicked,
to shackle their kings
and chain their leaders,
and execute God's sentence.
You faithful, this is your glory!
[Hallelujah!]

## Psalm 150

Praise! Praise God in the temple,
in the highest heavens!
Praise! Praise God's mighty deeds
and noble majesty.

Praise! Praise God with trumpet blasts,
with lute and harp.
Praise! Praise God with timbrel and
dance,
with strings and pipes.

Praise! Praise God with clashing cymbals,
with ringing cymbals.
All that is alive, praise.
Praise the Lord.
[Hallelujah!]